THE TRANSFORMATION

THE TRANSFORMATION

Healing Your Past Lives to
Realize Your Soul's Potential

AINSLIE MACLEOD

SOUNDS TRUE
Boulder, Colorado

Sounds True, Inc.
Boulder CO 80306

© 2010 Ainslie MacLeod

Book design by Karen Polaski

Printed in Canada

Library of Congress Cataloging-in-Publication Data
Macleod, Ainslie.
  The transformation : healing your past lives to realize your soul's potential /
Ainslie MacLeod.
     p. cm.
  ISBN 978-1-59179-770-8 (hardcover)
1. Parapsychology. 2. Reincarnation therapy. 3. Spirituality—Miscellanea.
I. Title.
  BF1040.M245 2010
  133.9—dc22
                                        2009052598

10 9 8 7 6 5 4 3 2 1

To my parents, Angus and Gwen, with all my love
"You're an oddity, but we love you anyway."

CONTENTS

ACKNOWLEDGMENTS

I'd like to express my deepest appreciation to my clients for their willingness to share their experiences, both past and present, in this book.

Once again, I'm especially grateful to my editor, Kelly Notaras, for her invaluable guidance and enthusiasm, to everyone at Sounds True for their efforts in bringing this book into the world, and to my agent, Eric Myers, for his thoughtful words of encouragement and wisdom.

I owe thanks, also, to my assistant, Kelli Nichols, and all my friends and family members for their support. Special thanks and big hugs to Lisa, Kyra, and Lucas for their patience and understanding while Dad was busy writing.

I'm particularly indebted to my spirit guides. And since it's common for them, during a session, to repeat a word or phrase three times for emphasis, I'd like to take this opportunity to do the same. Thank you, thank you, thank you.

THE TRANSFORMATION
A Spiritual Rescue Mission

WHEN THE PAST MEETS THE PRESENT

I used to cringe every time someone asked me what I did for a living. I'd mumble the word "psychic" so softly people would reply with a questioning, "psychotherapist?" or "psychiatrist?" unsure they'd heard me correctly.

In my last book, *The Instruction,* I wrote about how I used to describe myself as "The Reluctant Psychic." The reason was simple: I was embarrassed by what people would think about my unconventional career. I was worried they'd associate me with the charlatans and rip-off artists who give psychics a bad name.

With the help of my spirit guides I'd learned to make a strong connection with the spiritual universe. Yet my self-consciousness was such that I couldn't begin a conversation with the words, "My spirit guides tell me . . ." without blushing.

Then I started working with my spirit guides on issues of self-acceptance. It turned out I had some huge past-life fears surrounding judgment and self-expression. It not only explained my reticence, but also my aversion to public speaking and huge concern about how others perceived me.

Once I got over my fears, everything changed. I didn't care who knew. I was a psychic and proud of it. And after three decades of not speaking in public, you couldn't get me to shut up. I learned to embrace my calling, and that has led to a deep sense of self-acceptance and purpose.

Now when people ask me what I do, I can look them straight in the eye and say, "I'm a psychic," without the slightest hint of self-consciousness.

What I love most about being a (no longer reluctant) psychic is that it's never dull. I get to meet great people with fascinating stories to tell. I get to help them figure out who they are and what they're doing. And most interesting of all, I get to explore their past lives.

Though I'd experienced some extremely effective past-life regressions back in the late 1990s and knew their value, I was never particularly interested in doing it for others. To be quite honest, I found it kind of boring, especially when I could be channeling the same stuff my client would be getting—only a lot faster.

So, I slipped into the habit of telling people what happened to them in the past, rather than taking them through a lengthy relaxation and regression.

By now I've been all over the world and across time: Ming dynasty China, Renaissance Italy, Industrial Revolution Britain, the Wild West. In the thousands of past lives I've explored, there's hardly a corner on the planet I haven't visited.

The purpose of past-life regression is to clear baggage from the past and make way for a happier future. What I discovered was that exploring a past life the way I do is as healing and helpful as any regression.

But what has all this to do with the subject of this book? The answer is *everything*.

When I asked the spirit guides I work with what the purpose of this book would be, they told me they wanted to explain why the world is the way it is, why it doesn't have to be that way, and how spiritually conscious souls can be a driving force for change. No mention of past lives.

It was only when I got into the planning stage that I realized just how significant a role past lives would play in the upcoming shift in consciousness my spirit guides call the "Transformation."

I was pleased that my spirit guides wanted to talk about past lives. The subject had become such an enormous part of my work, and I was finding them so fascinating, I couldn't stop talking about them. I was grateful for a chance to share some of the astonishing adventures I've had with my clients and their many weird and wonderful incarnations.

But before I get sidetracked by my pet subject, let me explain why past lives have such significance and how they fit into the subject of the book.

We all have past lives. In fact, you might have a hundred or more incarnations behind you. And as you'll discover in the pages of this book, what we did or didn't get to do in our past lives impacts us in many different ways.

When your soul first left the Soul World (as my spirit guides like to call it) and came to the Physical Plane, it was on a mission. It was seeking knowledge. Since then, it has had many reincarnations. And though each lifetime has allowed it to evolve, your soul has encountered some significant barriers to growth along the way.

A major trauma in a past life can create a fear that will follow your soul across many incarnations. When an incident acts as a trigger, it can cause the fear to erupt, sometimes many lifetimes later.

During a session, I was talking to a woman named Alicia who lives in Southern California about a life she'd had in early twentieth-century Norway. As a young man in that life, she'd been heavily influenced by the hard-drinking father she worshipped, and she had died of hypothermia after passing out from the effects of an all-night drinking binge.

I'm familiar enough with lifetimes where there's been an extreme of temperature involved in the death to ask, "Do you have a problem with the cold?"

"Not really," Alicia said. "I live in San Diego, after all."

I was temporarily silenced. It had seemed a given.

"Oh, unless you mean at night," she said.

"You died at night," I reminded her.

"My husband and I have had to split the bed in half," she said. "He sleeps under a thin wool comforter that I share. On my side, I have a wool blanket underneath me and a king-size, heavy down comforter folded over so it's doubled. Between the two layers of the down is a double-folded blanket. I have a hot water bottle when my feet are cold, or sometimes fleece socks instead. Then I wear a long-sleeved T-shirt and leggings or sweatpants. And if there's the slightest chill, I can't fall asleep. And that's in summer."

Just to prove her point, Alicia sent me several photos. One shows the bed, as described, with the hot water bottle on the nightstand. Another is a picture taken by her husband. It shows Alicia taking a nap in the middle of the day. Through the window, the sun is shining. But Alicia is all snuggled up under the sundry blankets and comforters with her cats in her arms, and she's wearing a fleece jacket.

At the bottom of the e-mail were the words, "This better not show up on the Internet!"

"My husband finds it all insane, and I can't really blame him," Alicia said. "He feels my skin, and it's actually cold. He's been a lot better, though, since you and I spoke and he understands where it came from."

I asked her if she'd ever found a place that was warm enough for her. She said, "The Caribbean. It was the perfect temperature."

Since we spoke, Alicia has undergone something of a transformation. One night, she simply felt she didn't need all those covers. "I was toasty warm with just a single comforter," she told me. "We've had some chilly nights, and the windows have been cracked open, but I've been fine. I've started falling asleep very quickly, too, which is also new. My husband is happy that he's no longer sleeping with a heavily cocooned caterpillar."

Alicia has noticed a shift in her body temperature, too. "My hands used to be icy cold, but now they're always warm. And I can take sunset walks on the beach and not feel afraid that I'm going to die if I get cold. The change has been dramatic and freeing."

Interesting enough, you might say, but what's that got to do with the coming shift in consciousness?

Past lives affect us in many ways. What Alicia experiences at night is called a "resonance," a visceral reminder of what once happened to her soul. Resonances can be relatively minor, like Alicia's, or they can be large enough, as you'll discover later, to cast a giant shadow over someone's entire life.

Resonances signal the existence of a past life that's trying to get your attention. And once you recognize the symptoms of a resonance, you can get an idea of what kind of fear causes it.

Several of my clients have severe weight problems as a result of starvation in prior incarnations. They overeat in this life as a form of security in case of an event that will most likely never recur.

Past-life fears can cause huge blocks that prevent growth on the Physical Plane. Some people are virtually paralyzed by events that took place hundreds of years ago. These fears appear to have no obvious cause and often little in the way of symptoms, but they will surge to the surface when a trigger is encountered.

I have quite a number of clients who have been hanged in the past. They tend to avoid any kind of physical constraints around their necks, especially turtlenecks and jewelry. Sometimes the presence of this kind of reminder can create a panic reaction with little or no warning. One woman told me she's torn off necklaces. Another, whom you'll meet later in the book, said she can't bear even the weight of the sheet on her neck in bed.

Triggers can cause a dormant past-life fear to explode into life with volcano-like intensity. Many people know what it is like to have a partner cheat on them and to be astonished at the seemingly disproportionate reaction they have to it. But when someone's soul has been imprisoned and executed as a result of betrayal in the past, a trigger like infidelity can bring the fears surrounding the event alive again.

Overcoming these past-life fears is the key to spiritual growth and, as you'll see in the pages of this book, the fast track to a life of greater connection, fulfillment, and meaning.

Like my previous book, *The Instruction,* this book offers a system given to me by elevated spirit guides on what's called the

Causal Plane. It's a ten-step method in which I'll show you how to identify the blocks created by your past-life fears, how to turn each fear on its head to overcome its effects, and how to connect you with your soul's highest goals.

The ultimate goal is to overcome your fears and step into a life of greater spiritual fulfillment and deeper meaning. And, like all change, what you create within will eventually work its way out to impact the world around you.

LITTLE LOST SOULS

We humans have risen to become top dog on Earth. And we have the technology to prove it. We've built great big cities to live in, widescreen plasma TVs to keep us entertained, and we've been to the moon and back.

Yet, despite our phenomenal progress, we've created a world in which we allow billions of our fellow humans to go to bed hungry every night, while a handful of rich guys runs everything. And as a result of our detachment from one another, half of us are not entirely sure if waterboarding defenseless prisoners is torture or not.

In the space of something like 50,000 years, we've gone from cohesive, well-functioning tribes, in which we all took care of one another, to a fractured world in which we may go months without seeing our neighbors, where we face bankruptcy if we get sick, and where many of us are one paycheck away from homelessness.

And even if you're fortunate enough to have money in the bank, a well-paying job, and a family, you may still know what it is to lack real depth of meaning in your life.

You'd hardly know it from looking at us, but we are spiritual beings, programmed to be cooperative, nonviolent, truthful, and compassionate. Something has gone wrong, especially in the West, where we have higher incomes and more stuff than anyone else on the planet. You'd think we'd be walking around with big grins on our faces, in a constant state of gratitude for our immense good fortune.

But we don't. Costa Rica ranks number one in the Happy Planet Index, while America trails behind at number 114. Nic Marks, the person behind the Index, is quoted as saying, "There are a lot of people who are unhappy, particularly at the lower income end of the spectrum, but it is not only financial inequality, it is the longer working week, a lack of social cohesion through a sense of belonging to the community or the geographic area, indebtedness, low levels of volunteering and more passive lifestyles."

Marks' analysis is totally consistent with that of my spirit guides. Our lack of genuine happiness is largely a result of our detachment from each other and our self-imposed isolation.

Living in a dysfunctional world makes it harder to connect with our spiritual selves. Our souls are detached from our conscious selves, and vice versa.

The time has come for spiritually conscious individuals to start changing all this. It's time for those who are ready to reject the shallow materialism and greed of our modern world to step up to the plate and become, as Gandhi put it, the change they want to see. This radical shift in human consciousness is what my spirit guides call the "Transformation," and it's happening all around us, right now.

• • •

The last time our species underwent a transformation of this scale was approximately 55,000 years ago. This earlier transformation allowed our primitive ancestors to make a rapid shift from what my guides call "Stage Two Consciousness"—the kind seen in most large mammals—to what they call "Stage Three Consciousness," the kind humans enjoy today.

What occurred 55,000 years ago was a dramatic event for *Homo sapiens*. Stage Three Consciousness allowed us to develop a host of useful skills. We became more organized, learned to hunt better, and started having sex for fun. That led to an increase in our numbers and helped ensure our survival.

The tribe after the last Transformation was a place of far greater happiness and contentment than we might imagine. We worked together much more intuitively than we do now, and we took care of each other in a state of mutual cooperation.

Being more closely connected to our souls meant that we recognized our common humanity. Wars, when they did occasionally break out, were short and fought for practical rather than ideological reasons. Then, as now, we fought over access to resources.

On the whole, as long as resources were plentiful, there was no sense in taking more than your fair share. (When bananas grow on every tree, hoarding bananas makes no sense.)

It was only sometime closer to 10,000 years ago that things began to change for the worse. As our tribes grew to fill whole cities, artificial hierarchies sprang up as we lost our connection to one another.

Along with more formal religions and power structures came kings, priests, and other individuals who sought to take advantage of their position.

After thousands of years spent acting according to our souls' core values, we became, to some extent or another, trapped behind what my spirit guides term the "Illusion," the invisible block between our physical selves and our souls.

Under the Illusion, our traditions of cooperation and equality were cast aside in favor of greed and inequality. And as our physical world became more sophisticated, spiritual values such as truth, knowledge, and freedom were gradually replaced by hypocrisy, superstition, and coercion.

The purpose of the last Transformation was to bring our species together. By building strong relationships and communities, our souls made sure our species would survive and thrive for thousands of years to come. It meant that humans would be around long enough to learn increasingly complex lessons on the Physical Plane.

Now, as the negative impact of the Illusion threatens our very survival as a species, we're poised to make a leap similar to the one we made 55,000 years ago again.

Stage Four Consciousness will take us to a new level of awareness. It will reconnect us with our souls' core values, such as cooperation, equality, justice, and peace. And in the same way the previous shift in consciousness brought us together in a spirit of cooperation, the coming transformation will give us a renewed sense of belonging and shared purpose.

As we move forward into this great new future, this higher consciousness will help each of us to reunite with the tribe and embrace those core values that lie at the center of our souls. And as we learn to act with greater integrity and compassion, our lives will gain a renewed sense of purpose and meaning.

• • •

The Transformation, then, is a chance to be an active part of the greatest shift in consciousness in 55,000 years. And the good news is that all you have to do is be the person you really are—to connect with your soul's core values. Seems easy enough, right?

Not always. We must first free ourselves from the invisible grip of the Illusion. To do that, the key is to learn to live without fear.

Each of our incarnations puts us at risk of incurring soul-level trauma. In one life you might lose your entire family in a war. In the next you might be sentenced to imprisonment and torture. Every event that radically impacts your ability to complete your life plan (what your soul set out to achieve in that life) creates a soul-level fear.

The loss of your family will create insecurity about the future and perhaps irrational worry about losing your loved ones in this lifetime. Imprisonment and torture might give you a seemingly unexplained anxiety when confronted with people in positions of authority.

These past-life fears act as blocks to your spiritual progress by keeping you stuck behind the Illusion. But once you learn to overcome them, you'll step out of the Illusion into the light, open to achieve your true potential as never before.

And that's what the ten chapters in this book are all about. They will show you how to identify your fears and then how to overcome them to reach a higher level of consciousness.

The three steps to Transformation are:

1. Identify your past-life fear.
2. Find the motivation for change.
3. Connect with your soul's goal.

All past-life fears fall into one of ten categories. As you make your way through each of the ten steps in the book, you'll learn how to identify the fear by its symptoms, or "resonances."

Personal transformation is achieved by overcoming your soul-level fears. In doing so, you elevate your consciousness to Stage Four, resulting in a more fulfilling and meaningful life. (On a larger scale, each individual transformation elevates the collective consciousness, leading to a more spiritually conscious—i.e., Stage Four—world.)

To use a medical analogy, when a virus attacks your physical body, your immune system will react by sending antibodies to attack the cause of the sickness. In the same way, when a past-life fear is triggered, your soul reacts by offering you the motivation to stimulate recovery.

To take the medical analogy a little further, imagine you're suffering from a disease, but you don't know what it is. Will it keep getting worse? Will you die? Without knowing the cause of the ailment there's no way to treat it. Does it require medication or amputation? It's only when you know the cause of the ailment that you can treat it.

Similarly, when it comes to past-life fears, not knowing the cause or depth of the fear can be scary. But when you learn the cause, you can take appropriate steps toward healing.

In both cases, knowledge is power. It allows healing to begin. In the case of past-life fears, you are the healer. The cure is in your hands. If you choose, you can use the impetus for change to heal your soul and overcome the fears that block your spiritual evolution.

You might suffer from more than one fear at a time. Most people I work with are dealing with quite a few. They may all stem from one traumatic lifetime, or more typically, they have their origins in several different lives. Most fears will come and go several times over the course of your many incarnations.

When you connect with your soul's goals through the motivations, your fears will dissipate, and in many cases, simply disappear.

When you've worked through all of your past-life fears, you'll have undergone a process that would take most souls lifetimes to achieve. You'll have gone from Stage Three to Stage Four Consciousness, which is the next step in our species' evolution. If Stage Three took us to the moon, Stage Four will take us to the stars.

When we underwent the last Transformation, our Stage Three Consciousness gave us the ability for rational thought. Yet, we'd hardly have been considered great minds by today's standards. It took millennia to develop our current level of intellect. For most of that period we relied on our spiritual connection to guide us.

This time, however, we have the intellect. We just don't have the spirituality. Stage Four is the melding of intellect and spirituality.

Once you embody this Stage Four awareness, there's no going back (not that you would want to). You'll feel more connected to your fellow humans, and that will give you a deeper-than-ever sense of belonging.

Without your fears acting like a ball and chain, holding you back from achieving your true potential, you'll have the confidence to manifest your goals, to be all you were meant to be.

And what does it mean to be all you were meant to be? To put it simply, it means manifesting your true self—one that's both physical and spiritual.

Your personal transformation will imbue you with a sense of purpose and meaning. And when that happens, you'll act as an inspiration to others. Your transformation will raise the consciousness of those around you. Without even having to try, you'll become a force for change. You will *become* the Transformation.

USING THIS BOOK

There are a number of terms that you'll continually run into throughout the book. The following is a quick description of each.

The Transformation

This is the process through which humanity is set to undergo a shift to a more elevated consciousness and a world of greater cooperation and peace. On the individual level, the Transformation is the process of overcoming past-life fears to connect with your soul's goals and raise your consciousness.

The Collective Consciousness

This is the sea of souls, of which we're all a part. It is negatively or positively impacted by our behavior, which is why a small number of spiritually conscious souls can make a significant impact on the world.

The Soul World

This term is used by my spirit guides to describe the spiritual universe—the home to the Collective Consciousness, your soul, and your spirit guides.

The Illusion

The Illusion is an invisible barrier between this plane and the Soul World. Those who are "in thrall to the Illusion," as my spirit guides would say, are blocked to some degree or other from their spiritual selves. The cause is fear. Breaking through the Illusion is an essential part of the Transformation.

Stage Four Consciousness

The Transformation will take our species from a Stage Three Consciousness to the next (and final) level. Stage Four Consciousness creates a greater awareness of the importance of peace, unity, and other higher values by connecting us more strongly with our spiritual selves. It will help us create a world more conducive to these values, for ourselves and others.

This elevated consciousness has already been seen in people like Martin Luther King Jr. and Gandhi, and it exists in many who work to help create a better world, especially when they don't necessarily benefit themselves. (A person with plenty of health insurance who fights for universal health coverage is another example.)

As a species, our Stage Four Consciousness will continue to grow throughout the rest of our existence, and in doing so, it will ensure our survival.

Life Plans

Your life plan is a blueprint for this life that you create before you're born. In it, you have all the major goals and missions your soul wants to accomplish. It includes agreements with other souls to work on balancing karma from previous lives or simply to be together for the spiritual growth it offers.

Your life plan allows for total free will. It is only a rough guideline. Your soul will never, for example, choose the time and circumstances of your death or deliberately put you in harm's way.

Spirit Guides

Spirit guides are your support group in the Soul World. They understand your life plan, your agreements with other souls, and they know everything there is to know about your past lives. And to answer a frequently asked question: yes, we all have them!

The Tribe

When my spirit guides talk about reuniting with the tribe, they're not advocating a return to living in caves. They mean rekindling the awareness of our shared humanity that began at the time of the last Transformation, 55,000 years ago, and lasted until approximately 10,000 years ago, when the Illusion began to exert its influence.

Resonances

Resonances are reminders of past-life trauma. They can be mild, like an anxiety in the presence of men in uniforms, or they can color your entire life, like a fear of public speaking. Some resonances are physical, like sensitivity to extremes of temperature or unexplained pains.

Triggers

Past-life fears are triggered by events in this life. Losing loved ones in a previous incarnation can create a fear of Loss. In this life, the death of someone close can trigger the fear, creating symptoms such as uncertainty about the future.

Soul Ages

We are all at different points on our souls' evolutionary journeys. It means that some souls are older than others. Your soul age gives you your perspective on the world and shapes your beliefs. (A fuller explanation can be found in my previous book, *The Instruction.*)

Past-life fears affect young and old souls in different ways. Younger souls, with less experience on the Physical Plane, tend to be more in thrall to the Illusion. Their response to having a past-life fear triggered is often to hurt others as they were once hurt.

Older souls tend to internalize their fears, often manifesting unexplained physical reminders of the trauma.

Though there are five young-soul stages and five in the old-soul cycle, for simplicity, I simply refer to old and young throughout the book.

Karma

Though some believe karma to be about payback for earlier "crimes," my spirit guides describe it simply as a way to balance trauma from the past.

For an event to create karma, it must be significant enough to have blocked your ability to complete your life plan. This can happen through deliberate injury, disempowerment, or killing.

Spiritual Acts

Spiritual acts are ways of helping those less fortunate than yourself. The same motivation that enables you to balance the karma from a past-life fear can be used to help others who suffer as you once did. An organization like Amnesty International, for example, is full of people who have suffered imprisonment and torture in previous incarnations.

Through Spiritual Acts, you can accelerate your personal transformation.

• • •

Like a butterfly emerging from a chrysalis, when you step out of the Illusion and into the light of the Transformation, you will have undergone a radical and permanent change for the better.

The "Stage Four you" won't necessarily look any different. But you will feel and act differently. You'll find you have a higher than ever level of kindness and compassion, both for yourself and others.

As you become more loving, your relationships will be transformed. The changes you undergo will influence everyone you come into contact with. You'll be drawn to others and they to you. You'll become a walking example of what it is to be a spiritually conscious embodiment of the Transformation.

As you embark on your voyage of transformation, be assured that you have all the support of the universe behind you. Your spirit guides will encourage and guide you at all times. Your soul will do all it can to keep you connected to its highest values throughout.

I'd like to wish you bon voyage and good luck on your journey. You are a spiritual being in a physical body. May you bring the two into alignment and create a fabulous future of connection, fulfillment, and meaning.

CHAPTER ONE

YOUR SOUL'S EVOLUTION
A Voyage of Spiritual Transformation

THE COMING TRANSFORMATION

This book is a guide to becoming an active participant in the Transformation. In each of the next ten chapters, you'll learn everything you'll need to take your consciousness to Stage Four.

The process is simple. It is to discover your fears from the past and then use the motivation associated with each to connect you with your soul's highest values, or goals.

To demonstrate the process, let me give you an example from a session I had with a forty-eight-year-old woman in New York. Janelle had a past life, more than two hundred years ago, in which she was a young Londoner named Joseph. After enduring years of hardship and abuse in a London orphanage, he scraped together enough to pay for a passage to America. With his pregnant young wife, he set out in search of opportunity in the New World.

Once he got to Virginia, Joseph got himself a small piece of land at no cost, where he built a cabin for his wife and their newborn baby. The couple was grateful for the opportunity they'd been given, and they worked hard to make their little farm a success.

In a story that sounds like an episode from a Western TV show, the young man fell foul of a wealthy landowner who wanted his acreage. The landowner poisoned the family's well, killing the woman and her son. Joseph, though sickened, survived and tried to seek justice.

Unfortunately, the landowner had poisoned the minds of the populace, too. In trying to have the landowner prosecuted, Joseph found the tables turned on him. He was accused of murdering his own family. Though he was clearly innocent, the landowner was the one with the power and influence to decide his fate. To ensure no unpleasant facts were ever heard in a courtroom, Joseph was left alone in an unlocked cell. During the night, a lynch mob made sure he'd cause no more trouble.

When I've explored a client's past life, I always ask afterward if he or she can draw any parallels with this current life.

"Do you have any fear of being poisoned?" I asked Janelle.

There was silence.

I tried again. "Can you make any connection between that life and this?"

Again there was silence. Then, finally, Janelle spoke.

"I'm *paranoid* about being poisoned," she whispered.

I kind of laughed it off, saying that most people probably have an aversion to being poisoned.

"You don't understand," she said, "I'm totally paranoid. My husband has to taste *all* my food, and I check the seal on *every single* product that comes into the house."

What I'd run into was a particularly active resonance. Obviously, this past life was still dramatically impacting Janelle, even after several hundred years. When I interviewed her for this book roughly six months later, she filled me in on the details.

"When you asked me if I had a fear of being poisoned, I was in total shock," she said. "That's why I couldn't speak. I've thrown away so much food over the years, you wouldn't believe it. It's caused a lot of friction with my husband. I always had to be the one to open a package or container. If anyone else did, I'd throw it out. If anything was even close to its expiration date, out it went.

"When the kids came along, I began having terrible anxiety attacks. If the top of one of those little jars of baby food didn't pop with just the right sound, I'd throw it out.

"We were on a tight budget back then, and all our water came from a well. I spent a fortune on bottled water, even though I'd have the well tested every two or three months. I'd take a sample to the county even if it had already been tested. I wouldn't even bathe in the water if it hadn't been tested for a couple of months.

"Then there was the big Tylenol scare in 1982, when someone laced capsules with cyanide. I began having serious panic attacks. At least I could finally point to the Tylenol incident and say, 'Look, it does happen—it's not just my imagination.'

"It was around then that I started taking Xanax for the panic attacks. I was always having to breathe into a paper bag. Several times, my husband had to call an ambulance."

It appeared that when Janelle had used the word "paranoid," she wasn't kidding.

The terrifying events of that pioneer lifetime resulted in several fears being created. The biggest was what's called a past-life fear of Death. It occurs when death has been sudden, violent, and disruptive to the soul's life plan.

Janelle's fear shares one of the most common characteristics of any past-life fear: it's irrational. She's never been poisoned in this life, yet she's been exposed to what are called "triggers" over and over again. Every time a new product came into the home, every time she poured a glass of water, the event acted as a trigger, until the fear became disabling.

So, how is Janelle doing since I uncovered that past life for her? Well, to put it simply, she's cured.

"It wasn't an overnight thing," she told me. "It was a month later that I went to the fridge and poured myself a glass of milk. I walked away and suddenly realized I hadn't checked the seal."

The effect since then has been dramatic. Janelle has lost her fears, and she's no longer taking medication for her anxiety. She feels that simply knowing the cause was the first big step in calming her fear.

"I'm finally able to move forward. Until now, I was always too afraid. In fact, I'd get paralyzed by fear. Recently I lost my job. The old me wouldn't have been able to handle it. I'd have gone into a total panic. Now I'm not only able to deal with it, but my attitude has been 'Isn't this exciting! I'm looking forward to whatever's next.'"

Within a past-life fear of Death lies the motivation for change, in the form of an awareness of the importance of nonviolence. This karmic motivation can be used to balance the effects of the fear. It can cause the fear to dissipate and lead to the recognition that it's incumbent upon that person to help others, frequently those at risk of violent death in this life.

Overcoming the fear has allowed Janelle to be herself: a spiritually conscious old soul with a strong desire to see a more peaceful world.

"I have very strong feelings about violence and war," she told me. "I've always stood up for, and spoken out loudly against, anyone being treated unfairly. Cases that involve innocent people being put away or receiving the death penalty bother me so much more than it does most people.

"If I hear or read of police brutality, school bullying, or anything similar, I feel compelled to do something—even if it's just to write a letter to the newspapers."

Janelle's personal past-life experience has given her the impetus to help others (a Spiritual Act). "I've become a member of Amnesty International and hooked up with someone locally to get more heavily involved. I always speak out against war.

"I come from a family with members in the military, so I know how to be diplomatic, but I feel I have to express my opposition to violence of any kind more strongly now."

Janelle is also exploring new ways to help others. She has the ability to heal using her hands. Since losing her debilitating fear, she's been overcoming her reticence about using her gift.

"I know the more I practice, the stronger it gets," she said. "I can feel the energy like a palpable ball in my hands. I practiced on a puppy that went through surgery. The doctor was amazed. He said the puppy would be down for three days. He was up in a day."

Janelle is finding out what it is to be an active part of the Transformation. Overcoming her fears, speaking out for what's right, and being of service to others are three of the most direct ways anyone can elevate his or her consciousness.

What thrills Janelle particularly about her personal transformation is how fast it all happened. She noticed a change immediately after our session, and within a month, she was like a new person.

"I've put the fear into the past," she said. "It was quite simply the best day of my life when I poured that glass of milk."

• • •

What I've discovered in my work with past lives is something that may come as a surprise. It turns out we've all got past-life fears. Every one of us is impacted to some extent or another by our soul's past experiences. Not everyone has a paralyzing, seemingly irrational fear like Janelle's, but we all have some level of past-life fear within us.

Your fears can manifest as loneliness, inertia, procrastination, needless worry, jealousy, lack of self-acceptance or self-worth, intimacy issues, and a host of other symptoms you'll read about in the pages of this book.

We've all incarnated frequently enough that we have elements of all ten past-life fears within us. Some may affect us more than others. If you graded the fears on a scale of one to ten, you may have a couple of ones, several twos or threes, and maybe an eight or nine somewhere. Regardless of the strength of the fear, you can still make use of its related motivation to reach a state of elevated consciousness—a condition that will help you live a life of greater fulfillment and meaning.

HEALING YOUR SOUL

Fifty-five thousand years ago, we wrapped ourselves in animal skins, hunted with stone spears, and lived in poorly organized extended families led by the strongest and most aggressive males. We understood the world we inhabited about as well as a two-year-old understands the inner workings of the internal combustion engine.

Our lives were dull and monotonous. Our rate of progress was practically glacial. We had more in common with chimpanzees and gorillas than with modern humans.

But then something happened to completely change us. Almost overnight, we humans developed a whole new level of consciousness.

As a result of this shift, the destiny of our species was sealed. Our newfound awareness put us on track to become the dominant species on Earth.

The catalyst for this dramatic change in *Homo sapiens* was a Transformation. Not the one that's the subject of this book, but a previous event of similar importance.

This last Transformation took us from what is called Stage Two Consciousness, the kind you see in apes and other large mammals, to Stage Three Consciousness, which is present in all humans today.

This shift from Stage Two to Stage Three enabled us to become the creatures of reason we are now. We had brains with almost unlimited capacity. Now we could actually start using them.

LEVELS OF CONSCIOUSNESS

- **STAGE ONE:** Snakes, mice, insects, most birds
- **STAGE TWO:** Cats, dogs, apes, other large mammals
- **STAGE THREE:** Humans, whales, dolphins
- **STAGE FOUR:** Humans after completing the Transformation

Big changes started happening to our species as soon as the Transformation began. One of the most significant was that we began banding together in larger tribes. This was primarily for protection, but it helped prevent inbreeding and gave us a greater opportunity to learn from one another.

Our Stage Three Consciousness opened our eyes to our potential. It allowed each of us to recognize our individuality. Until then, our roles in our extended families had been determined more by strength than ability.

With our increased consciousness, we recognized that not everyone had the same traits. It became clear that some of us made better hunters or leaders, while others thrived in the areas of caregiving, teaching, or creativity.

As we learned to divide tasks according to abilities, we developed a deep sense of community. The survival of the tribe depended on the ability of hunters, for example, to stay focused and on their willingness to share their catch.

The spiritual and medicinal needs of the tribe were taken care of by the priests, shamans, and healers who had an easier connection to the other side than most. And caregivers manifested stronger-than-average nurturing qualities that made sure they wouldn't suddenly abandon those in their care just because they weren't family.

The tribe after the last Transformation was a place of cooperation and harmony. Food was shared equally, and each member supported the next, both physically and emotionally. Being freshly connected to our souls' core values ensured that no one took advantage of anyone else. There was huge stigma attached to any violation of these values, as they affected the well-being and sometimes even the survival of the tribe.

JUST HUMAN NATURE

The seemingly utopian world of the tribe is hard to imagine from our modern perspective. Yet, no matter how much I push my spirit guides, they still paint the same idyllic picture of mutual cooperation.

With the Illusion being virtually nonexistent until relatively recently, we were more deeply connected to our souls' core values: the goals I describe in the book. Cooperation was our natural way of being.

It's common, in our world, when someone displays greed or selfishness, to say, "It's just human nature."

But greed and selfishness are not human nature. They are aspects of the Illusion. Cooperation, like all the Goals, is an example of true human nature.

With everyone in the tribe having a purpose, it gave each person a sense of meaning in his or her life.

So what, you may wonder, went wrong? How come we can't seem to work together these days without at least one person trying to get more than his or her fair share? How come so many of us are ready and willing to exploit weaker members of society?

The answer is that we humans became in thrall to the Illusion, the invisible wall that separates our physical selves from our souls.

The Illusion is invisible and intangible, but it affects every one of us to a greater or lesser degree. It acts as a barrier to connection with the soul, and it separates you from the Collective Consciousness.

When you're separated from your soul, you lose the sense of belonging to the tribe that once gave your life meaning. This detachment from others is at the root of all the diverse problems of humanity.

It's why one human being can torture another, why our fellow citizens die for want of health care, and why we let corporations take the water out of our springs and aquifers for .000087 cents a gallon and sell it back to us for $7.50 to $11.50 a gallon.

....

ROBBING THE POOR

From behind the Illusion, other humans represent opportunities for profit. The poor, especially, tend to get the worst treatment from those who don't recognize their humanity.

At the time of writing, the U.S. government has introduced a bill to limit payday loans to a maximum annual interest rate of 391 percent.

That, apparently, is progress, and down from a recent high of 911 percent. (The irony that 911 is the number you call when you're being robbed was undoubtedly lost on those who set the rate.)

....

When we get caught up in the Illusion, we simply no longer connect to our souls as we should. In older souls, the result can be feelings of isolation, loneliness, and insecurity.

For younger souls and those more seriously in thrall to the Illusion, the lack of connection allows for greed and selfishness to thrive. Another person becomes the competition or someone to be taken advantage of, rather than a fellow soul who needs support.

The Illusion blocks empathy, which is why people who get caught behind it can behave callously toward others.

There are times when we all slip behind the Illusion as a way to protect ourselves from deep emotional pain. And when we do, we separate ourselves from our highest values. In extreme cases, that's why the person who is abused often ends up becoming the abuser.

The Transformation is all about returning to the values of the tribe. It's about getting to a place where we can see our shared humanity with the clarity we did 55,000 years ago.

When we learn to fully plug in to our souls again, we'll have the advantage of infinitely greater knowledge and understanding.

We can combine our twenty-first century brainpower with our souls' desire for connection to reunite with the tribe (which now numbers something like six billion) and radically influence the Collective Consciousness.

TRANSFORMATIONAL GOALS

If your soul has one purpose, it's this: to evolve. It wants to know what being a human is all about. So it comes to the Physical Plane repeatedly, each time attaching itself to a physical body for the duration of a lifetime to explore new lessons every time.

The soul has specific missions it uses to help give its lifetime a focus. A soul with a mission of healing, for example, will want to learn about being of service, helping other souls to complete their life plans, and of course, healing. We all have a combination of missions. They're narrow enough to give a life certain themes, yet broad enough to avoid limiting free will.

Beyond its specific missions for each lifetime, your soul is seeking something much bigger. Its grand purpose, if you like, is to unite with your Physical Plane self, through its ten transformational goals. Sometimes described by my spirit guides as "paths," or "core values," these goals are the key to personal transformation and are the ultimate lessons your soul is here to learn.

As the Transformation builds, and an increasing number of us connects with our goals, it will become easier for others to follow. (A rising tide lifts all boats, as the saying goes.)

A critical mass of Stage Four Consciousness will cause the process of Transformation to build momentum over the next generation or two. It won't, of course, happen without considerable resistance from younger souls, particularly those most in thrall to the Illusion, but as my spirit guides told me years ago, "The Transformation will happen on schedule, regardless of opposition."

Everyone, irrespective of their soul age, has the opportunity to achieve all ten goals. But even connecting with one is enough to cause significant personal change.

The ten goals, being our souls' core values, are universal. Though not always recognized or followed, they have always been with us and will continue to be with us throughout our existence. The only block to reaching the goals is fear, and showing you how to overcome those fears is the purpose of the book.

Connecting with the ten transformational goals is how, in this lifetime, rather than somewhere in the distant future, you can elevate your consciousness from Stage Three to Stage Four.

THE TEN TRANSFORMATIONAL GOALS

- Equality
- Cooperation
- Respect
- Justice
- Knowledge
- Understanding
- Truth
- Freedom
- Peace
- Love

Each transformational goal comes with its own payoff. When you embody your soul's goal of Equality, you'll recognize your true worth as a valuable member of the tribe, no better or worse than any other. This awareness will help to break down the Illusion and connect you more strongly than ever to your soul.

Arriving at the transformational goal of Cooperation will teach you that you're not alone. Embodying this fundamental spiritual value will give you the urge to participate more fully in the tribe.

When you embrace the goal of Respect, you'll feel better about yourself than you ever have before. You'll learn to take responsibility for your own decisions, and with that you'll develop a sense of self-respect that will stay with you for the rest of your life, and even impact future lifetimes.

The goal of Justice will ensure that you treat everyone you encounter with fairness. And since each of these goals is a two-way street, you'll find people will act more fairly toward you, too.

When you reach the goal of Knowledge, your innate curiosity will stimulate you to cast off beliefs and assumptions and instead seek out genuine wisdom.

Combining empathy and facts leads to the goal of Understanding, where you'll learn to look beyond the Physical Plane to gain deeper insight into your life and the people in it.

The goal of Truth takes you to a place where honesty becomes your default mode. Having overcome blocks to self-expression, you'll learn to voice your opinions with confidence and conviction.

When you embrace the goal of Freedom, you'll recognize the right of every person in the tribe, including yourself, to the maximum opportunity to complete their souls' life plans without interference.

When you overcome your death-related fears, you'll embody the goal of Peace. From that point on, you'll never sanction violence as a solution to any problem, either personal or global.

And when you embody the transformational goal of Love, you'll recognize that we're all connected through our Collective Consciousness and that it's incumbent upon you, as a Stage Four soul, to support the other members of the human tribe throughout the Transformation.

NO GOING BACK

Your soul's evolution is connected to the forward momentum of the universe. However different time may be on other planes, it still moves in a forward direction.

This means that when you reach your transformational goals, you're not going to wake up one morning and find you're back as you were. The Transformation is a game of Chutes and Ladders minus the chutes.

Once you embrace and embody your goals, you'll become a significant part of the Transformation itself. As your consciousness rises, you'll discover what it means to be a Stage Four soul acting at all times from your highest values. Without you even having to try, others will look to you as an example of what it means to be a spiritually conscious old soul.

• • •

The goals are, as I mentioned earlier, your natural way of being, which might make you wonder why we don't see a lot more of these higher values in the world around us.

Unfortunately, our world is one in which young souls have traditionally run the show. They're more ambitious, and there's always been a lot more of them. As a result, younger-soul values, such as "rugged individualism" and "dog eat dog" (both excuses for greed) vastly outweigh older-soul values such as cooperation and equality.

Since the more Illusion-based values are considered mainstream, it's easier for us all to slip into them. In doing so, we succumb to the Illusion, rather than taking the high road. When this happens, we're giving in to our fears.

How past-life fears manifest in a person is dependent on his or her soul age. Older souls internalize their fears. A fear of Loss, for example, will cause a sense of isolation, a reluctance to accumulate possessions or friends (the less they have, the less there is to lose), and a sense of insecurity about the future.

Younger souls externalize their fears. In the case of Loss, there's an attempt to cushion the fear of scarcity or further loss by accumulating more than is needed. Greed, conservatism, and a lack of cooperation with others are the markers.

However the fear manifests, it pushes the individual behind the Illusion, creating a block. (It's this block that must be overcome to break free of the Illusion and achieve your soul's goals.)

A past-life fear of Loss creates, among other things, a fear of insufficiency. It's the most significant source of greed. Behind the veil of the Illusion, you can justify taking a bigger share of the pie by saying, "If I don't take it, someone else will."

When you overcome the limiting effects of the fear and embody the higher value of Cooperation, such behavior is impossible. And when that happens, you'll find yourself actively motivated to work with others in a spirit of mutual support.

By investigating your own past lives, you can uncover the traumas that created the blocks you're currently experiencing. Once you understand the causes of these blocks to progress, you'll have taken the first step toward healing the wounds of the past and unshackling the invisible bonds of the Illusion that keep you from achieving all your soul wants you to in this lifetime.

PAST-LIFE FEARS

So, as we've seen, your soul's motivation is to evolve. And it does that by leaving its home on the Astral Plane to blend with your physical self on this plane and learning from all that you experience in this life.

This thirst for experience is why you're here. And, thanks to the principle of reincarnation, it's why you've been here before and why you'll be here again.

A one-time incarnation would do little to assist your soul's growth. You might turn up, keel over at the age of three, and head back from whence you came without really achieving anything you set out to do.

Instead, your soul keeps coming back here, going from one set of circumstances to the next. Like a human pinball, it bounces from location to location, gender to gender, picking up new understanding with every visit until it feels there's nothing much else to be learned.

Then, after a hundred-and-something incarnations, it shuffles off to the Astral Plane for the last time with the sense of satisfaction you get from a job well done.

....

THE ASTRAL INTERVAL

Between lives, your soul resides on the Astral Plane, which is the nearest nonphysical world to ours. It's where it reviews all it went through while it was here and makes plans for its next incarnation.

Each time your soul returns from its temporary stay on the Astral Plane, it brings with it a deeper understanding of what it means to be human. As a result of that knowledge, the older the soul, the greater the awareness that we humans are all connected.

. . . .

The process of reincarnation has been going on for millions of years. That doesn't mean your soul has been coming to this plane all that time. The oldest souls still currently incarnating have been doing so for something like five or six thousand years. That's about how long it takes to fit in a good 120 or so lifetimes.

With each passing incarnation, your soul ages. As it does, your perspective changes. Young souls, those who are roughly less than halfway through their many incarnations, still need to learn the big lesson: that we're all one. They see huge differences in others, especially if they're a different color, gender, or sexual orientation.

Older souls, having been around the earthly plane for so long, going from male to female in every variety of skin color and ethnicity, feel more connected to others regardless of their outward appearance.

There comes a point when nothing more needs to be accomplished. At that point, your soul leaves the Physical Plane for the Astral Plane, where it will continue to evolve in spirit, if not in body. (Stage Four Consciousness was previously part of the Astral experience. In the Transformation, it will happen on the Physical Plane.)

The problem with continually coming back to the Physical Plane is that, like a boxer coming out of the corner and back into the fight, your soul takes a fair old battering every time. The more lives you have, the more pummeling you're going to take.

These assaults on your soul result in trauma. And in subsequent lifetimes, the trauma manifests as fears. These fears may ebb and flow throughout many lives, depending on the triggers and how much you're able to follow your soul's motivations. (Many people reach their goals without ever consciously knowing that's what they're doing.)

Each lifetime spent in thrall to a particular fear is balanced by the motivation. To take the example of a fear of Loss again, a life as a miser will be karmically balanced by the motivation of Participation. It will impel you to connect with others and help a community in some way.

A practical example of how this process works might be one in which a robber baron from the nineteenth century becomes a community activist helping victims of corporate abuse.

Thanks to my spirit guides and the method they describe in this book, you can recognize your past-life fears from their resonances and begin working on them immediately. Your personal transformation can take place in this lifetime, not some time in the future.

There are ten fears that have their origins in past lives. Nine of these fears are the result of your soul's life plan being derailed. The tenth is related to the experience of death.

THE TEN PAST-LIFE FEARS

- Authority
- Loss
- Inferiority
- Betrayal
- Failure
- Intimacy
- Self-Expression
- Powerlessness
- Death
- Rejection

Unless this incarnation is your first, then you'll have past-life fears. (And if you're reading this, I can guarantee it's not your first time here.) You can't make it through more than a couple of lifetimes without some deep trauma to your soul.

We all have the ten fears within us. What is significant is the degree to which each of them is triggered.

Triggers are reminders of the past trauma. When you hit one, your soul goes on red alert, expecting a repetition of the event that originally caused the fear.

Take a past-life fear of Betrayal. This particular fear is the result of having your expectations in someone or some institution shattered. Let's say you were once betrayed by a jealous lover who had you arrested. Your life plan stops at the point of incarceration, causing a fear of Betrayal in subsequent lifetimes.

In this lifetime, that fear will lie dormant like a volcano waiting to erupt. You might have no idea it's there. You might wonder why people get so worked up about such things as infidelity.

Then you find your partner has cheated on you. The sleeping volcano of betrayal blows, and now you wonder why on earth you're so upset by it.

People in whom the fear is particularly strong are the ones who'll deal with an unfaithful spouse by changing the locks, reaching for a carving knife, or suffering some kind of emotional breakdown.

As you explore the past-life fears described in the following chapters, you'll no doubt recognize that some stand out strongly, and others less so.

You will have all ten of the fears somewhere in your soul, and it's important to deal with each one to reach its related transformational goal.

MOTIVATIONS

Motivations are karmic, meaning they balance the effects of a past-life fear. Your soul will respond to a fear being triggered in this life by offering the appropriate impetus for change.

When you act upon a specific motivation, whether consciously or unconsciously, it will take you to a transformational goal.

THE TEN MOTIVATIONS

- Identification
- Participation
- Self-Determination
- Fairness
- Curiosity
- Empathy
- Honesty
- Empowerment
- Nonviolence
- Forgiveness

To get a sense of how motivations work, I'll give you two examples—the first one using the past-life fear of Inferiority. This disempowering fear is the result of living a life according to the expectations of others.

Say you were born to wealthy parents in Prague a hundred years ago. You might think you'd have more opportunity than most. And that might be true, but societal and parental pressures could well end up being more limiting than liberating.

Instead of going to art school, which is what your soul had planned, you studied chemistry to please your father. "You'll never make a living as an artist," he would say. (This was a limiting belief he was responsible for instilling in you.)

So you end up in a job that offers little real satisfaction, but you put up with it because it's expected of you.

Then you meet someone you find really attractive. But Mom and Dad have other ideas. Under pressure from them, you marry a person you don't really care for, hoping you'll eventually fall in love.

You don't, of course. And at the end of your life, you look back and wonder why you never really felt genuinely fulfilled. Since you allowed others people's expectations to run your life, you die feeling disempowered—"lesser" than everyone else.

In this life, the fear is commonly triggered when other people try to run your life. Nine times out of ten it's a parent or a spouse. They either do things you should be doing yourself or coerce you to make choices that are contrary to your soul's life plan.

The danger is that when the fear is triggered, instead of standing up and demanding the right to self-determination, you fall into the submissive "default mode" you know so well from the past.

Once a fear of Inferiority is triggered, you might believe you have little control over your life. You might even see yourself as a victim, with no power to change anything. In extreme cases, people with this fear feel jealousy toward those they believe are more fortunate than they, not recognizing their own ability to have what they want.

The remedy for this fear is Self-Determination. Your soul provides the motivation for you to look at your life, determine whether it's yours or not, and take back control of your destiny. Self-Determination leads directly to the transformational goal of Respect.

The feeling of self-respect that results from following your soul's desires rather than those of your parents, your partner, or your peers gives you a profound sense of inner confidence.

By respecting yourself, you'll learn to respect others, and thanks to cause and effect, they'll respect you back. Pretty soon, you'll feel so empowered by the inner strength you've found, you'll never allow anyone to run your life for you again.

The other example I want to give is to show you how a motivation relates to the soul's connection to the Collective Consciousness.

A fear of Loss is caused when you lose everything you hold dear: a bomb destroying your home and killing your entire family in an air raid during World War II, for example.

In this lifetime, you might feel uncertain about the future. There may seem little point in planning for events that might well never happen. You become disempowered by the fear.

LITTLE TRIGGERS, BIG FEARS

When a past-life fear gets triggered, it can create a reaction that may appear a little out of proportion.

For one of my clients with a past-life fear of Rejection, a relatively trivial event caused a huge rift between her and her husband. He was late getting home one night, and she discovered he'd been out with some friends—and they'd ended up at a strip club.

My client's conscious self might have been saying, "For goodness sake, all he did was have a couple of beers with his buddies in a girlie bar on his way home." Meanwhile, her soul was crying, "Rejection! Rejection! Mayday! All hands to battle stations!"

In the tribe, the major fears we suffer as a result of past-life traumas were rarely allowed to build in the same way they do in the modern world.

Back then, the big difference was the level of support you could expect after a terrible loss. If you came home from the hunt and found your family dead and dying as a result of an attack by wild animals, you would have undergone all the same emotions you would now: grief, anger, sorrow, loss.

What would happen then is that the tribe would rally around you. In a smaller, more spiritually connected community, your loss was everyone's loss.

Recognizing your need for comfort and support, the other members of the tribe would have you eat and sleep with them for immediate comfort. (This was a common way of dealing with upsetting events like the death of a partner or the loss of children.)

Not having to worry about social mores, the tribe would nurture you, helping you to overcome the trauma. And if that required snuggling up at night with a bunch of friends, then that was what would happen.

Contrast this with one of the saddest triggers for a past-life fear of Loss in the modern world: the aftermath of the death of a loved one.

In our culture, the loss of a spouse elicits sympathy from friends and family, who offer consolation in the hours and days after the event. Then comes the funeral. The community turns out to pay their last respects. And that's often it.

The bereaved soul is left to carry on, sometimes entirely on his or her own. Everyone has to get back to their families and their work. Life must go on.

In the tribe, taking care of the bereaved *was* the work—at least for the helper and caregiver types whose purpose was to look after the needs of others. No one was left to grieve alone.

The recognition that we're all one was never so strong in our species. The tribe took care of one another in ways we can barely imagine. That sense of connection lasted from the beginning of the previous Transformation until gradually starting to dissipate around 10,000 years ago when our lives became more complex.

At the time that we went from being hunter-gatherers to having more organized agrarian lives, we began to detach from one another. As we lost our connection to each other, we became more in thrall to the Illusion.

That was when political and religious leaders began to abuse their authority, demanding monuments, temples, and more than their share of resources. Their Illusion gradually trickled down to influence the rest of the population.

As our tribes grew to fill whole cities, the Illusion gained even more strength. Greed and exploitation replaced altruism and cooperation. Detachment and disinterest took the place of connection and empathy.

IMPACT OF THE ILLUSION

This chart describes some of the more outward manifestations of the ten past-life fears. These symptoms are most commonly found in younger souls and those heavily in thrall to the Illusion.

FEAR	EFFECTS OF THE ILLUSION
Authority	Discrimination, abuse of authority, arrogance
Loss	Greed, exploitation, isolation
Inferiority	Victimization, jealousy, persecution
Betrayal	Cruelty, vengeance, mistrust
Failure	Assumption, blind faith, superstition

Intimacy	Indifference, callousness, lack of empathy
Self-Expression	Hypocrisy, dishonesty, bias
Powerlessness	Control, coercion, disempowerment
Death	Aggression, brutality, intransigence
Rejection	Detachment, sociopathic behavior, resentment

The current Transformation is poised to take us into a future of greater connection and meaning; at the same time it will return to the values that were responsible for our species' original success.

Throughout this book, each transformational goal, its related past-life fear, and its karmic motivation are expressed like this:

GOAL Respect

MOTIVATION Self-Determination

FEAR Inferiority

In the pages of this book, you'll find stories of past lives that I've explored with my clients. They're all there to help you identify your own past-life fears, understand the principle behind motivations, and show you how these individuals have used this work to achieve personal Transformation.

I was asked in an interview once why the past lives I talk about are so dramatic. "Don't we have pleasant lives in our past?"

The answer is yes. Uneventful lives do happen. We don't hear about them much during past-life explorations because they're not the source of traumas. You're hardly likely to incur a past-life fear from living happily in a time of peace and dying in bed surrounded by your loving family.

The lives I explore are the ones seared on your soul's memory so strongly your soul can't leave them in the past where they belong.

The fears are caused by something going wrong. In every case, a past-life fear is the result of either having your life plan derailed or of being killed—which is, of course, the ultimate derailment.

My clients have had past lives in all parts of the world. And since all my clients are old souls, they tend, at this later stage in their souls' development, to seek out interesting and often quite dramatic lives.

Rather than spending their three-score and ten in solitude, doing nothing, they're much more likely to have been drawn to a profoundly karmic relationship during a period of social upheaval for the lessons it offers.

• • •

One of my favorite illustrators, George Herriman, who created *Krazy Kat*, and one of my favorite poets, Don Marquis, joined forces in the 1920s to create *Archy and Mehitabel*.

The poetry is supposedly written by a cockroach (Archy) who lives in a warehouse and comes out at night to use an old typewriter. Since he's too small to use the shift key, Archy types in lower case without punctuation.

In the warehouse there's a cat (Mehitabel) who claims to have had many exotic past lives, and, as Archy puts it, "accuses herself of having been cleopatra."

However, when Archy asks Mehitabel a few probing questions about Cleopatra's legendary love interest, Mark Antony, all he gets are blank looks. Archy begins to wonder if Mehitabel is all she claims to be.

In my work, I went for a very long time before meeting any-one with the kind of past-life pedigree Mehitabel accused herself of having.

Most past lives are, as you'd expect, anonymous. But over the years, I've run into a few well-known people. I've met the painter Georges Seurat. When I told my client, he said, "I used to stare for hours at one of Seurat's paintings in the Field Museum."

"One of *your* paintings," I corrected him.

Another of my clients was the composer Hector Berlioz. And in Chapter Nine of this book there's a story about a gentleman named Francisco Ferrer y Guardia from Barcelona, whose life and death are well documented.

But most of my clients were once simply ordinary citizens liv-ing fascinating lives. The majority of the lives I've explored are quite recent (the last two hundred years), and that's reflected in the examples in the book. They're often a little "fresher" and more likely to still impact the soul, whereas the traumas from a lifetime a thousand years ago are more likely to have been resolved by now.

Though I think I've encountered only three lives that took place in Moravia (a region in the Czech Republic), two of them are cited in this book. This, and the frequency that World War I and Prussian troops appear, is coincidence rather than design.

My clients are predominantly women, but as you'll see from their past lives, they've been male as often as they've been female. The reason more women than men are drawn to explore their spirituality through a psychic is largely cultural.

A tragic consequence of our world's violent past is that rape and torture come up in past lives with depressing regularity. Almost all of us have been the victims of atrocities in times of war. If you're an old soul, with scores of lives behind you, it's virtually inevitable.

There's no escaping the fact that humans can inflict horrendous cruelty upon one another. I've spared most of the goriest details when describing past-life tortures and suchlike, but there are times when it's important to expose the reality of cruelty to help understand the present. I also feel it's important not to hide the truth of death and destruction behind bland euphemisms like "collateral damage."

There are books on past lives in which people spend an inordinate amount of time hunting down the person they once were. They seek out graveyards and parish records, hoping to validate the insights they received from a regression.

What I've found is that, though it can be exciting to find your name on a gravestone somewhere, it doesn't necessarily help you deal with the impact of the life itself.

I prefer to show my clients how a little research into the period in history or the geographical location can be much more useful.

What is most important is to recognize the signs of your past-life fears and use the exercises included in the book to heal your soul from the traumas of its previous incarnations. These exercises may seem simple in theory, but they are extremely powerful in practice. I ask that you suspend any disbelief you may have long enough to try them and see.

The ultimate goal of doing the work in this book is to connect with the transformational goals, and thereby transition from Stage Three Consciousness to Stage Four Consciousness—to take part in the Transformation that is happening all around us. Along the way, you will come to understand three "universal truths," that all consciousness is connected, that cause and effect are inseparable, and that all life is sacred.

A DECLARATION OF INTENT

The exercises that appear throughout the book were given to me by my Causal spirit guides. They're designed to stimulate the motivation related to each transformational goal.

In my spirit guides' world, nothing is mandatory. During my sessions, they offer suggestions, not orders (in fact, they begin almost every sentence to me with the words, "We suggest . . . "), and the same applies here.

All the exercises in this book are simply suggestions. Whether you follow them or not is your choice. But if you want the process to work, then I'd strongly urge you to take the time to complete them.

After you complete each exercise, it's always a good idea to thank your spirit guides and tell them "session over," to make sure you don't continue with your day in an altered state.

The first exercise is simple. It's to write a Declaration of Intent.

. . . .

DECLARING YOUR INTENT

The purpose of this declaration is to promise your soul that you'll do everything within your power to bring your conscious self and your soul into a place of harmony.

It can be one line or a paragraph, whatever works for you.

One of my clients wrote the following Declaration of Intent. I liked it so much, I asked her to let me use it as an example.

Dear Soul,

I promise to work diligently on achieving my life plan, so I can be in total peace and harmony with you.

With the guidance and instructions of my spirit guides, I will remain steadfast on my quest to live the life you intended for me.

You can borrow this, or create your own. I suggest you put it in a place where you'll see it at least once a day.

Dear Soul,

_____

_____

_____

_____

_____

....

Now that you've set the intention, let's get down to work and explore the first of the past-life fears and how you can overcome its effects to help you recognize your equality and increase your sense of self-worth.

CHAPTER TWO

THE SENSE OF EQUALITY
Overcoming the Illusion of Separation

GOAL Equality
MOTIVATION Identification
FEAR Authority

THE ABUSE OF AUTHORITY

There's nothing like a trial for witchcraft to create a long-lasting fear of Authority. Being hauled in front of a courtroom, facing terrifying accusations, and then being dragged off to be tortured and executed are major traumas to the soul.

I don't come across trials for sorcery too often in my work. And when I do, they don't seem to end in burning half as much as strangulation. Unfortunately, torture seems to be the common thread.

In a past life, Valerie lived in a small town in Cornwall, England. She was a young widow named Jane, whose husband had been drowned at sea. The first inkling she got that she might be about to face accusations of witchcraft came when the neighbors began shunning her.

Afraid for her life, Jane tried to leave the town during the night. Her attempt to escape only added to everyone's conviction that she was guilty. After a typically one-sided trial, in which ludicrous "evidence" of her guilt was presented, she was imprisoned, tortured, and hanged.

"I was born on Halloween," Valerie joked. "My mom used to call me her little witch." But the conversation turned more serious when she began to tell me how the life in Cornwall had impacted her in the present. Valerie had always been afraid of her neighbors. "They're all really good people," she told me. But they made her so uncomfortable that she would drive a mile down the road to jog or to walk the dog.

"Every evening the neighbors would hang out and chat," Valerie said. "My son called it the 'witching hour.' I'd have to wait until they went inside before I could even go to the mailbox."

Like many people who have been hanged, Valerie thought she had a thyroid problem. During our session she said, "I can't handle any pressure on my throat—not even a sheet across it. When I get stressed, my throat swells up and I choke."

Many people feel a big shift take place as soon as a past-life trauma is uncovered. When we next spoke, Valerie's throat issue had cleared up completely. "It happened instantly—as soon as you told me about that past life," she told me. And after a lifetime of being afraid of anyone in a position of authority—the school principal or superiors at work—she no longer experiences any stress from being in their presence. She recently relocated and hasn't the slightest worry about jogging in her new neighborhood.

Facing people in authority can be a huge source of anxiety for many people. I have a client who gets dry mouth going through Customs even though he has nothing to hide. Another client turns into a stammering wreck when she has to deal with her superiors.

And I have one who told me she bursts into tears when she gets pulled over by a cop.

When you encounter authority in this life, your soul remembers an episode in your past when a confrontation with those in a position of power massively impacted your life plan. It might well have resulted in imprisonment, torture, or death.

The fear puts you in a subordinate position. It diminishes your sense of equality. In older souls it can cause feelings of inadequacy or inferiority, or even the belief that you are less worthy of happiness or fulfillment than others.

In younger souls, this sense of inequality often results in discrimination based on race, gender, and religion. When these less experienced souls feel inferior, it's not unusual for them to redress the balance by finding someone "lesser" to dominate, thus elevating their own sense of worth.

THE ILLUSION OF AUTHORITY

When younger souls in thrall to the Illusion find themselves elevated to a position of authority, there's always a danger they'll unconsciously use it as payback for times when they, themselves, have felt abused.

It's why you get people like Texas Judge Sharon Keller, who refused to allow a new trial for a man convicted of rape and murder, even though DNA evidence showed he was not guilty.

"We can't give new trials to everyone who establishes after conviction that they might be innocent," she said.

The subtext reads, "I was just like him once in a previous life, and no one lifted a finger to help me."

After you overcome your fear of Authority, you'll get a feeling of equality, and that will create a deep sense of self-worth. It will allow you to be in the presence of any other person, regardless of his or her status, without feeling inadequate in any way.

Equality stems from the recognition that we're all souls on the inside. It is a natural result of breaking through the Illusion and seeing that regardless of your circumstances, you are intrinsically equal to every other soul on the face of the planet.

When you recognize that no matter how people present themselves they are no better or worse than you, and you'll see right through the Illusion of authority. Once this happens, it doesn't matter how imposing the uniform, how big the office desk, or how many credentials after the name. You'll simply see the person as a human being just like you.

Equality is a lesson that all souls eventually learn. It's achieved by continually returning to the Physical Plane, lifetime after lifetime, until you recognize that rank, status, and wealth have nothing to do with who you really are.

When your soul first arrived here at the beginning of its many incarnations, it found the world a scary place. It was noisy, brash, and on top of everything else, you looked around and saw superficially huge differences everywhere.

Discrimination means making a distinction about people, either favorably or unfavorably, based on their nationality, skin color, religion, class, or other superficial grouping, rather than on their behavior.

When you were a young soul, you were drawn to other humans who looked like you, spoke like you, and believed what you believed. Like all younger souls, you sought out the safety of the Illusion.

Acting more from a place of fear than love, younger souls want their gods to be strong, their churches authoritarian, their laws draconian, and their social structures rigid. As I discuss in *The Instruction,* it helps them to feel safe in a world that they don't fully understand.

In the young-soul worldview, there are huge differences between genders, races, religions, and nations. Stereotyping others makes younger souls feel superior in a world they've not fully learned to trust. Women are virgins or whores; anyone who doesn't follow the word of God is an infidel or heathen; members of other races may be backward, dishonest, arrogant, or stupid; and your country, whichever it might be, is specially blessed by God.

Over many incarnations, your soul bounces from one part of the world to the next, picking up experience as it goes. By the time it completes all its lives on the Physical Plane, it will have learned what it's like to have been male, female, affluent, poor, black, white, brown, Muslim, Christian, Buddhist, atheist, heterosexual, homosexual, and everything else that will help it to understand that no matter who we are, we are all equal.

And when it comes to authority, every one of us will learn important lessons in equality—both as perpetrator and victim of discrimination.

BREAKING THROUGH THE BARRIER OF ILLUSION

Only when we completely step out from behind the Illusion—the barrier between our physical and spiritual selves—will we truly recognize that we are all one. And we'll learn that when we mock another race, treat followers of another religion as inferior, or deny a particular group of people the same rights we expect for ourselves, we diminish ourselves.

Torturers can only brutalize another human being as long as they are unable to identify with the victim and his or her suffering.

Soldiers can only kill someone as long as that person is seen as a lesser human being. (Military training is dehumanizing for that very reason.)

....

DEHUMANIZING THE ENEMY

A soldier who steps out of the Illusion and identifies with the enemy is the last thing an army needs. He is trained to stay firmly behind the Illusion of discrimination. His world is designed to be one of rigid hierarchy, in which each person obeys the one above without question, and where the enemy is reduced to being a rag-head, a haji, a gook, a Jap, a Hun, or an animal.

....

Under cover of the Illusion, whole groups of people will confidently express their contempt for another group of people. And though it may make an individual feel more certain about his or her opinion when it's reinforced by a million other similar opinions, it doesn't make it right.

In 1959, Richard and Mildred Loving were arrested in Virginia. Their crime? Being married. The problem was that one was black, the other white. They were charged with a felony and forbidden to be together in that state for twenty-five years.

Public opinion at the time was strongly against interracial marriage. Georgia law declared that such unions were, "productive of evil, and evil only." Almost every state has had a ban on interracial marriage on its statute books at some time.

When the Mormon Church got behind California's Proposition 8, in 2008, its followers donated millions of dollars to change the state constitution to prevent gays and lesbians from getting married. The proposition was passed by a small margin.

There's nothing like having the backing of a large organization to validate a person's own bigotry. The power of authority to manipulate opinions and beliefs can never be underestimated.

A spark of intolerance toward another section of the community can be fanned into a raging firestorm by the voice of authority playing to popular fears. The part played by the Mormon Church was, quite simply, an abuse of authority.

Many Proposition 8 proponents believe that their opposition to gay and lesbian marriage was right. It was supported by the majority and enshrined into law, but that doesn't mean their behavior was supported spiritually.

Gays and lesbians may not have been rounded up and shot or sent to detention camps, but they were persecuted, nonetheless. It is no more spiritual for a church in 2008 to lobby against the rights of gays and lesbians than it was for a church to oppose interracial marriage in the 1950s. Discrimination is discrimination whether it's dressed up in the guise of "protecting marriage" or "protecting the white race."

The inability of some people to recognize the intrinsic equality of gays and lesbians made Proposition 8 possible. The same kind of discrimination kept a ban on interracial marriages on the books until 1972.

As the Collective Consciousness rises and more people step out from behind the veil of the Illusion, the opponents of same-sex marriage will, in just a few years' time, appear as antiquated and flat-out wrong as opponents of interracial marriage do to us now.

JUDGING A BOOK BY ITS
(SOMETIMES SHABBY) COVER

It was a blustery evening in San Francisco when I finally found a parking spot big enough for my '47 Chevy. I took the tartan blanket I used to cover the torn fabric on the back seat and rolled it up under my arm. I zipped up the old jacket I'd inherited from my dad when he started shrinking into old age and stepped out into the chilly summer night. (As Mark Twain reportedly said, "The coldest winter I ever saw was the summer I spent in San Francisco.")

I was a busy illustrator back then, living the bachelor life on a houseboat in the picturesque town of Sausalito, just north of the Golden Gate Bridge. I was in the city to attend a Learning Annex class on past-life regression, with a view to better understanding myself—and meeting women.

The registration form said to wear comfortable clothing and bring a pillow or blanket because we'd be lying down for much of the class while undergoing regression. I looked down at my old gray sweatpants flapping in the wind and figured they might be paint-spattered, but they certainly were comfortable.

I ran my fingers through my hair, trying to stop it lashing my face in the wind. I just needed to get some cash before heading over to the Crowne Plaza Hotel for the class. After popping into a café to pick up a coffee to go, I spotted an ATM across the road.

There's something I've noticed happens a lot with me. I'm always inadvertently cutting in front of people in line. I'm the guy who wanders up to a vacant ticket office only to be told there's a line. I'll turn and see two hundred people who weren't there a moment ago, scowling menacingly at me.

This evening was no exception. I walked up to the machine and stood, hunched up against the wind, a few feet behind a cute blonde in a business suit. After a minute or two, she took her cash, popped it in her purse and turned, looking startled to see me standing there. I gave her a smile and made toward the ATM. "Get away from me!" she barked.

I was temporarily stunned. I stepped back a few feet and babbled something incoherent like, "I . . . bu . . . bu . . . ah . . . " She looked me up and down in disgust and strutted off, casting a backward glance every so often to make sure I wasn't following her.

I shuffled up to the ATM and took my wallet out of my pocket, trying not to spill my coffee or drop my blanket. A voice behind me said sharply, "Hey, there's a line!"

I looked behind me and saw three or four people waiting at the curb. Sheepishly, I went over and joined them. I smiled apologetically to one of them, and he quickly looked away.

Five minutes later I walked across to the hotel, and that was when I caught sight of myself in a shop window. If I'd been asked to illustrate a homeless guy for the cover of the *Bay Guardian,* I wouldn't have had to look far for reference. It was me.

My hair, which I'd grown long, was everywhere, and my rosacea had flared up earlier that day, giving a blotchy effect to my complexion. My clothes were old, dirty, and ill fitting. On top of that, I looked like I had my bed rolled up under my arm and a begging cup in my hand.

Suddenly it all made sense. That woman had thought I was a homeless person. And it struck me that she had behaved so rudely not because I was standing a little too close to her, but because she had a problem with who I was. "That stupid, ignorant &%^\$#@!" I muttered to myself. If anyone had witnessed my little outburst it would only have confirmed any preconceptions they might have had about me.

I was angry. To begin with, I had a kind of "how dare she treat me like that" attitude. Then it morphed into a kind of "how dare she treat *anyone* like that" attitude. In a matter of seconds, I became a defiant champion of the city's scruffy underclass.

Later that evening, after a regression to a town in thirteenth-century Bavaria and a lesson in not going back to a destructive relationship out of guilt, I passed a panhandler on the way to my car.

"Spare a little change?" he asked.

"Here," I said, handing him a twenty-dollar bill.

As I walked away, I thought to myself, "We underdogs need to take care of each other."

This experience reminded me that we humans have a tendency to make snap decisions based on superficial impressions. Judging people by appearances is far from spiritual. By remembering that we're all souls beneath the skin, we can learn to recognize the humanity in all of us.

LITTLE FLEAS NEED LITTLER FLEAS

It's an unfortunate aspect of the Illusion that no matter where we are on the socioeconomic ladder, we can always find someone to look down on.

India has its caste system, where Brahmins look down on the Kshatriyas, and they look down on the Vaisyas, who in turn look down on the Sudras. And everyone looks down on the outcasts, the Dalits. Even within the Dalits there's a hierarchy, in which Bhangis are regarded as outcasts among the outcasts.

In Britain a person who would regard the caste system as absurd will judge others by their accent and schooling. Eton graduates look down on Winchester graduates, who look down on grammar school graduates.

In America, it's got a lot more to do with money. The Rockefellers look down on the Vanderbilts, who look down on . . . okay, only kidding. But there can be little doubt that America has its own class system, and it's one based on the almighty dollar.

The more people are in thrall to the Illusion, the more they perceive differences between themselves and others. Depending on how strongly they're affected, they can manifest symptoms ranging from mild social snobbery to overt racism.

Looking down on another human or group of humans gives many individuals a sense of superiority. Whether the reason for feeling superior is economic, racial, religious, gender-based, or tribal, it's always in direct conflict with the soul's goal of Equality.

Your soul sees every other soul as an equal. Obviously there are Physical Plane inequalities. Queen Elizabeth is doing vastly better in many ways than the panhandler I encountered in San Francisco. Yet she has a soul that is no better or worse than any other soul, and she deserves to be treated as such.

SOUL-LEVEL EQUALITY

The belief that certain groups of people are better or worse than others is purely a result of the Illusion. There is no "master race" or "chosen people."

Advocates of white supremacy or believers in a superior caste, better class, or any other kind of exceptionalism, are simply in thrall to the Illusion. We are all equal on a soul level.

Under the influence of the Illusion, younger souls particularly use a position of authority to get a transient feeling of superiority from abusing that authority.

One night in London during the 1980s I parked my car in a temporary lot on a construction site. An elderly man in a peaked cap took my money and reminded me to be back before he locked the gate at midnight.

At the stroke of twelve, I came trotting around the corner, hoping I hadn't left it too late. In the distance I could see the attendant closing the gate. I got up to him and panted something about how glad I was to have caught him before he went home.

"Sorry, Mate, we're closed," he said, turning the key in the padlock. A few feet away I could see my car sitting there, the only vehicle left in the place.

"But surely you can let me get my car out," I gasped.

"You'll have to come back in the morning," he said, turning his back on me. I couldn't quite believe he was being so petty. I thought perhaps he didn't understand the situation.

"That's my car right there," I said.

"And it'll still be there in the morning," he laughed.

I spent the next two or three minutes arguing with him. I was livid. He was calm and, in my opinion, really enjoyed watching me getting mad.

There's a word they use in Britain for someone like him. It's "Jobsworth," and it's one I used several times (though it was undoubtedly counterproductive) in my futile attempts to get him to see reason.

A Jobsworth is someone, usually a petty official, who refuses to bend the rules, claiming, "It's more than my job's worth." Though I don't recall my adversary actually using the phrase, he clearly wasn't going to break the rules for me. And that was that.

What really got to me was how he found the situation amusing. I can still picture the smirk beneath his little gray mustache. I walked home fuming about his intransigence and even called a girlfriend to tell her about this grave miscarriage of justice. At the time (1:30 a.m.), she seemed oddly unsympathetic.

The old guy behaved like a real jerk, but you know what? So did I. Would the situation have been different if I'd been more respect-ful? I could have treated him as a fellow human being instead of calling him by the pejorative "Jobsworth." I could have been more sympathetic to an elderly man who'd been standing in the cold for hours waiting to go home. It might not have changed the outcome, but it would definitely have stopped me from diminishing myself by forgetting our shared humanity.

....

IDENTIFICATION EXERCISE 1
TEN PEOPLE JUST LIKE YOU

The exercise that follows is deceptively simple. It's designed to remind you that we're all equal. You can have fun with it—I did. But it has a serious aspect to it, too. It will stimulate the motivation of Identification and help you to see that we're all souls beneath the skin.

Invite your spirit guides in with the following request: "I call upon my spirit guides, acting in my highest interest, to help me reach the transformational goal of Equality."

- Make a list of ten people, famous or otherwise.
- Close your eyes and picture them, one at a time, in their underwear.
- In your journal, write a "brief" description of the kind of undies each one is wearing.

Horace Mann said, "Education is the great equalizer." And maybe it is. But so is picturing your boss in Mickey Mouse boxers.

After completing this exercise, one of my clients wrote to me saying, "This was a very sneaky way of the guides coaxing me to accept my body! Forcing myself to look at ten naked people made me realize that I do accept my body more than I ever did before. The exercise also showed me that I could look at these other bodies with acceptance—not comparing, resenting, or wishing. They are what they are, and so am I."

Petty or unreasonable behavior from a Jobsworth who has achieved a position of power can trigger deep resentments within us. A past-life fear of Authority can be triggered by such an encounter. It may be related to a trial for a trivial offense that resulted in harsh punishment many lifetimes ago.

A run-in with a Jobsworth can be frustrating. But it can be so much worse when lives are at stake. Imagine a mother facing bureaucratic intransigence and indifference while searching for her missing son during Argentina's "Dirty War" of the late 1970s.

The karmic consequences of the abuse of authority are significant, which is why I come across it so often with my clients. It takes courage to stand up to authority. But when you do, and you allow your soul to be your guide, you make a huge leap in terms of your spiritual evolution.

During a past-life exploration, I took a nurse named Vanessa on a journey to South Africa during the Second Boer War, sometime around the year 1900.

As a young Dutch man in that life, Vanessa was forced to witness the horrors of war at close hand. When he and a group of fighters raided a small farm, his best friend was shot and fell to the ground with half his head missing.

The young man knew in that instant that he couldn't take another life. Inside the farmhouse, two children and their badly wounded mother huddled in a corner. Two older men, his superiors, told him to shoot them. He dropped his rifle and silently refused to obey the order.

After repeatedly, and angrily, demanding that he kill the family, one of the men, his uncle, shot him in the head, then turned his gun on the mother and her children.

The trauma of his friend's death had connected him instantly with his soul's core value of Equality. He identified with the mother and children as fellow humans, not the enemy.

Suddenly, he was, as my spirit guides put it, "following orders higher than military." There was no way he could kill another person, even when his own life was at risk.

Vanessa has some strong feelings about the abuse of authority in this present life. Like many people with similar past-life experiences, she automatically supports the underdog. At the time we spoke, she was looking for volunteer nursing opportunities abroad, a reaction against the for-profit system she felt she could no longer be a part of.

A lesson learned over a century ago in South Africa impacts her to this day. She saw, in a flash of awareness, the equality that unites us on a soul level, and recognized that when authority is abused, there is no spiritual imperative to obey.

SUPPORTING YOUR FELLOW SOULS

The antidote your soul offers to cure the effects of a fear of Authority is the motivation of Identification. It impels you to see yourself and every other person on the planet as equals.

It will allow you to identify with the underdogs. That will give you the impetus to help them, as you hope would happen if your positions were reversed. Doing so leads to strong feelings of increased self-worth and an immediate dissipation of the fear itself.

The moment I told Meredith that she'd had a life as a young, male Spanish architect she said, "I always wanted to be an architect!" Uncovering what happened in that life made a huge impact on her. She said it had been like "drawing a card and jumping four steps."

Meredith told me later, "Understanding the source of my fears has absolutely altered me. I've really settled down. I've even lost weight since we talked. What's weird is that I kind of remembered this stuff, but until I got confirmation, it didn't seem real."

The architect, Federico, made a huge mistake in his twenties that would ultimately ruin his life. He took government money he'd been given to design a new building and spent it on women and rich living. It wasn't long before someone noticed he hadn't put pen to paper.

With the authorities after him, Federico hightailed it to Cuba, where he lived for the next fifteen years. When he felt it would be safe, he returned to Spain around the age of forty, disguising himself by shaving off his beard and wearing spectacles. Unfortunately, he was soon recognized and arrested.

The authorities were merciless and threw Federico into a prison cell to await trial. He'd died in prison in his previous life and had developed a huge fear of incarceration.

After being held in a relatively large room, Federico was transferred to a tiny cell following the court's sentence. When he saw the cramped, dingy cell that was to be his new home, Federico's fear spiraled into full-blown panic, and he died of a heart attack, which, mercifully, saved him from decades of isolation and deprivation.

When I asked Meredith if anything resonated strongly with her, she said, "I was watching a TV show about a prison, and I told my husband, 'I'd die of a heart attack if I was ever imprisoned.'

"I can't stand bear hugs or having my arms pinned down," she continued. "I've always felt that I'd die if I were handcuffed."

In this life, Meredith makes sure she doesn't fall foul of authority. "I've never taken so much as a pencil from a job," she told me.

SPIRITUAL ACT 1: SUPPORTING THE UNDERDOG

Spiritual Acts are things you do to help those less fortunate than yourself. More specifically, they are ways to help people who are going through negative experiences you yourself have experienced in previous incarnations. Spiritual Acts are major steps in healing your soul from the effects of past-life traumas.

The motivation of Identification urges you to remember that you're no different from the next person. When you come across someone who's suffering as you did, perhaps many lifetimes ago, your soul will remind you that you were once like that

Energetically, when you carry out a Spiritual Act, you offer love. And due to the reciprocal nature of Spiritual Acts, you get love back. (That's why giving feels as good as, or even better, than receiving.)

By supporting the underdog, you help both of you to grow. A Spiritual Act might be a small act of charity or something you devote your life to.

There are many organizations such as Food Not Bombs and Oxfam International that actively assist life's less fortunate individuals and families. You should have no difficulty finding one that resonates with you and that could use your support.

I told Meredith how a past-life fear of Authority motivates people to support less fortunate members of society.

"I'm a real champion of the underdog," she said. "I work at a construction company where I've spent years watching my boss lie, cheat, and hold off paying people until they settle for seventy-five cents on the dollar.

"I've stayed in the job to make sure there's someone there to look after the contractors' interests. There's been so much drama over the years. I'd fight and yell trying to get my boss to do the right thing. I've even taken twenty-dollar bills out of my own pocket and stapled them to paychecks with a note of thanks."

Meredith's concern for others is evident in her activities outside of work, too. "I used to cook meals for the homeless, and I set up a group to help kids at grade school who'd lost parents through death or divorce. I support an organization that helps homeless kids. I buy food and bedding for them.

"I'm always giving money to people. I feel we're all just a few steps from homelessness. The other day I was in the mall with my husband. I gave someone a dollar, and he said, 'There's five-hundred thousand people in the mall. You can't give to them all.'

"I said, 'I can try!'"

RECOGNIZING YOUR EQUALITY

The Nobel Prize-winning physicist Richard Feynman (who is one of my heroes, as you'll discover at the end of the book) was raised by a father who taught him important lessons in equality.

When Richard was a little boy, his father would sit him on his knee while he read the *New York Times*. "Now look at all these humans," he'd say. "Here's one human standing, and all these others are bowing. Now, what's the difference? This one is the Pope.

But he has the same human problems. He eats dinner like everyone else. He goes to the bathroom. He's a human being."

Feynman's father knew what he was talking about. He was in the uniform business. He saw five-star generals in their BVDs.

When you get to know someone as a friend, you start to see him or her as an equal. The exercise that follows will stimulate your motivation of Identification and help you recognize that celebrity, like rank and status, is part of the Illusion.

....

IDENTIFICATION EXERCISE 2

PLAYING WITH CELEBS

This exercise is about visualizing yourself sharing an activity you enjoy with a celebrity you admire. The purpose is to see yourself as his or her equal. It will help you to accept that you are no less important a human being than anyone else.

It goes like this: Choose a celebrity with whom you share an interest. Then visualize yourself hanging out, playing, and generally having fun with that person.

I'll give you two examples to give you an idea of how this works.

Example 1

Interest: Golf

Celebrity: Tiger Woods

Visualization: Close your eyes and picture yourself playing a round of golf with Tiger. Imagine laughing over some silly jokes, discussing your vacation plans, showing each other photos of your family, and giving one another tips on how to improve your game. (Try not to mention the scandal that rocked his career at the end of 2009. He's still touchy about it!)

Example 2

Interest: Singing

Celebrity: Madonna

Visualization: Close your eyes and picture yourself onstage with Madonna, taking turns singing verses, and joining together for choruses. Laugh and hug backstage as you compliment each other on a great show before dashing past the paparazzi and adoring fans into the back of Madonna's limo.

Step 1: Choose an interest.

Step 2: Choose a celebrity.

Step 3: Close your eyes and say, "I call upon my spirit guides acting in my highest interest to help me visualize playing with_____."

Step 4: Picture a location where you're most likely to meet your celebrity. Begin by hugging that person like an old friend. Start having fun!

Step 5: When you've finished, give your celeb a big hug and invite him or her to play with you again sometime.

It's through firsthand experience that the soul learns that the president of the United States is not intrinsically more or less valuable a human being than a janitor in Kiev or a prostitute in Kowloon.

And it's this deep sense of equality that makes it possible to undertake the next significant part of your soul's voyage to Stage Four Consciousness: Cooperation.

CHAPTER THREE

THE REWARDS OF COOPERATION
Building Spiritual Bridges

GOAL Cooperation

MOTIVATION Participation

FEAR Loss

I WORRY I COULD LOSE EVERYTHING

Shortly after she became the mother of twins, Carlotta would wake up screaming several nights a week, often more than once, having dreamt that something terrible had happened to her children.

"It was this constant, nagging fear," she told me. "It got my husband rattled, too. He always said I was psychic, so when I started having the dreams, he thought they might be premonitions."

Fortunately, Carlotta's dreams were not glimpses of the future but reminders of a past life in which her entire family was slaughtered, in their home, by Viking raiders.

The fear created in that life was one of Loss, and it was triggered by the appearance of the twins. It's a fear that's surprisingly common. Very few of us are untouched by its long-lasting impact on our souls.

Do you have an underlying feeling of uncertainty about the future? Do you worry you could wake up and everything you have could be gone?

A fear of Loss has its origins in a previous lifetime in which you lost your nearest and dearest, your home, your community, or even your way of life. It can manifest as a mild sense of insecurity or a constant, nagging worry about losing your job or home.

In some people the fear can trigger nightmares about losing their children or partner, or a reluctance to take risks in case something terrible happens. They may become anxious when their spouse is late arriving home. Their deep sense of uncertainty can be immobilizing.

If a catastrophe in a previous incarnation left you without security, sufficiency, or love, then a fear of Loss will result. Perhaps you had to go it alone, lacking adequate food or shelter, with no other humans to call upon for support. In this life you'll have the awareness that anything could happen.

The triggers include such things as unwelcome change in childhood (divorce, relocation, or losing a family member). And the fear can surface in adulthood when you lose a job or a partner, or when someone you love dies. It can even be triggered by losing a beloved pet.

Though one significant incident is often all it takes to bring it into play, multiple triggers can cause the fear to keep increasing. Being an army brat who has to continually move from one place to the next is just the kind of upbringing to make a past-life fear of Loss take center stage in your life.

....

LOSING YOUR SENSE OF PERMANENCE

Richard Feynman, the physicist I mentioned in Chapter Two, worked in Los Alamos on the development of the nuclear bomb during World War II.

When he returned to "civilization," he would sit in a restaurant in New York and picture the kind of damage a Hiroshima-size bomb would inflict on Manhattan.

Feynman's work at Los Alamos and the recent death of his wife had conspired to trigger his past-life fear of Loss. He said, "I would see people building a bridge, or they'd be making a new road, and I thought, they're *crazy,* they just don't understand, they don't *understand.* Why are they making new things? It's so useless."

. . . .

By far the most common resonance associated with a fear of Loss is the need to "travel light" through life. I have clients with this fear who own virtually nothing; their underlying feeling is one of "the less I have, the less I have to lose."

In extreme cases, people with this fear will have a natural tendency to become reclusive. They don't want to get too attached to people for the same reason they don't like to have too many possessions. Having close friends means risking huge emotional upset if you lose them.

Needless to say, the fear is irrational. It's purely a result of experiences that happened long ago in your soul's past. There is, however, a cure.

The cure for a fear of Loss is the motivation of Participation. The more you get involved with others and work toward a common goal, the more you connect to the transformational goal of Cooperation.

When you do this, you cause the fear of Loss to dissipate. You'll find yourself with less anxiety about the future, and you'll be better able to reach out to others for support when you need it.

....

SIGNS OF A PAST-LIFE FEAR OF LOSS

A fear of Loss creates a feeling that you could lose everything almost overnight. (Roughly eight out of ten people with this fear prefer to have as little in the way of material possessions as possible.) The following quotes are from clients of mine who manifest this fear:

- When people come to my house, they ask, "Does anyone live here?"
- I was terrified something awful would happen to my kids.
- I hate stuff. It makes me anxious.
- I've never saved for a rainy day.
- My hero was Robinson Crusoe.
- I don't get attached to things.
- Everything I owned could have gone in one bag.
- I used to say the fewer people I love, the less I have to lose.
- When the phone rang at night, my body would turn to water.
- I'm a minimalist.

One of my clients asked me if I could tell her anything about her adult son. My spirit guides said he had a huge fear of Loss. When I described the typical symptoms, she said, "From the time he was a little boy, he never wanted Christmas presents. He still doesn't. He's a total minimalist."

There are, of course, exceptions to the rule. Some souls with a past-life fear of Loss become packrats and hoard possessions as a kind of security blanket.

....

When you overcome a fear of Loss, you lose the sense that all you have could evaporate overnight, and it becomes a lot easier to plan for the future when you feel secure about there actually being one.

It's through the motivation of Participation that you'll gain the sense of being connected to the Soul World. You'll become less an observer of life and more actively involved in shaping your own life. You'll lose the sense that you have no one to rely on but yourself.

In a world of increasing uncertainty, the fear of Loss is surfacing like never before. In older souls, the fear creates doubt and worry. In younger souls, and those heavily impacted by the Illusion, the fear results in increased self-interest, greed, and the accumulation of wealth.

In those souls, the idea of cooperation may seem absurd. They measure achievement and success in material terms. Lacking the ability to see themselves as part of the Soul World, they hoard money and possessions for fear of not having enough. Cooperation means sacrifice, and that's something they won't do willingly.

• • •

Approximately 55,000 years ago, when *Homo sapiens* made the last great Transformation from a Stage Two to a Stage Three Consciousness, cooperation was as natural as breathing. Our survival had everything to do with our ability to work together peacefully.

Despite what you might imagine, life in the tribe back then was not all pushing, shoving, and "might makes right." Our species never would have made it to this point if it had been.

If the biggest and strongest (adult males) had feasted themselves on the day's kill around the campfire, while the weaker ones (women and children) were forced to rely on any scraps that came their way, the tribe would soon have died out.

When we underwent the last Transformation, we were very much connected to our souls, which meant that we acted according to our souls' core values more than we do now. Seeing the world through the lens of Cooperation meant everyone worked together for mutual benefit.

Cooperation is our natural state. It's what drew our primitive ancestors together to form tribes, and it's what made that communal kind of living successful.

As the Transformation picks up speed, Cooperation will once again unite us as it did in the past. This time, thanks to our greater intellect and soon-to-be-stronger connection to the Soul World, the Illusion will dissipate, making the change permanent.

Cooperation can be seen everywhere in nature: from the tiny bird who steps inside the jaws of a crocodile to scavenge scraps of food from between its teeth, to the colonies of ants in which each member has a specific role in the running of things.

Whether Cooperation is symbiotic—in which lunch is offered in return for dental care—or simply to ensure the survival of the species, it's an integral part of most creatures' hard wiring.

As a core value, Cooperation was first introduced to us in its current form during that last Transformation. As our species grew into its new consciousness, the core value of Cooperation allowed us to create well-functioning tribes in which everyone pulled together in an atmosphere of mutual support.

This "all for one, one for all" attitude lasted for thousands of years and was one of the major secrets of our species' rise to success.

What changed, and why Cooperation is no longer our default mode, was that the Illusion began to exert a stronger influence. In our world, there's far less Cooperation and a lot more self-interest and greed because of it.

Cooperation is, in some ways, the most significant of the ten core values. When our innate sense of being in this world together began to erode under the Illusion, it opened the door for all the other core values to become blocked.

As our species evolved, we began to make a huge impact on the world around us. Yet, as we did, we gradually lost the very thing that allowed us to thrive for so long.

The more we humans became disconnected from one another, the more we began to slip behind the Illusion. And, of course, vice versa. Instead of sharing what we had, we became protective of what we considered to be ours and envious of what others had.

The result of this lack of mutual Cooperation was isolation. Certain individuals learned to take advantage of others and gain more of the tribe's wealth for themselves. But it came at a cost. No longer cooperating equally, sharing the good times and the bad with everyone else, those individuals lost their connection to the tribe.

In a community in which everyone supported the needs of the tribe, each person had a clearly defined purpose. This gave our lives meaning, and it's one of the major reasons why regaining connection with the tribe is so important.

Once the Illusion took its grip, isolation grew. Feeling less connected to the needs of others led to greed and the accumulation of more than was needed for one's self. Blinded by the Illusion, our ancestors were unable to imagine the long–term consequences of short-term greed.

Now, 55,000 years after the first big shift in consciousness, the current Transformation will draw us back into the tribe by helping us see ourselves as part of the whole. When we do, we'll finally break the grip of the Illusion and realize that if our species has a future it must be one of Cooperation.

KICK THEIR ASS AND STEAL THEIR GAS

The spiritual perspective on the issue of Cooperation is that if we could share our wealth more equally, we'd all feel a lot more secure as a result. Yet, for those who are stuck behind the Illusion, their sense of entitlement makes sacrifice an abomination.

You may have noticed that certain people have a huge sense of being special. They don't feel they have to abide by the rules they set for others. They seem to believe that what they want is what they should get. And it doesn't just happen on an individual level. It can happen to whole nations, too.

On a peace march shortly after the U.S. invasion of Iraq, I saw a sign that read, "Kick Their Ass and Steal Their Gas." It was carried by someone protesting America's attack on Iraq, and it was, of course, meant to be ironic.

But kicking their ass and stealing their gas was exactly what was happening. According to Paul Wolfowitz, the U.S. deputy defense secretary at the time and one of the prime architects of the war, Iraq is a country "swimming on an ocean of oil."

Of course, you're hardly likely to get the American population to rally behind a war by telling them their troops are going in there simply to steal that country's resources. You'd have to do better than that.

In the film *Why We Fight,* which explores the reasons for America's invasion of Iraq, there's a series of scenes in which various individuals try to answer the question, "What are we fighting for?" No one seems sure.

"I honestly don't have an answer."

"Continued freedom?"

"I think for ideals and what we believe in. At least I hope that's what it is."

"I'm not sure if we're fighting for the oil or not."

Much of this confusion is due to the fact that lies had to be created to cover the real reasons for the war. Was it because of 9/11? Saddam Hussein using weapons of mass destruction (WMDs) on his own people? Connections between Iraq and al-Qaeda? The need for regime change? The threat of an imminent mushroom cloud? Uranium from Niger? Stopping the spread of terrorism? No wonder people are confused.

According to Wolfowitz, "For reasons that have a lot to do with the U.S. government bureaucracy, we settled on the one issue that everyone could agree on: weapons of mass destruction."

But what gives the people of one country the right to march into another country and steal their resources? Spiritually, of course, the answer is clear: nothing. It only appears reasonable to those who can't see beyond the Illusion.

. . . .

WHEN THE ILLUSION BLOCKS EMPATHY

Back in 1996, Madeleine Albright, who was then the U.S. secretary of state, told interviewer Lesley Stahl that the sanctions, which had caused the death of 500,000 Iraqi children, were "worth it."

To be fair to Ms. Albright, she did apologize later. (Not for the sanctions responsible for half a million dead children, but for what she said.)

Not everyone involved thought the price was worth it. Two major figures, United Nations Assistant Director General Denis Halliday and his successor Hans von Sponeck disagreed strongly. Halliday resigned after thirty-four years of service saying the sanctions amounted to genocide.

Von Sponeck resigned after thirty years; he described the effects of sanctions as "deliberate strangulation."

From behind the Illusion, the death of half a million children might be "worth it." It might be hard, however, to find a grieving Iraqi mother who shares that sentiment.

....

When you're trapped behind the Illusion, people of other cultures are perceived as lesser beings. And if they're inferior, that makes you superior. When you combine that sense of superiority with the greed inspired by a fear of Loss, then the result is a belief that your needs outweigh those of anyone else.

In other words, being caught up in the Illusion makes it easy for one lot of people to exploit another. When whole groups of people come together under the bogus unity of the Illusion, they may exploit anyone who doesn't fit into a narrow spectrum of what they regard as "normal."

This happened in Nazi Germany where Jews were persecuted by those who considered themselves part of the "master race." It happened in South Africa under apartheid. It's happening in Israel where Palestinians are treated as less than equal.

And, however hard it may be to accept, it's happening in countries like Iraq, where the U.S. military is used to suppress objections to the theft of the country's oil, and in Afghanistan where, again, U.S. forces are employed to ensure access to oil and gas from the Caspian Basin.

Our capitalist system is built on greed and inequality. It allows for massive wealth for the few at the cost of massive poverty for the many. It is not designed to be fair. It is, unfortunately, the antithesis of Cooperation—one the most fundamental of the soul's core values.

Wall Street, for example, is an institution built on a foundation of greed. It wasn't set up to ensure everyone got a fairer shake or to redistribute the nation's wealth so everyone could benefit from

America's good fortune as one of the richest countries in history. Its purpose is to enrich the rich.

If you wanted to find an institution that is intrinsically at odds with the goal of Cooperation, Wall Street would be it.

In the 1980s movie Wall Street, the character Gordon Gekko coined the phrase "greed is good," a message that many of those behind the Illusion have taken to heart.

The solution to building a world free from greed is not some form of communism. It's a better form of democracy—one that favors individuals over soulless corporations. It's one in which wealth is more evenly distributed, and workers have greater ownership of the businesses they make possible.

In a Stage Four world, there will be no banks with the power to trash the economy through greed and recklessness. There will be no for-profit health-care system raking in billions of dollars while cooking up reasons to deny benefits. There will, in fact, be no capitalist system.

The world as we know it is straining under the weight of the Illusion. It quite simply has to change.

....

I'VE GOT MINE

When younger souls, and those most in thrall to the Illusion, have their past-life fear of Loss triggered, they tend to become reluctant to share what they've got. Curiously, the more they actually accumulate, the more unwilling they become to make any sacrifice.

When these people get really rich, they oppose taxes, take advantage of offshore tax dodges, and hire high-priced lobbyists and tax lawyers to rig the system in their favor. That is why Warren Buffet, the second richest man in the world, pays tax at a lower rate (17.7 percent) than his secretary (30 percent).

....

Another sign I saw on a peace march read, "How Did Our Oil End Up Under Their Sand?"

Good question.

When a country goes to war it's never for access to resources or to expand its empire. It's always to "spread democracy," "bring freedom to the masses," or "stop the spread of Communism, Socialism, terrorism," or some other threat to "our way of life."

And a war couldn't possibly be about oil. Only a cynic would dare suggest something as crass as that. That kind of naked greed would be totally unacceptable.

Yet, wherever the troops go, big business follows. Nothing is as profitable as war. Whether you're a corporation benefitting directly by starting a conflict, as United Fruit did in Guatemala, or indirectly by providing arms and resources, like Halliburton or Raytheon, war is good for the bottom line.

That brings us to the question, "How *did* our oil end up under their sand?" What quirk of fate resulted in the West's most desirable resource being buried deep underground in the Middle East?

After launching a war that has killed, at the time of this writing, more than a million human beings, Western companies are well on their way to taking over the production and shipping of Iraq's oil.

Though the official (and constantly shifting) reasons for the war in Iraq were to prevent the use of WMDs, to topple an evil dictator, and so on, the war turns out to have been about oil all along. (This is not a surprise to anyone who has studied Iraq's historical exploitation by the British and other imperial powers, or who has read the Downing Street Memo.)

....

THE DOWNING STREET MEMO

These minutes of a top-secret meeting between U.S. and British officials a year before the start of the Iraq War (in 2003), show that military action was inevitable.

The minutes include the phrase, "The intelligence and facts were being fixed around the policy." In other words, the decision had been made to invade Iraq. All that was required was the excuse.

According to one British official quoted in the memo, "It seemed clear that Bush had made up his mind to take military action, even if the timing was not yet decided. But the case was thin. Saddam was not threatening his neighbors, and his WMD capability was less than that of Libya, North Korea, or Iran."

The memo also includes the shocking statement, "Bush wanted to remove Saddam, through military action, justified by the conjunction of terrorism and WMD."

Remember, despite being phrased in the past tense, the minutes were written in 2002.

The karmic consequences for all those involved in manufacturing the Iraq War will follow their souls for many lifetimes to come.

....

Needless to say, America's oil didn't really end up under Iraq's sand; it just sometimes seems that way. But if you're a six-hundred-pound gorilla and someone over there has a banana, then what are you going to do? You're going to take it.

And if someone is sitting on top of 112 billion barrels of crude oil, what then? Sadly, those in thrall to the Illusion, fearing loss, simply take it.

This exploitation of others is not just a modern American phe-nomenon, of course. Throughout history, powerful countries have sought to dominate weaker ones. Under the effects of the Illusion, and the feelings of superiority it brings, technologically advanced countries have always believed in the civilizing effects of empire.

In other words, we may be taking your cotton, gold, tea, spices, tobacco, labor, land, and whatever else we can get our hands on cheaply, but we're giving you our religion, values, and (usually rather one-sided) laws. And you'd better be grate-ful for it.

As a result of the Illusion, technological superiority (big-ger guns and more effective forms of transport, for example) has always been equated with being more civilized—at least by those who see the world from behind the Illusion.

What has happened in Iraq and Afghanistan in recent years has happened throughout history. Alexander the Great, the Romans, the Mongols, the Ottomans, and dozens of other mighty empires plundered their way across the known world, justifying their greed, as imperial nations still do, by promising to bring with them a bet-ter way of life.

The Brits ran India for more than two hundred years with a mixture of arrogance and racial superiority. And today, as then, wherever the empire goes, exploitation is sure to follow.

What if no individual or group of individuals sought to domi-nate others? What if nations worked together to ensure adequate food, shelter, water, and working conditions for all, instead of looking after the interests of their most affluent, as happens now?

What if we returned to the way we were in the tribe, when we shared our wealth and resources? What if taking care of the less fortunate members of society was our priority?

The answer is that everyone would benefit. Cooperating with others, rather than taking advantage of them, would cause the Collective Consciousness to rise. That would lead to a greater sense of spiritual fulfillment and less reliance on the transient high of materialism.

As the Transformation carries us into a higher level of consciousness, more people will learn to draw out the motivation of Participation to reach the goal of Cooperation.

OVERCOMING THE DEMONS OF THE PAST

To give you an example of how the fear of Loss can be used as a force for good, I'd like to introduce you to one of the most complex and intriguing individuals of the twentieth century: Leo Szilard.

Szilard was the genius who discovered the secret of the chain reaction that led to the development of nuclear power.

At the end of World War I, the young Szilard left his home in Budapest to escape rising anti-Semitism and settled in Germany. There, he studied and worked with other great scientists, including Albert Einstein.

While in Berlin, he witnessed the rise of fascism under Adolf Hitler. Again facing persecution as a Jew, he fled to London for safety. Shortly before the outbreak of World War II, Szilard arrived in America, where he eventually became a citizen.

Leo Szilard had previously lived a life in which he'd lost everything. Several centuries earlier, an invading army had destroyed his home and killed many members of his family.

In this life, Szilard's fear of Loss was triggered by the loss of his mother and the continual uncertainty he faced. Fleeing from one country to the next, never having any sense of security, left him unable to trust that one day would follow the next, or that he wouldn't just lose everything overnight.

As a direct result of his fear of Loss, Szilard spent most of his life in hotel rooms, even turning the lobby of one hotel into his office.

He would spend hours every morning in the bathtub, where he'd do his best thinking. And just a few feet away, beside the door to the room, were two packed suitcases. With little in the way of personal possessions, he was ready to move at a moment's notice. (In fact, he did just that during the Cuban Missile Crisis, when the fear of Loss kicked in, and he hightailed it to Switzerland for safety.)

Szilard had a soul mate named Trude. They knew each other from their early days in Berlin. Yet it was decades before he showed any sign of commitment. Even when he and Trude finally married, he still spent most of his time away from her.

By distancing himself from Trude and having no possessions, he had nothing to lose. The fear was irrational, but the loss he'd experienced centuries before had risen to the surface. In an obstinate old soul like Szilard, it wasn't going to disappear in a hurry.

Szilard's soul instilled in him an urge to be involved in the world. Through participation, he'd learn that he could receive the support of others. What happened, in practice, was that he slipped in and out of the Illusion through most of his life.

In my previous book *The Instruction,* I mentioned how many great scientists (the ones who are able to make huge leaps of imagination) have a combination of the Thinker and Creator soul type influences within them. Szilard was one of those.

He famously thought of how to create a chain reaction while watching traffic lights change on London's Southampton Row. (Some of his colleagues dispute the veracity of this story, claiming that the idea that someone as impatient as Leo Szilard would wait for traffic lights to change was absurd!)

Like many old-soul Thinker types, Szilard was an atheist. (Religious dogma doesn't speak to such skeptical, rational individuals.) Yet, his spiritual connection to the Soul World caused him to go from helping invent a weapon of mass destruction to becoming a vocal and influential proponent of nuclear disarmament.

Though his petition to President Harry Truman—begging him not to use atomic weapons on Japan—fell on deaf ears, Szilard continued after World War II to lobby against the use of such weapons and especially to keep atomic energy out of the hands of the military.

His most significant karmic legacy can be seen in his brainchild, the Council for a Livable World, a nonprofit organization that works to reduce the danger of nuclear weapons.

Szilard's sincere attempts to balance the karmic debt incurred by the use of the atomic bombs on Hiroshima and Nagasaki have resulted in a legacy more positive than negative. His soul will, however, be impacted by this very karmically active life for many incarnations to come.

KINDRED SPIRITS

As the level of the Collective Consciousness rises, like-minded souls will gravitate toward each other. My spirit guides describe this process as finding "kindred spirits," something more than just congregating together for comfort. Older souls, particularly, will look for a way to share their spiritual growth and to work with others to a common end. In that way, each of us can leave a karmic legacy, however small.

The motivation of Participation involves just that. You can't play an active role in the Transformation by sitting on top of a mountain—or even hiding in the splendid isolation of a gated community. You need to get out there and be with your fellow souls, your kindred spirits.

In *The Instruction,* I described how souls of a certain age are drawn to certain parts of the world. Whole communities and even countries have a certain flavor—one based on their soul-level outlook on the world.

As the soul ages, it goes from a place of self-interest to one of greater altruism. An old-soul community tends to be more progressive, and it will take better care of minorities, the elderly, and its children.

Younger-soul countries and communities are usually more conservative and religious and place less emphasis on equality. Being more in thrall to the Illusion, and consequently more fearful, they usually spend a lot more on their military than their schools.

Lillian lives in a small, conservative, southern U.S. city, in a state renowned for being solidly Republican and Baptist. Since her husband's work took her to the area several years ago, Lillian has felt like she's never really been part of the community. When we spoke, I uncovered a big past-life fear of Loss that had been triggered by the move.

The origins of the fear stem from a lifetime in the Balkans, many centuries ago. Lillian was a rugged male named Boris, whose horse-riding skills were legendary. The young soldier attracted the attention and admiration of the prince of the municipality, and he was made a general.

The prince, who was physically weak, admired the young man's physique and would organize wrestling matches between his hero and other soldiers.

Boris was ordered to take up arms to crush a revolt. He refused to attack, claiming it was a strategic decision. In reality, he was reluctant to shed blood unnecessarily. The second time he tried the same excuse, the prince was livid.

After being thrown into a dungeon and blinded, Boris was brought before the prince on his hands and knees. The prince beat the defenseless Boris with his fists and ridiculed him for his "cowardice." Boris later died under torture.

This past life has left Lillian with certain resonances. She hates being ridiculed and has always dreaded being put on a pedestal.

"If anyone ever says, 'You're so great,' I feel obliged to take myself down a peg. I immediately react with self-sabotage," she said.

Many fears were created in her lifetime as Boris. The fear of Loss was the result of losing a number of his friends, staff, and fellow brothers in arms. The prince had them all tortured and executed, too. At the time of his death, Boris felt their loss acutely.

Now that she's in a new part of the world, Lillian's fear of Loss has been triggered by the changes. The tendency for many people with this fear is to allow themselves to become isolated from their community.

"I don't fit in too well," she admitted. "I don't really feel safe telling people much about myself. I do energy healing, and I'm an environmentalist. At work, they ridicule me. I'm called a 'tree hugger,' and they make fun of my vegetarianism.

"The other day, my workmates were discussing torture, saying they thought it was a good thing. I was shocked that anyone would openly express such opinions. It saddened me and made me realize we have a long way to go as humans."

My spirit guides ended the session by encouraging Lillian to seek out kindred spirits—those people who share her interests and values. It would help to overcome the fear of Loss and inspire the karmic motivation of Participation.

During our next session, Lillian couldn't wait to tell me about her encounter with like-minded souls. "It was one of the greatest experiences we've had since we moved here. I discovered a psychic fair was in town, so I dragged my husband, Paul, along to check it out. I had no expectations, but we had a fantastic time. We talked to lots of people; in fact, we spent an hour and a half at the first booth alone.

"It was such a relief not to have to worry about people thinking we're crazy. We could talk about spirit guides, belief systems, books we've read. It was like being around family.

"We spent all afternoon there. When we left, Paul stopped and patted his pockets. He said, 'I feel like I've left something behind.'

"I said, 'Yes, you've left all your negative baggage!' There's another event later in the year. We'll definitely be there."

Stimulating the motivation of Participation has helped Lillian get back into the world. She's become involved with the Southern Poverty Law Center, a civil rights organization that battles white supremacists and the Ku Klux Klan through legal action.

"I got a flyer in the mail that said if you donate a certain amount, they'll put your name on a wall, stating that you believe in equal rights for all," Lillian told me.

"I wanted to make a stand. The Southern Poverty Law Center goes to bat for folks who get put in jail unjustly, and it helps to get the right legal support for the accused. Donating to this cause makes me feel good about myself, like I'm really helping someone."

....

SPIRITUAL ACT 2: MITIGATING LOSS

In your past, there are lives in which you've lost your parents, your children, your family, your friends, and even your home. The Spiritual

Act that heals your soul from such traumas is to help those who've suffered loss in this life.

There is no coercion or expectation connected with a Spiritual Act. How much you decide to devote yourself to one is totally up to you. Whether you mail a small donation or dig people out of earthquake rubble is your choice.

In the case of loss, the Spiritual Acts that heal are ones that help such people as orphans, the bereaved, the homeless, and victims of natural disasters.

If you know someone who has suffered a loss such as the death of a spouse or even a pet, you can help him or her avoid becoming isolated—the biggest risk associated with loss—by simply keeping in touch.

Many couples come together to work on karma. And sometimes they just like being with each other. For Ava and Brian, it's a little of both. In their relationship, the key word is "cooperation." When I first spoke to Ava, my spirit guides told her she had a recurring dream. She knew immediately what they were talking about. It was not simply a dream. It was a past life the couple had in a Soviet gulag when they were brothers named Nikolai and Viktor.

Ava was the older, Nikolai, and Brian was Viktor, the younger by about five years. They were dissidents who'd been sent to Siberia for their crimes against the state.

The brothers decided they were going to escape. The camp wasn't particularly well guarded. It didn't need to be. There was nowhere to go even if you did get out. Had the pair known how futile their escape was going to be, they would never have considered it.

Nikolai stole food from the kitchen, while Viktor begged him to leave. But Nikolai knew they'd need the food if they were to stand any chance of survival.

In her dream, Ava remembers stuffing a bag with food, while her brother urged her to flee. "I see this playing out this time around," she said. "Brian thinks I have no sense of time. I'm always trying to cram so much in before we leave. His anxiety is out of all proportion."

The brothers headed south. They didn't last long. The temperature at night would drop so low that they eventually died together from the effects of hunger and exposure.

"Brian had surgery recently, and he's lost a lot of weight," Ava told me. "I get so stressed when he doesn't eat. In fact, I get really angry."

When I first spoke to Ava, my spirit guides said they knew of no other couple with as many past lives together. "That confirmed what we always felt," she said. "It's not logical how we came together. I was between my sophomore and junior years in high school. He was twenty-five. But we bucked all the trends, got married five years later, and weathered all life's storms to stay married—twenty years this year.

"Cooperation has been the theme of our relationship. We didn't always get support from outside, so we looked to each other for support. Though we have a shared mission, we also have individual needs for expression. When I was in school, he worked. When I started working, I supported us both so he could pursue his art.

"Understanding that past life has helped make sense of the present. I'll be standing in the kitchen holding a carrot, with terror in my heart, when all I have to do is fix dinner. And there he is, petrified that we'll both be shot if we don't hurry, when all we need to do is lock up the house and leave for the party.

"I always wondered why I had to be the one doing everything. I felt I had to be the one to provide. I couldn't ask him for help.

"It has really helped to know that when we're in the middle of an argument, we can put it in perspective by remembering it's not coming from current circumstances."

Ava and Brian lost each other in Siberia. And given their many lifetimes together, it probably wasn't the first time. But they've learned the value of Cooperation and used it to enhance their lives both individually and together.

Brian told me later, "When we talked about having died together out in the cold, we burst out crying. We knew it was true. It has helped us to understand that by dying together then, we are zealously determined to keep each other alive now."

These kindred spirits are raising their daughter in an atmosphere of love and security. After a lifetime that ended in a prison camp, it's important to them she never has to go through the isolation and loss they experienced. "The house is her home," Ava told me. "We want to make sure she has a strong foothold in this life."

IT TAKES A KNITTED VILLAGE

What do Mohandas Gandhi and Martin Luther King Jr. have in common? There are many answers, but the one that's relevant to this chapter is that they both show us that true spirituality and a desire for social justice are inseparable. Their messages were ones of unity and cooperation.

As highly evolved old souls, Gandhi and King elevated the Collective Consciousness. They saw clearly that real change comes from working together. Significantly, both were what my spirit guides call "Transformers."

Your soul is a social and political animal. Gandhi threw the British out of India. King was responsible for the biggest shift in consciousness in America's history. They were both fully connected to their souls' core value of Cooperation. They used that awareness to unite like-minded, spiritually conscious souls to actively participate in overcoming oppression and discrimination.

The idea that spirituality is marked by a detachment from the real world is a fallacy. And those two rabble-rousers prove it.

Yet, you don't have to be a Gandhi or a Martin Luther King Jr. to make a difference—to leave a karmic legacy of your own. You can do it in small ways. To give you an example, let me take you to the charming little English village of Mersham.

A group of retired ladies got together and began knitting a three-dimensional scale model of their village, which included the local pub, the original Norman church, and even a cricket team on the village green. The task took twenty-three years, and when it was finished, they sold it off in bits to raise 10,000 pounds to restore their village hall.

Obviously there's a big difference between leading a civil rights movement and knitting a bunch of houses, but what each has in common is that it brought people together in a spirit of cooperation, to achieve a higher purpose.

....

PARTICIPATION EXERCISE 1
DONATING A LITTLE TIME

This exercise is designed to help you engage the motivation of Participation and get you moving on the path to a life of greater involvement and increased meaning through the goal of Cooperation.

We all have busy lives, but you may be able to find a couple of hours on a Saturday morning or a little time after work, perhaps one night a week, to help out your community in some way.

Ask around and find an organization that could use a little help. I have clients who volunteer in soup kitchens and food banks. Two of my clients got together to spend evenings with children in a local hospital. In institutions and organizations, individuals with an increased focus on cooperation are coming together with a shared sense of higher purpose to challenge traditional working methods. Whether they know it or not, they're seeking the goal of Cooperation.

....

PARTICIPATING IN LIFE

To find the impetus to make cooperation a part of your life, it's essential to get involved. The motivation of Participation is the key.

This next exercise is to remind you that there are plenty of opportunities out there to find people like you: ones who share your interests and values.

....

PARTICIPATION EXERCISE 2
FINDING KINDRED SPIRITS

Bring in your spirit guides with the following request: "I call upon my spirit guides, acting in my highest interest, to help me reach the transformational goal of Cooperation."

- Make a list of ten ways to find kindred spirits: people with similar interests and values.
- Highlight the three possibilities that most appeal to you.
- Participate!

Some people like the idea of joining a book group; others are inspired by joining a bowling league. Use your imagination. The ideal is to find a group that meets at least once a week, so you have a regular opportunity to participate in it.

The universe is moving in a forward direction. Your soul is growing and continually evolving. There's no reverse gear that will suddenly catapult us back to the Dark Ages. It's a case of onward and upward.

A person living in fourteenth-century London would have had difficulty imagining a world without witch burnings, the heads of traitors on spikes at Tower Bridge, and child prostitutes on the streets.

Similarly, it can be hard for us to imagine a world much different from the one we're in. But as the Collective Consciousness grows, change becomes imperative.

As the Transformation picks up speed, its forward thrust will make us ever more eager to work together with one another. Spiritually Conscious souls will begin forming more influential groups as the need to participate pushes humanity into a new level of cooperation.

A sign that the Transformation is truly gaining momentum can be seen in the global movement for social change and justice. From farming cooperatives to Jane Goodall's Roots and

Shoots organization that inspires youth to become a force for change, it seems that cooperation is recognized as the key to creating a better world.

Cooperation teaches us the importance of working together. It shows us that two heads are better than one and takes us toward the next goal: Respect.

CHAPTER FOUR

THE ACHIEVEMENT OF RESPECT
Finding Your Inner Strength

GOAL Respect

MOTIVATION Self-Determination

FEAR Inferiority

THE IMPORTANCE OF BEING YOU

Do you feel listless, lacking in direction? Are you waiting for someone or something to come along and drag you out of your inertia?

Do you have plenty of plans but just can't seem to get started? Do you know what it is to feel a victim of circumstances, disempowered by unexpected blows like financial loss, separation, or some other disappointment?

If you do, it's very likely you've got a past-life fear of Inferiority, and something has triggered it in this lifetime.

The past-life fear of Inferiority is the result of having lived your life according to the whims and desires of others. At the time of death, you'll have looked at your life, compared it to others, and found it lacking. Perhaps you felt you could have done more or that someone else got what you should have had.

....

SLIPPING INTO SUBMISSION

While you're on the Physical Plane, your soul will always urge you to manifest the real you, not someone else's idea of who you should be.

Living your life according to someone else's wishes takes your soul back to a time when you had no free will. When you face triggers in this life, the default mode can manifest as passivity, codependence, submission, self-hate, or resignation.

Learning that you have the power to transform your life through the motivation of Self-Determination is the cure. When you live your own life, you walk tall and hold your head high, and that leads to unlimited self-respect.

....

Ariana grew up in a family of eight, where she wasn't always heard. She would try speaking up, but soon learned what it was like to be without any real voice.

In her past, I discovered a lifetime in Germany at the beginning of the twentieth century. She was a boy named Axel, whose mother died when he was two. He was raised by his father, a drunken bully who criticized everything his son did.

Axel would go within himself for safety, afraid to interact with a father who might turn on him at the slightest provocation. His hobby was one that required patience and introspection: he made detailed models of battleships. At least he did until his father destroyed them all in a drunken rage.

Axel grew up obese and nearsighted, and he suffered from obsessive-compulsive traits. He would toy with a piece of string, endlessly tying and untying knots in it. He went to college to study chemistry but dropped out after a year. He felt too insecure to interact socially with other students. As he grew steadily more self-conscious about his nervous manner, attending classes became a kind of torture.

Instead of returning to his home, he went to live with relatives in the town of Kassel. He was a little happier there, until a false accusation completely derailed what was left of his life plan.

When he picked up a wallet from the floor of a restaurant, Axel was accused of having stolen it. He was arrested, tried, and sentenced to two months in jail. Emotionally ill-equipped to deal with prison life, he started to crack up. He was afraid of the other prisoners and disgusted by the filth and smell of the place.

Most of all, he was terrified of what his father would say about it. In the depths of depression, he hanged himself with his shirt.

After I'd finished exploring that tragic life, I looked for the most obvious resonance in Ariana first. "I don't suppose you wear turtlenecks?" I suggested.

"I hate turtlenecks or anything that chokes me," Ariana said. "It's not good; I'm a singer. The slightest stress and I get hoarse."

The past-life fear of Inferiority had many triggers in Ariana's childhood. "I had older siblings who did everything for me. They thought they were helping me, but I ended up being helpless. And with so many other kids around, I was never heard.

"Understanding this past life explains so much. I always had a feeling I had a past life like that. So much of that life is with me in this one. I don't build ships, but I've always isolated myself from the outside world through music and writing. I feel I was an amazing, creative person in that life. Seeing that has helped me to trust my own strengths. I'm learning now to become more empowered and stand up for myself."

The inner Motivation that overcomes the fear of Inferiority is Self-Determination—the urge to live your life by your own rules, without being negatively influenced by others.

Self-Determination connects you to the transformational goal of Respect. When you take charge of your life, you feel positive about yourself. This creates self-respect, and when you respect yourself, you'll respect others.

A past-life fear of Inferiority is triggered in this life when you allow someone else to manipulate you or to control you in some way. It results in feelings of victimization. In fact, when the fear is triggered, you'll often hear someone complain of being a victim of circumstance.

When it kicks in, the irrational soul-level fear is that overcoming whatever's currently happening to you is beyond your control.

RESONANCES FROM A PAST LIFE
OF INFERIORITY

- Feeling stuck
- Waiting for something or someone to come along and change things for you
- Feeling a victim of circumstances
- Feeling lesser than others
- Lack of self-respect
- Letting other people run your life
- Comparing yourself to others
- Feeling you should be more like someone else
- Jealousy of others' happiness
- Agreeing to something just to avoid conflict

Proactivity is a word my spirit guides use a lot. They encourage us all to be more involved in shaping our lives, especially when it comes to following our souls' desires.

My spirit guides often talk, too, about doing the right thing. That means that when you have a choice of whether to be proactive and take action in accordance with your soul's desires, or to take the passive route and do nothing, your soul will always urge you to choose the former.

Self-Determination imbues you with self-respect and gives your soul the message that you respect it, too.

You have a life plan. You're here to follow the route-map your soul created for you before you came into this incarnation.

Following your life plan is not a question of sitting back and letting life happen around you. It's about proactively going out there and making it happen *for* you. It's about Self-Determination: living your life your way, not according to someone else's idea of how you should be.

ESCAPE FROM VICTIMIZATION

"Clueless" is just one of the words used to describe Eric Abbott, an English sailor whose lack of preparation and knowledge has nearly cost him his life on numerous occasions.

Armed only with an Automobile Association road map, his attempts to navigate the Irish Sea have been a disaster. And the cost to the Coast Guard and lifeboat services has been huge. Mr. Abbott claims he goes to sea alone to "find himself." Unfortunately, it's usually up to others to find him.

Most people who set sail do so with charts, a radio, and a compass—not Mr. Abbott. As a result, he's always having to rely on others to come to the rescue.

In a past life, he might never have had the opportunity to take responsibility for himself. In this life, there's a part of him that's stuck in the past. He acts without considering the consequences, and he expects someone else to race to the rescue when he screws up.

Self-Determination is about planning ahead and taking responsibility for reaching your destination. In *The Instruction,* I told how my spirit guides had observed that many people spend more time planning their Thanksgiving dinners than they do planning their whole lives. My guides are big into planning. In fact, during a session with a client, they'll often repeat the words "plan, plan, plan" for emphasis.

If you set out into the future armed only with a ten-year-old road map and high hopes, you may find what you're looking for, but it's going to be largely a hit-or-miss affair. On the other hand, if you have a clear sense of where you're going, and you know the steps you need to take to get there, your chances of arriving in one piece are infinitely higher.

Becoming proactive about manifesting your future can be transformative. Most important, as I've already discussed, it can radically enhance your sense of self-respect. Every time Mr. Abbott has to be fished out of the ocean, his soul takes a knock.

He might have plenty of bravado and a boatload of arrogance— when asked if he had a skipper's license he replied, "I don't need one; I'm far more intelligent"—but there's little respect there, either for himself or for others.

If Abbott had self-respect, he wouldn't put himself through the indignity of being continually rescued, and if he respected others, he wouldn't risk their lives calling them out to help him.

The motivation of Self-Determination leads to the transformational goal of Respect. The more respect you have for yourself and others, the easier it becomes to take control of your life.

Because the past-life fear of Inferiority can take you back to a time when you had no personal power, it can sap all the fight out of you when it gets triggered.

You might otherwise be perfectly confident and able to run your life according to your own inner sense of what's right, but when Inferiority strikes, it can stop you in your tracks. Like the kryptonite that turns Superman into a weakling, Inferiority can rob you of your power.

When a fear of Inferiority strikes, you may spend a lot of time comparing yourself with others. You may dwell on negative thoughts: "My friends are all married with kids. I should be married with kids at this point in my life, too." Or you may put down others to boost your own confidence: "Poor Jennifer. She looks like she dressed in the dark." You might even fish for compliments by putting yourself down: "Why am I so stupid?"

Being so busy comparing your life to others can lead to self-absorption, and that can bring out the "inner bitch" like nobody's business.

Years ago, I was in a pub in Scotland when two friends announced their engagement. The woman beside me didn't even offer a smile before turning to her partner and saying, "So, when are you going to ask me, then?"

If you're constantly comparing your life to someone else's, you're taking your eye off the ball in a big way. This life is yours. And if you still haven't had a proposal, and you're two years older, and you think you really should have been married by now—so what! Don't allow your jealousy to put a damper on someone else's happiness. Do something to change your situation.

When you gain control of your life, you not only respect yourself, but you respect others, too. Did the woman in the pub feel a strong sense of self-respect? I doubt it. If she had, her first thought wouldn't have been about her place in the scheme of things. She would have shown respect for the newly engaged couple by sharing in their happiness.

Respect for others comes naturally when you respect yourself. And when you respect them, they respect you. It's circular. It's all a matter of shifting out of a place of submission, defeatism, or resignation.

Self-Determination is the fast track to respect for yourself and others. But what, exactly, does it mean to act with respect?

Self-respect doesn't mean going through life with your nose in the air, looking down on others. That's called self-importance, and it's what happens when someone (particularly a younger soul) with a past-life fear of Inferiority gets caught up behind the Illusion.

You don't have to lose your sense of humor to act with dignity. In fact, it can help to do quite the reverse.

And what if it is someone else who's laughing at you? What if you're held up to ridicule? A couple of telling examples come courtesy of comedian Sacha Baron Cohen, best known for his film roles as Borat and Bruno. As Ali G., he plays a breathtakingly ignorant TV interviewer who claims to be the "Voice of da Youth." The subjects of his interviews are unaware that they're being set up.

Ali G. asks former astronaut Buzz Aldrin, whom he refers to as Buzz Lightyear (a character from the movie *Toy Story*), "What was it like *not* being the first man on the moon? Was you ever jealous of Louis Armstrong?"

Aldrin politely replies, "It was *Neil* Armstrong, and no, I was not jealous."

Then he asks, "Do you think man will ever walk on the sun?"

Aldrin tells him that's not likely.

When Ali G. asks, "What 'appens if they went in winter when the sun is cold?" Aldrin smiles and patiently explains, "The sun is *not* cold in winter."

In another interview, Ali G. meets a bad-tempered Andy Rooney. "Does you think the media has changed since you first got in it?" he asks.

Rooney muses on the question. "*Does* you think the media has changed?" he says. Then he repeats it as he feels it should have been posed. "*Do* you think the media has changed?"

"Whatever," Ali G. replies, feigning disinterest.

But Andy Rooney has a point to make. "No, it's English. '*Do* you think the media has changed?'"

Less than a minute later, Rooney stands up complaining, "I can't do this. I can't waste my time."

End of interview.

The difference between the two interviewees is like night and day. Buzz Aldrin maintains his dignity and sense of humor throughout, no matter how absurd the question. By acting respectfully, even though he was being made fun of, his demeanor was guaranteed to gain the respect of viewers.

Rooney, on the other hand, comes across as self-important and humorless—a condition that doesn't command respect in anyone.

DEVELOPING SELF-DETERMINATION

The motivation that overcomes inferiority from the past is Self-Determination. Sometimes a child will come into the world with guns blazing, clear from the start about where to go and how to get there. For others, the feelings of resignation and submission are hard to shake off.

When I first spoke to Karen, she was in a dead-end marriage that had no chance of survival. She'd been struggling with one of the biggest effects of a past-life fear of Inferiority: a deep-rooted sense of, well, inferiority.

Karen needed help in finding the courage to leave the relationship. To reassure her, my spirit guides said, "You're going to meet your soul mate sooner rather than later." In my experience, that means months, not years.

The feelings of inferiority that have dogged Karen stem from a life in Prague, in what's now the Czech Republic. As Rosa, she was the daughter of a strictly orthodox Jewish family. Rosa was expected to marry a local man she despised. In such a strict family her protests were ignored.

When she was fourteen, the rabbi sexually abused her. Rosa told the family. For reasons that are impossible to understand in our time and culture, they forced her to apologize to *him*. Not surprisingly, her trust of people was nonexistent.

Rosa married the man her family chose for her. He was also abusive toward her. She became sullen, rarely speaking in case she incurred his displeasure. They had one child, a girl, which was something of a disappointment to her family. A year later, she died while giving birth to a second child.

Even as Rosa struggled to bring her baby into the world, her family berated her for not trying hard enough. They made it clear they thought she was a poor wife.

Rosa died feeling a victim of everyone around her. She never learned to stand up for herself. And because she was so disempowered by her family, the result was a fear of Inferiority.

Karen has struggled in this life with throwing off the effects of her past in Prague.

"I totally connected with everything you told me," she said later. "All through my childhood I felt inferior. I always thought I had to please everyone. But since we explored that past life, I've been learning to take my power back."

Karen's empowerment had begun three years earlier when she created a "serenity room" as a kind of refuge from the marriage. "I read every book on self-esteem and loving yourself," she said. "I decided I wanted to be a healer. Taking control of my future gave me confidence."

Karen felt that understanding her past life was the key to freeing herself from its effects. "I believe that the more you understand, the more you put everything in its place," she said. "As soon as I had that knowledge, it took the chains off me."

But what of the soul mate who was to arrive sooner, rather than later?

"I've found my soul mate," Karen told me. "Our energy together is ridiculous. I've never felt anything like it before. It was totally meant to be."

The story of how they met is an example of the power that draws soul mates together.

"Four months after I separated from my husband, my soul mate tracked me down online. We had fallen in love when we were both fifteen. Then we went our separate ways. We lost touch, but what's funny is I always told people I'd marry him.

"So we met up, and I found out Chris had always told people, 'There's this girl called Karen. I'm going to marry her one day.'"

When I finally met Chris, he pulled out a faded photograph from his wallet. It showed a young Karen at a party on the night they met. He had carried it with him for almost two decades.

Reuniting with her soul mate has helped Karen completely overcome her past-life fear. Now she's using the motivation of Self-Determination to its fullest extent.

"Before I met him," Karen said, "you encouraged me to write a list of twenty things I wanted in a relationship. Well, he's everything on the list. Not only that, but I said I wanted to be back in the town where I grew up. That's where he lives.

"Chris is supportive of everything I want to do. And I want to be a healer. With him, I feel I can complete my soul's mission and focus on what I can give back to the world."

When Karen and I last spoke, she told me how both their children from their previous marriages live with them. "It's been a year now, and we have our dream home, and all four of us are doing so much better than we were prior to this change," she said. "We're all flying to Disneyland for our first Christmas holiday as a family."

....

SELF-DETERMINATION EXERCISE 1

CREATE A SUPER-YOU

Invite in your spirit guides with the following request: "I call upon my spirit guides, acting in my highest interest, to help me reach the goal of Respect through the motivation of Self-Determination."

Close your eyes, and begin the exercise.

- Visualize yourself as a superhero, complete with a super-suit of your own design. (A cape is optional. Contemporary superheroes don't seem to feel the need.)
- Picture yourself in a super-pose, flexing your muscles of steel, a confident super-smile on your face.
- Imagine yourself in a situation where you normally wouldn't feel confident, standing up for yourself.

- Say aloud: "I am Super-_____ [your name]."
- When you've done this, thank your spirit guides and tell them, "Session over."

Whenever you find yourself in a situation where you feel disempowered, picture your super-self and remember your secret identity. It will help prevent you from falling into the trap of submission.

· ·

As long as she can remember, Suzanne has felt that life doesn't owe her anything. "I was so goal-oriented that when I was a little kid I vowed, 'Twenty years from now I want to be able to say I went to college on a soccer scholarship,'" she recalls.

This need for Self-Determination stems from a lifetime in Dundee, Scotland, sometime in the early twentieth century. Suzanne was then a young woman named Rhona, the daughter of an elder of the Presbyterian Church. Her father was sanctimonious, selfish, and controlling. He made her a virtual slave.

In this austere household, Rhona was made to wear plain clothes and cut her hair short. Her father didn't want her to look attractive to men. By the time she was in her late teens, the spirit had gone out of her. My guides described her as having "no ability to smile."

When Rhona struck up a friendship with a young man, her father was determined to stop it going anywhere. He took the lad aside and threatened to kill him if he didn't get lost. Rhona never saw him again and never knew why.

She looked after her father until he died when she was forty. Soon after, she met the second man in her life. By then, she was emotionally cold and sexually closed down. He thought he could change her.

Their marriage was unsatisfactory for both of them. He finally left for Canada, suggesting he'd send for her. He never did.

What hurt the most was that Rhona never knew why he went. He'd never told her what was bothering him about the relationship. In her mind, he was just like the young man, twenty years earlier, who'd simply disappeared without explanation.

This lifetime in Dundee was a classic example of one in which a soul's life plan is derailed by another person's expectations. Rhona's father had robbed her of her ability to live the life her soul intended.

So, when Suzanne came into this world, her soul made every effort to be sure that she's the one running the show.

"My mom always told me I was unique," she said. "I certainly always felt different. I was so driven. I had to get As. When I got a B+ in second grade, my dad found me hiding the paper in a planter. They told me they'd be proud of me if I got a C—that it was okay not to be perfect. They had no expectations, and they wanted me to ease off the throttle and enjoy my childhood."

There are two strong resonances that stem from Suzanne's past life in Dundee.

The first is the importance of Respect, which is the transformational goal associated with a fear of Inferiority.

"I do appreciate when people acknowledge my achievements at work," Suzanne told me. "It's the only kind of praise that I can say makes me feel good. It comes from a place of respect. I like to gain respect through my actions—not smoke and mirrors, or my words, but actions. It infuriates me if I'm disrespected.

"In competitive sports I never wanted to be a star, but I ended up in that role. I credited every accolade to my teammates. I knew my success depended on them. I respected them, and they respected me."

The second resonance is a huge need for explanations. "I've always lived inside my head," Suzanne said. "Even as a child, I asked "why" all the time. At work I get irritated when management puts out a directive initiating widespread change but doesn't explain why.

"I've always sought whys, especially when I went through my divorce. I wanted to know why our marriage failed, so I wouldn't have to go through it all again."

Suzanne is a learning to use her intuition to help answer some of those whys. "I've learned that I need to use my gut more," she said. "When I got married, a voice said, 'Don't marry him,' but I did. On the morning of the wedding, my feet were ice cold. I had to soak them in a basin of hot water. When my dad walked in, he asked if I had cold feet.

"I said, 'No, I have to get married,' but I was denying who I really was. I knew I was making the wrong decision, but I didn't trust my intuition.

"The life in Scotland taught me that if you live a life denying who you are, you never get a chance to experience what you're here for."

I asked Suzanne if she'd noticed any changes since we uncovered her past life in Scotland.

"There was an immediate shift," she said. "People from my past began reconnecting, and strangers would come up and talk to me out of the blue. I used to put out this 'don't come near me' vibe. This shift has been so powerful I'm just blown away. I used to get this ridiculous anxiety if anyone showed the slightest interest in me. All of a sudden I had three people wanting me to meet their friends. I've been on several dates, and there's been no anxiety."

To build an unshakable level of self-respect, you need to take responsibility for your life. The motivation of Self-Determination is the way. It means not waiting for someone else to make things happen for you; it means rolling up your sleeves and making them happen for yourself.

Recognizing that you have a choice in every situation is a major step toward the goal of Respect. Making the right choice every time begins by asking yourself, "Am I doing the right thing?"

DOING THE RIGHT THING

When the motivation of Self-Determination gets fired up within you, you'll recognize that you have not just the choice to get out of a rut, but the chance to change the course of your life.

Like an ostrich pulling its head out of the sand, you'll blink your eyes a couple of times, look around to get your bearings, and see that you have unlimited choices before you.

You can take the active path, or you can do nothing and wait for someone else to make the decisions for you. The choice is entirely yours. Being an active participant in your own life means, of course, being proactive. And being proactive means you always have a choice whether or not to do the right thing.

Your soul knows the difference between right and wrong. It works silently in the background, continually mapping and remapping your course, gently keeping you on the right track.

When you act according to your soul's wishes, you'll do the right thing, regardless of social mores, prevailing custom, or even the law. The law, for example, is seldom a reflection of your soul's core values. It is a man-made set of rules that frequently favors the rich over the poor and men over women.

Just because the law says panhandling is illegal, for example, it doesn't mean your soul agrees. From your soul's point of view, helping out a destitute fellow human with a little spare change is a Spiritual Act. And that means it is always encouraged.

This inner sense of what's right and what's wrong is your soul's subtle way of making sure you do the right thing as often as possible.

When you pay attention to that small, still voice, you'll be in harmony with your soul, and that helps make you feel good about yourself.

Say you find a wallet lying in the supermarket parking lot. You can keep it, and nobody will ever know. Or you can turn it in and hope its owner returns to claim it. What are you going to do?

The closer you are to your soul, the more likely you are to "do the right thing," which, of course, is to do what you can to reunite it with its owner.

Conversely, the farther you are from your soul—or to put it another way, the more you're trapped behind the Illusion—the easier it is to simply stick the wallet in your pocket and keep on going.

Assuming that you're in tune with your soul and return the wallet, you'll find yourself rewarded with positive emotions that emanate directly from your soul. It's as if your soul is saying, "Good job! You did the right thing."

People are always asking me how they can tell if they're following their soul's guidance. The answer I tell them is, "Does it feel right? Does it make you feel good? Do you feel you're doing the right thing?"

In the case of "doing the right thing," the positive emotion you'll feel relates directly to your soul's third transformational goal: Respect.

Since our exploration into her past life in Scotland, Suzanne has embraced Spiritual Acts with open arms. "I was always the one to step back and watch others," she told me. "But now I'm bold and acting. I began with random acts of kindness, but soon I started getting involved in my son's school. I raised funds from corporations, and I wrote to senators and even the president.

"I used to help out by cutting a check. Now I'm developing a science curriculum for kindergarten classes and finding all sorts of ways to give kids opportunities they wouldn't otherwise have had."

. . . .

SPIRITUAL ACT 3: TEACHING TO FISH

One surefire way to get to a place of self-respect is to use your own past as the impetus to help others. It's done, as you might by now imagine, through Spiritual Acts.

Healing a life in which you've had no opportunity to exercise self-determination happens quickly when you take steps to help those who suffer as you once did.

The motivation of Self-Determination should give you a strong clue as to the kind of Spiritual Acts that will help you on your path to Transformation. By helping others to achieve Self-Determination, you'll be helping yourself. It's very much a case of teaching someone to fish, rather than simply giving him or her a fish.

This can apply to raising or mentoring children, supporting a sick relative, or contributing to a charity that helps people to improve their own lives.

. . . .

One word of warning: when you undertake Spiritual Acts that you hope will empower someone, it's important to be careful to avoid doing things for them that they should be doing for themselves.

One of my clients, Sarah, was married to a man who grew up in a home where his adoring grandmother provided every meal and made sure everything from his laundry to his school homework (really!) was done for him. In the marriage, the husband expected Sarah to take the role of his grandmother. Unfortunately for him, she did.

When they divorced, he ended up alone without the basic skills to properly take care of himself. And instead of developing them, he stayed in a state of mild depression, looking for someone who'd take care of him.

"His home is filthy, and he doesn't seem to care," Sarah told me. "When our daughter went to visit, she was supposed to stay for a week. I got a tearful call from her at midnight begging me to come and take her home. She couldn't bear the smell."

Though the women in his life thought they were helping this man, they had, in fact, disempowered him.

THE POWER OF CHANGE

So much of what happens to you in this life is not a result of inescapable destiny. It's up to you. If you react to every negative experience by shrugging your shoulders and saying, "I guess it was meant to be," then you're doing nothing but disempowering yourself. By recognizing that no one is going to pull you out of any crisis but yourself, you're on your way to Self-Determination.

Becoming proactive about your life means getting involved in shaping your destiny. It means taking charge of manifesting the kind of life you want. It means creating clear goals and, most important, achieving them. And it means pushing any feelings you might have that you're a victim of circumstance into the past where they belong.

• • •

Many years ago, I worked as a cartoon illustrator in London. After a long day in my studio, I was walking home from the Tube station when I stopped outside my flat. It was late and I was ready for bed, but I couldn't seem to summon the enthusiasm to climb the steps to the front door.

If you've read the introduction to *The Instruction,* you'll know that there was an extended period of time when I was so much at sea, I made the sailor with the road maps look like Columbus.

When it came to choosing relationships, I made every mistake known to man. With abysmally low self-respect and a huge past-life fear of Inferiority, I was a walking example of someone in victim mode.

I'd been living with a young woman for several years, but the relationship had deteriorated badly. I was regularly working twelve or more hours a day to fund the business I'd set up for her, yet she was obsessed with the idea that I was cheating on her. When I'd have found the time, heaven knows.

A few months earlier, I'd asked her to leave. She was furious. She'd refused to budge, saying, "You've hurt me—now I'm going to stay and hurt you." I was living in a nightmare and couldn't see the slightest glimmer of hope for the future.

Being continually ground down, my past-life fear of Inferiority had taken a firm hold of me. I walked with a slouch, felt permanently depressed, and when people asked, "How are you?" I'd automatically answer, "It's a dog's life."

So, there I was, standing at my front door. I had good reason to be nervous. The night before, I'd arrived home to find her in the middle of the living room, staring at me with her steely blue eyes, her pupils like pinpoints. I was a little unnerved. I'd seen that look before, and it always spelled trouble.

"That girl called," she told me, her lower lip quivering with suppressed emotion.

"What girl?"

"You know the one," she said. "I know you're still seeing her."

It took several questions before I could figure out who she was talking about. I barely knew how to respond.

"I haven't seen her in five years," I gasped. "We split up long before I met you. She doesn't live in this country anymore. She doesn't even live on this continent!"

If that was supposed to reassure her, it didn't.

"If I had a pair of scissors, I'd stab you," she hissed through clenched teeth. Trembling with rage, she turned toward a pile of dressmaking stuff on the floor. We both spotted the scissors at the same time. Before she could get her hands on them, I turned and shot out the door.

Whether she would really have stabbed me or not, I don't know. I certainly wasn't taking any chances. I'd recently begun to joke with a friend that one day I'd end up dying at her hands, accused of some imaginary crime I could never have predicted. Suddenly, it was no longer quite so funny.

So, I found myself, twenty-four hours later, standing outside my own flat, not knowing what I'd find when I got inside. Would she be hiding behind the front door, packing a pair of pinking shears, or would she be curled up on the sofa watching TV like nothing had ever happened? Based on past performance, either scenario was possible.

I decided to do what generations of Scots before me have done when faced with such a dilemma. I went to the pub.

Half an hour later, I was standing at the bar in the Leinster Arms, musing on the fact that two-and-a-half pints of Guinness hadn't taken even the slightest edge off my anxiety. I was slightly concerned, too, that the bar was closing in a few minutes, and I was still stone-cold sober.

Suddenly, I had a flash of insight. I put my glass down on the bar and stared into it. I realized I had a decision to make. I could continue as I was going, living with a volatile, sometime scissor-wielding maniac and gradually slipping into alcoholism in an attempt to calm my anxiety. Or I could shape up, ship her out, and start living a better life.

The choice, I recognized, with a jolt, was entirely mine to make.

I left the rest of my beer and went for a long walk. By the end of an hour, I felt energized and excited, and I had hatched a plan that I put into action the next morning.

My girlfriend was in bed when I got home, so I felt relatively safe. I slept like the proverbial log. The moment the sun came up, I bounced out of bed (or the sofa, to be more precise). Instead of starting the day in my customary gloom, I was like a man on a mission, which to a very great extent I was. I chose to wear a suit and tie, rather than jeans and T-shirt, and I went straight out and bought a notebook and pen.

Half an hour later, I was in the ritzy Café Royal, situated on London's famous Regent Street. I ordered a coffee and a bottle of Perrier, and I began making plans for my future.

The first decision had been made the night before. I was going to give up smoky pubs for a while in favor of more upmarket venues like the Café Royal. Feeling like an explorer taking his first step into uncharted territory, I opened my notebook and wrote: "I want to live in America."

Several other points followed in quick succession. They included "Talk to U.S. immigration lawyer," "Give up beer," "Lose potbelly," "Eat better," and "Swim every morning."

The list included getting rid of the girlfriend—a goal I'd set before (the time she point-blank refused to put her book down and get me another blanket while I was in the teeth-chattering chill of a chicken-pox-induced fever) but hadn't followed through on. This time I meant business.

Taking charge of my life like this was empowering. With my newfound sense of clarity (something that lasted long after that fateful night in the Leinster), I felt as if I could see into my own future. I didn't know how I was going to do it, but I was determined to seek out a new life in the States.

What happened to me at the bar of the Leinster Arms in Notting Hill was something that puzzled me for the next few years. I was aware that I'd had some kind of an epiphany. I didn't, however, understand it until I began working with my spirit guides.

There are times in your life when the soft voice of your soul, amplified by your spirit guides, can break through the Illusion and make itself heard. For me, that moment in the Leinster was one of those times.

It happens often when there's nowhere left to go but up.

To cut a long story short, I got fit, dumped the girlfriend, and made plans for America. The last part was proving tricky, though. I saw a lawyer who told me that although I was working for U.S. clients, moving there was going to be a lot more difficult than I imagined.

Strangely, I wasn't discouraged. I felt in my bones that no matter how daunting the immigration process might be, I'd end up in America.

....

FEASIBLE GOALS

There's something exciting about creating a goal and seeing it manifest. What I've learned from doing this is not to be afraid of coming up
with a big goal. Even if you can't see how it could ever happen, you've
nothing to lose by putting it out there.

As long as your goal is in your highest interest, the universe will get
behind you. If it's not, you may find yourself wasting a lot of energy.

If your goal is to have a fleet of Cadillacs, so you can drive a different
car every day of the week, then good luck to you. You'll need it. But if
you're planning to use them to start a luxury-car rental business, then
you're a lot more likely to get the support you need.

....

In the next year, I fell in love with and quickly married a glamor-
ous New Yorker, not for a green card, but 100 percent for love.
The whole courtship and relocation to a new country felt like the
most natural process in the world.

From that morning in London's Café Royal to the time I first
climbed the stairs to our Manhattan apartment, I'd felt an absolute
sense of purpose, and my self-confidence was at an all-time high.

What I learned from discussing the experience with my spirit
guides was that I'd connected emotionally with my own future,
and that was why I felt so certain I'd end up where I did.

The planning I did was at the urging of my soul. It helped
to firm up the goals and create the impetus that would make
change inevitable.

The one, single-most important thing I gained from taking
control of my future was self-respect. As I began taking the steps
necessary to achieve my goals, I felt a confidence I hadn't really

known before. I was no longer a victim of circumstances; I was master of my own destiny.

I was shaping my own life and receiving positive emotions as a result. I found myself walking taller, smiling more, and generally acting and feeling like a person with self-respect should.

Before my epiphany in the Leinster, I'd fallen into the trap of victimization. I was depressed and felt powerless. It was taking that 180-degree turn and recognizing that no one was going to get me out of the rut but me that gave me the impetus to change the direction of my life.

FROM SMALL THINGS, BIG THINGS COME

Now I'd like to help you get to the same point I did after my epiphany in the Leinster Arms. The difference is that you don't have to hit bottom, as I did, before hearing the voice that gives you the choice between self-destruction and empowerment.

The approach is the same whether your life is a mess and your partner is a homicidal maniac, or if things are okay and you'd just like your future to be a little more fulfilling.

In the exercise I'm going to show you, you'll discover a technique for creating tangible goals for the future and turning those goals into reality.

When my spirit guides first suggested this exercise, I asked them what level of goal they meant. They said, "Change your hairstyle; cook something you've never cooked before."

Several of my clients have reported, "I changed my hairstyle like your guides suggested. I feel great!"

What I did in the Café Royal, you can do too. The first step is to find your own little Café Royal. I suggest you go somewhere a little ritzy, so you feel like you're doing something special (which you are).

....

SELF-DETERMINATION EXERCISE 2

TEN GOALS IN TEN WEEKS

Bring in your spirit guides with the following request: "I call upon my spirit guides, acting in my highest interest, to help me reach the goal of Respect through the motivation of Self-Determination."

- In your journal, write ten small goals.
- In a calendar, or on a sheet of paper, place one goal in each of the next ten weeks.
- Complete each goal.

One of my clients reported that for the first few weeks she set intentions to select a paint color for the bedroom, try a new restaurant, and try a new recipe.

"I realized that all I had to do was visualize the intention, then all I needed to manifest it would be right in front of me," she said. "The inspiration for the paint color revealed itself in a magazine, and the new recipe came from a conversation with my mom."

Another client started taking a different route to work, began volunteering at church, and found that her small goals had begun shifting into bigger goals.

....

The big lesson here is about setting intentions and following through with them. With every one you complete, you're going to feel increasingly able to bite off more. So, when you've done ten weeks, start all over again. But this time, up the ante a little. Make your goals a little grander, and see what happens.

The practice you get from completing small goals will help you when it comes to creating bigger plans for your life.

Self-Determination, as we've seen, results in self-respect, but it also increases your respect for others. It's often said that you can't love others without first loving yourself. The same applies to respect.

When you embody the goal of Respect, you'll have higher expectations about being treated fairly. And you'll recognize that others also have that right.

This recognition will help you to reach the next of the ten goals. Through the motivation of Fairness, you'll seek out a future of greater justice for yourself and your fellow souls.

CHAPTER FIVE

THE EXPECTATION OF JUSTICE
Identifying with the Underdog

GOAL Justice

MOTIVATION Fairness

FEAR Betrayal

THE SHOCK OF BETRAYAL

We all have expectations when it comes to other peoples' behavior. We may say things like "I have no expectations," but we do. It's part of the human condition.

A past-life fear of Betrayal is all about expectations. If someone stabs you in the back, metaphorically or literally, you're going to feel (among other things) a sense of betrayal. Why? Because you expected something better of that person.

We all associate betrayal with the kind of scenario where someone you know does something treacherous behind your back, but the origins of a fear of Betrayal go beyond that. The fear is caused by a betrayal of trust, whether it comes from a spouse, a friend, or an entire community.

In the tribe, after the last Transformation, we had an expectation of fairness from others. We'd scratch their backs and expect a scratch in return. But we also expected fairness from our leaders. In disputes over property, we'd look to them for justice. Any abuse on their part was a huge assault on our soul's core values.

Having betrayal in your soul's past means you've literally been betrayed, either by a person or a group of people. In many past lives I've explored, a fear of Betrayal has been created not so much by a single person, but by injustice in a court of law or tribunal of some kind.

A common manifestation of this fear is an inability to trust someone after they've been disloyal.

Marie had a shock when her husband had an affair just three months after they tied the knot.

"It must have affected you very deeply," I said.

"I had a nervous breakdown," she explained. "He told me he never thought I'd be so upset. We've been together twenty-one years now, but I've never regained my trust in him. It's never been the same since he betrayed me."

The cure for a fear of Betrayal is found in the motivation of Fairness. You can use it to reach the transformational goal of Justice.

The goal of Justice is a way of making sure you treat others fairly. This can range from giving your children equal attention to ensuring that when you get selected for jury duty the defendant is treated with the utmost fairness.

REAPING, NOT SEWING

Horatio Bottomley was a swindler and fraudster. He began work as a courtroom shorthand writer and eventually became one of Edwardian England's most notorious crooks. In an endless series of Ponzi schemes, where he used investments from one business to cover the losses on the last, he bilked thousands of people out of their savings.

Bottomley, like many of his ilk, masked his true intentions by wrapping himself in the flag and nationalistic fervor. He founded the *Financial Times,* a journal that still exists, and a jingoistic weekly magazine called *John Bull.* The former helped him promote his dubious schemes, and the latter featured regular competitions (such as predicting the results of soccer matches) whose entry fees supported Bottomley's penchant for champagne and gambling. (He once lost a fortune backing his own horse—whose name just happened to be Ainslie!)

After a spell as a member of Parliament, Bottomley came up with a scam involving the sale of bonds. Despite going to great lengths to hush up the fraud, he was tried and convicted, and he spent the next seven years in His Majesty's Prison, Maidstone.

While Bottomley was in jail, he finally found himself engaged in honest labor. A prison visitor, said to have been a fellow MP, spotted him sewing mailbags. "Ah, Horatio," he cried out, "Sewing?"

To which Bottomley glumly replied, "No, reaping."

Thanks to the laws of karma, you eventually reap what you sow. And though it may not happen in this life, your soul will always seek out ways to balance injustice from the past.

An unfair trial and imprisonment is a surefire way of having your life plan derailed. And even when imprisonment is an appropriate sanction for bad behavior, cruel and unusual sentences are never without karmic consequences.

• • •

When I interviewed Julia for this next story, she told me she felt that other past lives we'd explored had greater significance than this one. My spirit guides disagreed, assuring her that the strong visceral reaction she had when we uncovered this life was a sign of its importance. She had to agree that she might still be processing it.

This story is one in which betrayal comes in the form of a stab in the back from a lover. The tragic consequences that followed are one reason why Julia's reaction to the event was so dramatic.

In the lifetime we were working with, a talent for music led Julia, who was then a young man named Emile, to being hired as a court entertainer for the Dauphin, the young heir to the French throne.

Emile had a normal upbringing in a small town outside of Paris. His parents were comfortably off and raised him with a good education, making sure to encourage his musical abilities.

Emile was a born performer. He was funny, charming, and mischievous. These qualities endeared him to the young prince, but they engendered strong feelings of jealousy and contempt in other members of the court who sought the royal child's favor.

Though Emile was an intelligent young man, he was particularly naïve and gauche when it came to relationships. He was no match for the Machiavellian machinations of the more experienced members of the court. He was regarded by his peers, and particularly his superiors, as a fool—much like the part he played while entertaining the Dauphin.

Emile fell in love with an attractive and worldly courtesan named Louise. Together they had a brief sexual relationship. For Emile, it was his first. For Louise, it was simply one of many.

They were careful to hide their friendship from her lover, an official in the court who was known for his jealousy and explosive temper. He was already deeply envious of Emile's popularity with the Dauphin, and that made the lover particularly dangerous.

Louise was older, more experienced, and a master manipulator. She made fun of Emile behind his back, laughing at his inexperience and lack of sophistication. She made a big mistake, however, when she told a fellow courtesan about the relationship.

This other woman was jealous of Louise and used the opportunity to her advantage. In an attempt to ruin her competitor's career at court, she alerted Louise's lover.

He was furious and threatened to have Louise thrown out of the court. Out of concern for her survival, the terrified woman agreed to turn on Emile and help rid the court of this competitor for the Dauphin's attention.

Louise and her lover both accused Emile of treason, citing his family's associations with a group of the king's enemies. The hapless Emile was arrested and thrown into prison, where he was tortured and eventually executed.

Julia's reaction to this lifetime was telling. When I told her about Louise's denunciation of Emile, she blew her top. Until that point she was quietly making notes. Next she began demanding, "Who was that woman?" She was really mad.

When we talked about it later, Julia said, "I had a huge reaction. It was weird—it's just not my personality to go off like that."

A fear of Betrayal is one that's hard to conceal. If you have it, you'll have major loyalty issues. If you're open to your soul and its influence, you'll be highly loyal.

And you might react with Julia's level of passion when someone betrays you. It's not unusual for people with this fear to have, at some point, completely cut others out of their lives for their disloyalty or even their perceived disloyalty.

....

THREE STRIKES RULE

If you have a fear of Betrayal, you'll recognize the strong emotions disloyalty stirs inside you. It's common to deal with the fear by refusing to have any further contact with the person who has shown disloyalty.

I once asked a client if she related to the idea of "three strikes and you're out."

"Three strikes?" she asked. "You've got to be kidding! One strike— that's all I give!"

Since then, I must have heard that same response to my question at least a dozen times.

....

There was a strong physical resonance for Julia from that life in France, too. Since Emile was a musician, the torture inflicted on him included having his hands mutilated.

"I have no small-motor control in my hands," Julia said. "My six-year-old has more legible handwriting than I do."

Julia has strong feelings about justice in this life. "In first grade I was a bit of a bully. Then I realized I could use my strength for good or bad. I decided then that I wanted to fight for justice—just like Richie Cunningham's character in the *Happy Days* TV show.

"My dad was a good teacher about betrayal and having expectations of others. I always expect everyone to behave in an honorable way. I believe it's a hidden agreement between souls."

At the end of the interview, I asked Julia how she was feeling about her life in France now. "I have a lot of anger about that past life," she admitted. "I'd happily throw that woman off a bridge if I met her in this life." As Julia said, she's still processing this one.

As an interesting footnote, I got an e-mail from Julia a couple of months later. "I was helping my daughter with her lowercase letters," she wrote. I picked up a pencil and *Kablamo!*—my writing had changed! My husband commented that you can read my handwriting now. It's round, and the angles are different. It's like an adolescent girl's. And my hand feels relaxed. Before, my hand used to hurt, and my writing was so intense that you could turn the sheet of paper over and read it like braille!"

The betrayal in Julia's life in France was literal. She was denounced by someone she loved. For another client, Kirsten, the fear was caused by a false accusation of theft and exacerbated by being let down by everyone she trusted.

Kirsten is an old soul who spent a happy and comfortable life as a cook in a castle in Moravia several centuries ago. When I began exploring this life with Kirsten, the first thing that resonated with her was the word "castle."

"I've always wanted to live in a castle," she said. "I built my home with stone floors and walls. It's kind of unusual in southern Texas."

And when I told her she'd been a cook, she laughed and said, "I've always said I was once the peasant who works for the people in the big house." The big house, in this case, was a castle.

"You were falsely accused of stealing food," I told her. "You were dragged in front of some kind of a court and then taken away and executed."

It was not just the false accusation that triggered Kirsten's fear of Betrayal, but losing trust in the entire system. She became a victim of harsh laws that were never really designed to protect the innocent.

Like everyone with a fear of Betrayal, Kirsten has strong views on loyalty. "It shocks me when someone is intentionally disloyal," she said. "I would never do that to anyone—not in a thousand years."

That life—particularly the execution—has triggered other fears, too. Powerlessness, authority, and particularly judgment are all issues stemming from that one experience. It was no surprise to hear Kirsten say, "In my world, everything has to be fair."

After our session, Kirsten searched the Internet for the Moravian castle using some architectural details my guides had given her. (The castle had unusual turrets, with roofs that were flattened instead of round.)

"I felt a real sense of urgency to find it," she said. "It was four in the morning when I saw a picture and recognized it right away. Since I've always wanted to live in a castle, I've had a picture of it on my vision board for years. I put the two pictures together and they were identical."

A few months later, I asked Kirsten how uncovering her past life affected her. "Learning all this stuff has been like opening a door and finding all the reasons why. It really has meant everything to me. My two friends, who are also clients of yours, feel the same way. It's like we've grown so much. And whenever one of us gets fearful, the other two will remind her that it's an irrational old fear from the past."

....

FAIRNESS EXERCISE 1

CREATE YOUR OWN MANTRA

Kirsten told me, "When I get a knot in my stomach and realize it's a past-life fear surfacing, I say to myself, 'Kirsten, calm down. They can't kill you again. Calm down; it's just an old fear.'"

You can do the same. Simply find a word or a phrase that helps you to remember your fear is from the past and has no place in your current life.

....

The motivation of Fairness has grown increasingly stronger in Kirsten. She's become even more outspoken on issues of justice than she was before.

"I call people on injustice all the time. We had some folks over for dinner, and they were talking about another couple, making him out to be the heavy and her the victim. Finally, I had enough. I shouted, 'Stop it! Have any of you thought about this? Do you have all the information you need to judge him? Can you see his point of view?'

"My husband asked, 'Whose side are you on?' I said, 'That's the whole point. I'm not taking sides.'"

There are some interesting resonances from the life in Moravia that have surfaced in Kirsten's life. The connection with stone walls and floors, for one. Kirsten loves the feel of her stone walls. "I rub the stone all the time. It feels wonderful."

In that life, Kirsten had worn an apron in her work. As strange as it may sound, she loves aprons in this lifetime. "When I wear an apron, I feel creative. I made one for myself when I worked in a frame shop. I just had to have one," she said.

Since uncovering the life in Moravia, Kirsten has recognized something significant. "When I was going over that past life, it hit me that I'm living the second half of that life that was taken away from me. And I am so much enjoying it."

When Kirsten first described her wonderful stone house, I asked her if she cooked. She told me she had a big, well-equipped kitchen but never felt the desire to cook.

Well, that's all changed. "I've found I can really cook," said Kirsten. "And when people say, 'Wow, you're a great cook,' I reply, 'Yes, I was a chef in a past life.'"

THE KARMIC MOTIVATION OF FAIRNESS

The key word when it comes to betrayal is trust. If you're in a position of authority—anything from a parent to a president—then you have a responsibility to others.

Sadly, many people in authority lose their connection to the Soul World and betray the trust expected of them. It's hardly surprising, then, that I often find a past-life fear of Authority along with a fear of Betrayal.

If you were dragged before a court during the Spanish Inquisition, then you might well have a fear of Authority. When authority has betrayed its implicit trust and imposed an unnecessarily harsh sentence on you, then lifetimes later it might cause you to become a nervous wreck when you're pulled over by a uniformed officer.

Being treated as less than equal and having your trust in the fairness of those in authority broken is a common double whammy. On a soul level, the expectation is that those in authority will treat you like an equal. A lack of respect for you as a fellow soul is a massive betrayal of trust and an assault on your core value of Justice.

A past life of betrayal teaches your soul big lessons about doing "the right thing." Being continually exposed to the fear of Betrayal over many lifetimes, you finally learn the importance of treating everyone else justly.

In his book *We Die Alone,* author David Howarth tells an astonishing story of survival and endurance. During World War II, a group of Norwegian patriots left the Shetland Islands, at the very northernmost tip of Scotland, on a mission to destroy an airfield in the icy fjords of Nazi-occupied Norway.

On their arrival at their destination, a remote village on a rugged part of the Arctic coastline, they made contact with a shopkeeper who British Intelligence assured them was a trusted ally and would do anything he could to help them.

The man they encountered was nothing like they expected. Their presence made him anxious, and he made all sorts of excuses to avoid being involved in their plan. It turned out that the man they should have met had died several months before. The shop's new proprietor had the same name and hadn't felt any need to change the sign above the door.

After the men left, the shopkeeper made a decision that would seal the fate of the mission. The story goes that he worried the patriots were, in fact, German soldiers testing his loyalty, and that if he failed to report them, he and his wife might end their days in a concentration camp. He chose to report then to the authorities.

Later the next morning, the Norwegians discovered they'd been betrayed. All but one was killed. The man who escaped, Jan Baalsrud, discovered later that his comrades had been executed by German soldiers.

Let's take a look at the karmic consequences of such betrayal. After a number of subsequent lifetimes, in which any act of disloyalty will immediately take their souls back to the snow-covered northern wastes of Norway, the souls of the men who were executed will learn that minor acts of betrayal are not going to automatically lead to death.

Those who follow their souls' guidance will have a heightened sense of loyalty toward others. Knowing that like attracts like, their souls will work overtime to make sure they bring loyalty into their lives.

The ones who get caught up in the Illusion may be embittered by further betrayal. They risk becoming mistrustful. When that happens, they'll exude "mistrustful vibes," and that, unfortunately, will draw betrayal, the thing they most fear, toward them.

In the meantime, each of these souls will have a hair trigger when it comes to issues of betrayal and injustice. Like many people who have suffered as they once did, they may react with "fight or flight" when they perceive disloyalty toward them.

The shopkeeper is reported to have fretted all night over his decision to betray the men. Yet, when it comes to the possibility they might have been Nazis in disguise, the answer, my guides say, is obvious.

"He knew they were Norwegians in the same way you would recognize genuine Scots by cultural and historical references," they told me.

By betraying the men, the shopkeeper "did the wrong thing." Aligned more with the Nazis than the patriots, he hoped to ingratiate himself with the occupiers.

Betrayal, as a fear, is the result of an expectation or trust being broken when it leads to an individual's life plan being severely impacted. To put it simply, the patriots had an expectation. The shopkeeper had a choice. The choice he made resulted in death. The result: a fear of Betrayal for the souls who were executed, and eight years of hard labor and a significant karmic debt for the shopkeeper.

MANDATORY MINIMUMS: MAXIMUM INJUSTICE

In 1973, in an effort to deal with the rise in drug use, New York governor Nelson Rockefeller introduced tough Three Strikes Laws, aimed at taking repeat drug offenders off the street. The laws were unusually severe. Selling two ounces or possessing four ounces of "narcotic drugs" resulted in an automatic sentence of fifteen years to life.

In 2009, New York governor David Paterson said, "I can't think of a criminal justice strategy that has been more unsuccessful than the Rockefeller drug laws."

Since their inception, the laws have resulted in appalling misery for many of those convicted, as well as their families. And they did nothing to curb drug use.

In addition, the Rockefeller drug laws are often described as racist. The shocking statistics reveal that African-Americans and Latinos make up 23 percent of the population of New York State, yet they comprise 91 percent of those locked up for drug crimes.

ONE LAW FOR ALL

When you're caught up in the Illusion and your empathy is blocked, it's easy to think that the answer to crime is to "lock 'em up and throw away the key"—unless you suddenly find yourself, or a family member, in court. That's when every attempt is made to ensure leniency.

In 2002, when Noelle Bush, daughter of Florida governor Jeb Bush, was caught forging prescriptions, she was lucky. She received ten days in the slammer and rehab, amidst a flurry of requests for leniency. Had she been poor and black, she'd have been locked up for years.

In New York, vicious murderers have regularly received significantly lesser sentences than low-level drug dealers, thanks to the Rockefeller laws. In federal prisons, drug offenders do more time than rapists.

Why do Rockefeller's laws apply to drug users and not, say, white-collar criminals? White-collar crime costs the country billions of dollars more than drug-related street crime. Why not apply the same sentencing to a crime like insider trading?

When you're caught behind the Illusion, you relate to those who most resemble you. Rockefeller could most readily identify with affluent, educated, Caucasian males—just like him.

He had no ability to identify with people of color, the poor, the uneducated, the disadvantaged, and those whose behavior ran counter to his very narrow view of what was and wasn't acceptable.

In 1971, during Nelson Rockefeller's tenure as New York governor, riots broke out in Attica Prison in protest of the "ruthless brutalization and disregard for the lives of the prisoners," and in response to the murder of prisoner and author George Jackson in California's San Quentin prison. Hostages were taken and buildings set on fire.

Ignoring requests from officials and inmates, Rockefeller refused to meet and talk with Attica prisoners about their grievances. Instead, from his estate hundreds of miles away, he called in the National Guard.

A helicopter dropped tear gas on the compound. State police, guardsmen, and prison officers used machine guns and shotguns to fire indiscriminately on prisoners through the thick fog of gas. Ten hostages and twenty-nine prisoners died. All the hostages were killed by the authorities.

Would Rockefeller have refused to negotiate with the prisoners if they'd been Wall Street executives doing time for securities fraud? Would he have ordered them to be shot? Would he still have described the work of state troopers as "a superb job"?

Would he have allowed the torture and mistreatment of prisoners that occurred in the aftermath of the Attica assault?

It's a very good bet that had the prisoners been from the same background and ethnicity, they would have been treated very differently.

LEGISLATING MORALITY

Throughout history, laws have been mostly created by affluent or socially privileged males. As a result of the Illusion, poor people, women, and minorities have always tended to come out the worst off.

You only have to look at laws against prostitution to see a striking example of the old maxim, "One law for them; one law for us."

Prostitutes make up a fraction of those involved in the crime of prostitution. In other words, it takes two to make selling sex a crime: a buyer and a seller. Yet it's the seller, not the buyer, who feels the full weight of the law when the two get busted. Approximately ninety prostitutes are arrested for every ten customers.

Should they be arrested at all? Like the prohibition of alcohol in the early 1900s, laws against the sale of sex are ultimately ineffective because they deny human nature. People want to alter their consciousness, and people want to get laid.

Arresting a woman, who may have little choice of profession due to coercion or poverty, is a harsh way of dealing with the crime. And arresting a customer who might simply need a little physical comfort in the midst of an otherwise isolated life seems similarly unfair.

During the Transformation, attitudes toward prostitution, as with many other consensual crimes, will begin to undergo a big shift. How much more enlightened might it be to recognize human nature for what it is and work to make the lives of sex workers safer and happier?

For all the arguments pro and con (and there are many), there's one big reason prostitution is illegal: because it offends the sensibilities of younger souls.

As I described in *The Instruction,* young souls have problems with sex. Their lack of experience on the Physical Plane manifests as a kind of Puritanism. That's why ineffectual "abstinence only" policies exist. These may not do a thing to stop teen pregnancies, but they feel a lot more comfortable to younger souls than the more successful methods of education and accessible contraception.

A researcher from Johns Hopkins found that teens who took the pledge of abstinence behaved no differently from those who didn't. They began having sex at the same age and had a similar number of partners. The big difference is that they were much less likely to use contraception, particularly condoms.

Pretending that the sex urge—which keeps the world turning—doesn't exist, younger souls make themselves feel morally upright. The laws they enact make prostitution more—not less—of a problem. It's these very laws that keep pimps in power, prevent sex workers from getting regular medical checkups, and make it easier for prostitutes to be abused by their customers.

Some people go into prostitution by choice, in which case they have a right to exercise their free will. Others are coerced or forced into it through necessity. Either way, no one should have to face punishment for it.

Author Peter McWilliams wrote the definitive work on the subject of the hypocrisy and unfairness of consensual crimes in his book *Ain't Nobody's Business If You Do*.

Tragically, he became a victim of the very laws he tried to eliminate. After developing cancer and contracting AIDS, he was arrested for conspiracy to cultivate and distribute medical marijuana. Though California had legalized medical marijuana, McWilliams was arrested under federal law.

In court he was not allowed to use a medical marijuana defense or to mention his illness. He was also prohibited from smoking medical marijuana while awaiting sentencing.

Unable to use marijuana to curb the nausea from the medication he was taking for his illness, he choked to death on his own vomit.

Prosecutors claimed to have been "saddened" by news of Peter McWilliams's death (probably not quite to the degree experienced by his mother).

AN EYE FOR AN EYE MAKES US ALL BLIND

It's ironic that the institutions charged with dispensing justice are the ones most often guilty of crimes of injustice. These are crimes committed by courts, governments, and institutions of all kind. They may be legal, but they are spiritually unjust.

Behind the Illusion, a person is capable of inflicting cruel and unusual punishment on other souls. In courtrooms throughout the world, justice plays second fiddle to the rule of law, expediency, discrimination, and vindictiveness.

In Somalia, a petty thief undergoes multiple amputations; in Thailand, a drug courier is shot; in Texas, a guy who steals a Snickers bar receives a sentence of sixteen years under the state's three-strikes laws. ("It *was* a king size," assistant district attorney Jodi Brown told the press.)

....

CRIMINAL INJUSTICE

California's Three Strikes Law was intended to keep violent repeat offenders off the streets. If that was the intention, it's been a dismal failure. The people whose lives have been ruined by this cruel, fear-based response to crime have mostly been petty offenders.

Robert DiBlasi is a married man with two children. He's doing thirty-one years to life for the theft of a pack of AA batteries that cost $2.69.

Rene Landa is serving twenty-seven years to life for stealing a car tire.

Ruben Arriaga was sentenced to twenty-five years to life for the theft of drill from Sears that cost $70.

The citizens of California must sleep easier knowing these menaces to society are safely locked away pretty much forever.

No matter how noble their intentions, everyone responsible for the negative consequences of such draconian laws will carry a karmic debt. For those who simply voted for the measure, the debt will be small. For those who enforce it, especially when they have the option not to, the debt will be significant.

....

Judicial sentencing is an accurate way to determine the soul age of a nation or region. Younger souls, with fewer lifetimes of experience behind them, tend to be less able to empathize with victims of injustice and more fearful about becoming a victim of crime.

The idea of locking bad guys up and throwing away the key makes perfect sense to young souls. (As long as they're not the ones being locked up, of course.) And when a person's empathy is blocked by the Illusion, justice becomes more about retribution than fairness.

Ruth is dealing with the challenge of having her oldest son in prison for using drugs. His incarceration has triggered in her a previously dormant motivation of Fairness: Ruth has become a one-woman fight for justice.

When Keith was arrested for possession of drugs, it stirred up a traumatic past life in which Ruth was a boy born into slavery in the South. During his short life, he witnessed countless acts of injustice and cruelty, and he had every form of indignity imposed on him. The unfairness created a burning resentment inside him.

When the boy's father was unjustly accused of rape, he threatened one of the accusers, earning himself a severe whipping. The injury was compounded when he witnessed his father being lynched. His anger was now virtually uncontrollable, and for his owner's safety, he was sold.

After he attacked his new master, he was branded and permanently shackled. He died not long after from disease at the age of just nineteen.

It's hardly surprising that such a harsh past life would stir up deep anger in Ruth now. She might never have really felt its impact had Keith not been arrested, but when he became the victim of a cruel and deliberately heartless system, the motivation to help him (and others like him) kicked Ruth into action.

The motivation of Fairness turned an otherwise mild-mannered, soft-spoken soccer mom into a fearless fighter for justice.

"I've always stood up for the underdog; I've always been a rebel in that way," Ruth said. "A lot of people haven't had all the chances I've had, and I'm not afraid to stand up for them."

Keith had never committed a violent crime. He'd had a few misdemeanor charges for possession of pot, but this time it was for methamphetamine, and they really threw the book at him. "He needed treatment, not imprisonment," Ruth said, echoing the sentiments of my spirit guides.

He was locked up in an overcrowded and insanitary prison, along with some of the most violent criminals imaginable. On top of a stiff sentence, both Keith and Ruth had to deal with official obstruction and intransigence, which turned something as simple as a prison visit into a nightmare.

"One time I went to visit my son, and they said he was on lockdown. I demanded to see the warden. I found out later they were lying—he wasn't on lockdown at all. Later my son told me he'd heard a guard say some lady was giving them some lip. 'I knew it had to be you,' he said.

"I can get a little feisty. The prison had the phone company block calls from the prison to my home. I went straight to the prision administrators and complained," she said.

Keith got out of prison and was drug free and doing great until the police raided the house he lived in, after a complaint from a neighbor, and found some drugs on a roommate. It was a violation of his parole, and he found himself in trouble once more. Facing another long sentence, he decided to become a fugitive.

"When guys get out of prison, it's impossible to find a job," Ruth said. So when Keith discovered that no one wanted to hire him, he made plans to start his own business.

All Ruth knows of Keith's whereabouts is that he's somewhere in North America setting up his own business. He's off drugs and planning to turn himself in when the business gets going. He wants to have something to come out to.

Ruth channeled her karmic energies into becoming a volunteer with the Insight Prison Project, an organization dedicated to empowering prisoners by creating rehabilitation programs.

"I got involved after talking to a man who saved my son from being forced to stab someone," she said. "He told the other prisoners, 'Leave him alone. He's a kid and he's getting out soon.' He may have saved Keith's life.

"Through the project, I would get a group of ten or twelve prisoners to work with victims of a similar crime—a kind of surrogate healing. The prisoners have to be accountable for the crime they committed and be aware of how the crime affected the person they hurt and everyone else involved. One guy, who had murdered his girlfriend, had a list of three hundred people he'd hurt."

SPIRITUAL ACT 4: SPREADING FAIRNESS

We all have had lives in which we've been the victim of betrayal, whether it's a draconian sentence for a trivial crime or the inability to receive justice for crimes committed against us.

Ruth has been able to harness the impetus from her past life to give her the energy to help her son. Apart from helping him, she has also given her life a sense of meaning.

You, too, can help yourself and others by Spiritual Acts that bring a little more fairness into the world. To do so, look for ways to help victims of social or judicial injustice. I have, for example, a client who helps indigent families find accommodations; another helps victims of violent crime get treatment. Both are using the motivation of Fairness to heal themselves while benefitting others.

Because of Ruth's own past-life experience as a victim of injustice, her son's ordeal has triggered the motivation of Fairness more strongly than it might otherwise have done. She responds to the plight of ex-prisoners with a compassion that comes from having suffered in similar ways herself.

"When prisoners get released, they enter a world of corruption, dishonesty, and lack of accountability," Ruth said. "One of the men I worked with got out after thirty years. It took him months to get a driver's license because he didn't have a credit card. Everything he tried to do, the bureaucracy put him through hoops. Even then, no one would hire him.

"I feel so strongly about helping these men," said Ruth. "After working with them, I'd have any one of them in my home. I've given thousands of dollars to the Insight Prison Project, and when I sell my house, I'm going to give a whole lot more."

The motivation of Fairness is never as strong as it is in those who've had their trust in humanity betrayed.

FIGHTING FOR JUSTICE

In 1984, in Bhopal, India, toxic gas escaped from a Union Carbide plant. It blanketed the surrounding area, causing hemorrhaging, choking, and blindness. According to one survivor, "People were defecating and urinating in their clothes. They didn't want to live." Thousands of men, women, and children died in terror and agony.

The company had ignored warnings from inspectors and had refused to implement their safety recommendations. On the night of the disaster, none of the plant's safety systems was working. The gas escaped and began killing without any warning. At least half a million people were poisoned.

Doctors were hampered by Union Carbide's refusal to reveal the nature of the gas. In the years since the incident, tens of thousands of people have died, babies have been born with terrible deformities, and cancers and respiratory diseases are continuing to take their toll.

REMINDERS OF PAST INJUSTICE

When you've been the victim of injustice in a previous lifetime, your heightened sense of fairness will automatically cause you to side with the "underdog." When you see someone being the victim of authority or injustice, your soul will nudge you in the ribs and say, "Remember when we were like that?"

Union Carbide's executives were charged under Indian law, but they refused to turn up in court. The company was sued for compensation. They offered a fraction of what was required to pay for medical treatment and to help those who can no longer work or feed their families.

To this day, the water in Bhopal is heavily contaminated by Union Carbide's chemicals and has been declared unfit for drinking. Yet, Union Carbide, now owned by Dow Chemicals, has done nothing to relieve the situation, despite having annual profits in the billions of dollars.

Dow's karmic debt, like its profits, is enormous. But thanks to shareholder pressure and the greed of the company's top executives, it will not be balanced in this lifetime.

Yet, already, the power of karma is creating the impetus for change. Survivors of the killing are becoming a voice of change, not only for the Bhopal victims, but for people worldwide who are exploited by ruthless corporations.

Two of the survivors, Rashida Bee and Champa Devi Shukla, have become a force to be reckoned with. They were winners, in 2004, of the Goldman Prize for Environmental and Human Rights.

These two courageous old souls have taken on the mighty Dow Corporation with some success. They've organized hunger strikes, protests, and rallies credited with causing a drop in Dow's stock price.

What gives these two women the impetus to help their fellow victims? It's not just their own plight. They have the heightened awareness that comes from having undergone lessons in betrayal in past lifetimes. They may be recalling events that occurred hundreds of years ago; they may have been the victim or the perpetrator.

Their soul-level memories encourage them to access the motivation of Fairness to summon the impetus to help their kindred spirits.

The urge to help their fellow victims was triggered by the injustice the women saw in Bhophal. According to Rashida Bee, "Some of my family members were missing for days. I had to look at thousands of bodies to see if they were among the dead."

It's through the goal of Justice that these courageous souls are making the shift from Stage Three to Four.

By harnessing the motivation that lies within them, Bee and Shukla have become champions for human rights. They're acting in harmony with their souls against an organization that has no soul. And that has given their lives a higher purpose. They have reached into their souls' past and drawn out the energy to create a positive force for transformation that will influence generations.

BUILDING A SENSE OF JUSTICE

It's easy to be tough on crime when you're not the one facing years in the slammer. The purpose of this exercise is to stimulate your motivation of Fairness.

FAIRNESS EXERCISE 2

TEN SENTENCES FOR TEN CRIMES

Bring in your spirit guides with the following request: "I call upon my spirit guides, acting in my highest interest, to help me reach the goal of Justice through the motivation of Fairness."

- Make a list of ten crimes, such as DUI, selling marijuana, home burglary, or rape.
- Considering each crime, one at a time, write what you believe would be an appropriate sentence for the crime.
- Now do the same, picturing yourself as the perpetrator in front of the judge.
- Again, write what you believe would be an appropriate sentence.

There's no right or wrong answer. It's simply a way to get you thinking about justice from a different perspective.

The Transformation is elevating our Collective Consciousness and taking us away from primitive emotions such as revenge. It won't be long before the idea of locking up fellow human beings for punishment or retribution—rather than rehabilitating them—will seem as antiquated as putting citizens in the stocks and cutting off their ears.

As the Transformation builds, the desire to act in a more elevated way will affect each of us. One area where this shift will be most noticeable will be in our impetus to learn. The next chapter explores the coming emphasis on the pursuit of knowledge and the way it will rapidly speed the shift to a Stage Four Consciousness.

CHAPTER SIX

THE SEARCH FOR KNOWLEDGE
Making Up for Lost Time

GOAL Knowledge
MOTIVATION Curiosity
FEAR Failure

THE URGE TO KEEP LEARNING

Curiosity motivates us to learn. It puts questions into our heads that we then feel the urge to answer. And where does this curiosity come from? It flows directly from the soul.

As you know, your soul comes here to find out what it means to be a spiritual being in a physical body. Like a shark that has to keep swimming in a forward direction to survive, your soul has to keep learning to evolve.

Though the desire to learn is stronger in some souls than others, there will always be a sufficient number of highly curious individuals to ensure continual growth of the Collective Consciousness.

When a lifetime ends prematurely, it creates a soul-level feeling of disappointment at the time of death. You might have died of typhus at age six and missed out on a career as a teacher. Or perhaps you drowned at age twenty, never having had the family you planned to raise.

Having lost years, or even a whole lifetime of learning, your soul will want to make up for lost time in this incarnation.

People with a past-life fear of Failure have a thirst for knowledge. They'll listen to National Public Radio, watch the Discovery Channel, read nonfiction, and attend workshops and classes. This is a generalization, of course, but it's surprising just how many of my clients recognize these few simple markers.

The fear causes anxiety—a worry that you're not going to complete your life plan again. It can create a sense of urgency and a pressing need to get things done sooner rather than later.

Unfortunately, procrastination, the legendary thief of time, very often has a fear of Failure at its root. The result is that nothing gets done. You might develop a case of "what's-the-point-itis" or, if you have a present-life issue with restlessness, start running around like a headless chicken: plenty of activity but no real progress.

If you have a past-life fear of Failure, you might have real problems beginning a task. Then, once you do, you may become obsessive, feeling you must get it finished urgently. Some people swing between the two.

A lot of people with this fear are afraid of making decisions in case they make the wrong one. Nila is one of them.

In Nila's recent past, she was a five-year-old boy named Manuel who lived with his father and stepmother in Mexico City. He'd been put in their care after his birth mother had to spend time in a mental institution.

When Manuel was told he'd be returned to his mother, he was distraught. He didn't want to leave the home he loved to be with someone who was volatile and distant. Hoping to make himself sick so he could stay, he drank a toxic liquid he found in the garage. He burned his esophagus and died in great distress with damage to all his major organs.

When I told Nila about what had happened to her, she saw the resonance with this life immediately. In fact, it couldn't have been more obvious.

"When I get stressed, or when I'm around a chemical cleaner like Comet, I stop breathing," she said. "My throat just closes up. Usually, I can get a little air through my nose, but one time in the shower, I couldn't get any air at all. I was hysterical—I thought I was dying.

"My husband has had to call 911 a few times, but after a minute or two I'd be okay, and he has had to call them back. I cough a lot after and can't talk. I gasp and my eyes water, and I'm hoarse for a couple of hours. I've been to doctors, but they can't find anything wrong."

As I said earlier, a major manifestation of the fear has been a problem making decisions. Like a lot of people with a deadly mistake in their soul's past, Nila fears the consequences of making the wrong choice. I asked her if she recognized that symptom.

"I can't make decisions! I hate to make them," she said. "I'll just kind of surrender."

Since the big mistake she'd made in Mexico had been to ingest the substance that killed her, I asked if she had problems with giving her children medicine, or with taking remedies herself.

"I was so afraid of making a mistake, I used to write down everything I gave the kids," Nila answered. "I was terrified they'd get kidney failure from too much Tylenol or something. I never take conventional medicine myself—just natural herbs and supplements."

Nila had just left her husband, and I asked her how she'd made that decision.

"It was tough," she said. "I wanted to leave him for years, but I just couldn't act on it. Then I found out he'd cheated on me, and he lied about it, over and over. I might have gotten over the unfaithfulness, but it was the lying that got me. I lost all respect for him. We tried staying together for the kids, but I got so depressed I wished I were dead. Then I realized that if I didn't leave, I wasn't putting the kids first."

Nila has recently filed for divorce and quit her job, which she feels are positive changes in her life. "I'm finally making really good choices about my future," she told me. "And I haven't had any more problems with my throat. Now, after fifteen years of a bad marriage, I'm resurfacing, stronger than ever. I feel happy; I feel in control. I feel like a weight has been lifted."

Like so many people with a past-life fear of Failure, Nila had been reluctant to leave her marriage, no matter how unhappy she was, in case it turned out to be a mistake. Overcoming her fear has given her the opportunity to achieve her potential in this life.

. . . .

SIGNS OF A PAST-LIFE FEAR OF FAILURE

People with a fear of Failure are all impacted in different ways by their souls' irrational concern that this life could end at any time. Though the soul-level anxiety is related to premature death in a prior incarnation, this is not to be confused with a fear of Death, which we'll look at in Chapter Ten.

As we saw earlier, people with a fear of Loss might have a heightened concern that they could lose their children. And, sure, it could happen, but the odds are no higher than the next person's.

With a fear of Failure the same applies. That individual's chances of not completing his or her life plan are not significantly greater than anyone else's. (And having this fear is most certainly not a sign of a potential early demise.)

Making up for lost time in a previous incarnation gives almost everyone with this fear a need to keep learning.

The following are all quotes from clients of mine who have a fear of Failure:

- I'm going back to college to get my master's degree.
- I'm scared of making a decision in case I get it wrong.
- I feel there's never enough time.
- I worry I won't complete my life's purpose.
- I love taking classes.
- I only ever read nonfiction.
- I go to bed stressed out that I didn't get enough done in the day.
- I feel like I'm in a holding pattern.
- I struggle with procrastination.

The fear of Failure is, of course, irrational. Your soul bases its belief on past performance, not the future. You could live to be a hundred. And once you can convince your soul of that, you can actually achieve more than you would otherwise.

There's one important thing you need if you're going to connect to your goal of Knowledge, and that's to overcome the effects of the Illusion.

The key is to use the motivation—in this case, Curiosity—to help you attain the goal. Thanks to the principle of cause and effect, the more knowledge you obtain, the more you stimulate the curiosity within you. And the more you stimulate the curiosity, the more you'll be compelled to obtain knowledge. It can become self-perpetuating.

Once you get into the cycle of knowledge and curiosity, your soul senses forward movement, and the fear of Failure dissipates. As long as you keep learning, you're making up for lost time. Your soul can breathe easy.

So, if you're in a holding pattern, uncertain which way to turn, and you have a pressing need to keep learning, a fear of Failure is the most likely culprit.

A fear of Failure can make it hard to get motivated. What if it's the wrong choice? What if there's no time to retrace your steps and start out on another path?

MINDLESS ACTIVITIES

A client asked me, "Why can't I lie on a beach reading a celebrity magazine like everyone else?"

If you've had a significant past life in which you died without completing your life plan, you'll have missed out on a big chunk of Physical Plane experience.

Having a sense of unfinished business means that in your leisure time you'll find it difficult to just switch off and do nothing.

Each summer, the museums and galleries of Europe are packed with individuals who want to take a break but keep learning. These are the types of people who would rather attend a workshop than take a cruise with nothing to do all day. (One of my clients with a very strong fear of Failure recently returned from an all-expenses-paid cruise and described it as a "floating prison.")

If you have a fear of Failure, lying on a beach with a celebrity magazine may have to wait for your next lifetime.

THE KARMIC CONSEQUENCES
OF ASSUMPTION

It's easy to confuse beliefs and assumptions with knowledge. The difference is that knowledge leads to a higher level of consciousness, whereas assumptions block spiritual growth. To become a spiritually conscious Stage Four soul, you need to make sure you can tell the difference.

A great physicist, possibly the greatest of them all, was Sir Isaac Newton. The famous story goes that one day he was sitting beneath a tree when an apple fell on his head. In that moment, he realized that falling objects are drawn to the Earth, which led to his discovery that objects throughout the universe, like stars and planets, must act upon every other object the same way.

Newton made a permanent impact on the world because he followed his soul's innate curiosity to search for facts. He was interested in knowledge, not just finding a way to back up preconceived beliefs. He set out to prove his theories rather than base them on assumptions.

For centuries, human understanding had been held back by a rigid conservatism. Aristotle's descriptions of an Earth-centered universe and Galen's works on anatomy were accepted without question for almost 1,500 years.

Before Newton, there was no understanding of the way the world worked that didn't involve religion. Newton's "mechanistic humanism" explained the world in natural terms. His investigative methods opened the doors to scientific discovery.

It was Newton and others who relied on experimentation and observation instead of speculation, who laid the foundations for science as we know it.

Karmically, Newton was responsible for a huge shift in both his own consciousness and our Collective Consciousness. His work in mathematics and physics has impacted every one of us whether we know it or not.

....

NEWTON'S LAW OF KARMA

According to Newton's third law of motion, for every action there's an equal and opposite reaction: a prime example of cause and effect.

It could also describe the laws of karma. When you take a life, you'll return in another incarnation to save a life. If you've limited someone's free will, you'll balance the karmic debt by one day giving that soul opportunities they might not have had otherwise.

Karma is about balance, not an eye for an eye. (If you kill someone, they will not be obliged to kill you at some later date.) Every karmic debt created must be, at some point, repaid. The way that's undertaken depends on the kind of karma.

Negative karma is the result of interfering with a person's ability to complete his or her life plan. Positive karma is created when you help someone who wouldn't otherwise complete his or her life plan to do so.

....

A negative reaction against the pursuit of knowledge comes from those who fear it. And, sadly, there are many people who do fear knowledge and the illumination it brings. Instead, they prefer to hide in the darkness, very often in the company of others like themselves, safe from any challenges to their worldview.

The good news is that this fear-based reaction to the pursuit of knowledge is part of the Illusion. While knowledge, being one of the soul's goals, is subject to the continual forward movement of the universe. In other words, during the Transformation, knowledge will always trump assumption, no matter how much resistance there is against it.

To put it yet another way, resistance to knowledge is doomed to failure. Why? Let me give you an example.

Galileo, another great physicist, was also an astronomer and mathematician. Einstein described him as the father of science. Galileo's problems began when he rejected the conventional view that the sun, the moon, and the stars revolved around Earth. He reckoned Earth circled the sun. It was an opinion that would cause him to be dragged before the Inquisition, threatened with torture, and forced to spend the remaining years of his life under house arrest.

The belief that Earth stayed still while all the other heavenly bodies moved around it had been Church doctrine for centuries. Any suggestion that it worked in another way threatened the Church's power. Yet, eventually that institution had to review its position.

Even today, the Creation Museum in Ohio presents as truth ideas that completely ignore modern scientific understanding. The museum explains that the world is just a few thousand years old, that humans and dinosaurs coexisted until recently, and that dinosaurs, despite their vicious looking fangs and claws, were herbivores. It even displays a lifelike triceratops with a saddle, implying that dinosaurs had once been domesticated.

Disney movies tell us that wooden puppets can become real boys if they tell the truth, that fish will travel thousands of miles to save a single offspring, and that toys come to life when you're not looking and can negotiate the streets of a big city without anyone noticing.

The difference is that no one is pretending *Pinocchio, Finding Nemo,* and *Toy Story* are real. Creationists, on the other hand, claim that the biblical story of Genesis is fact and should be taught in schools alongside evolution.

Belief and facts are two different things. You might believe the world is flat, but if you keep sailing, you're never actually going to find the edge. If you believe you're invisible, you might remove your clothes in a crowded mall, but chances are you're going to be detained by security.

The idea that the world is only a couple of thousand years old, and that dinosaurs and humans recently coexisted, may help to explain away inconsistencies between science and religion. But it's a belief and has no basis in reality.

There is no spiritual growth in belief. The goal of Knowledge, on the other hand, takes your soul on the fast track to a Stage Four Consciousness.

The Church eventually had to accept that Galileo was right. Earth does revolve around the sun, not the other way around. In the face of overwhelming evidence that the sun lies at the hub of the solar system, the Church had to change its mind for the sake of its own credibility.

To do otherwise would have risked going the way of the dinosaurs. (The real ones—not the ones with saddles.) And when the pursuit of science became a less dangerous pursuit, it opened the door to greater fact-based research.

Knowledge banishes assumption, the blissful state of having belief without substantiating facts. Beliefs, especially those you adopt from another source without engaging your intuition, can lead to spiritual stagnation. That's something your soul desperately seeks to avoid.

WHEN YOU ASSUME . . .

In an episode of the classic TV series *The Odd Couple,* character Felix Unger conducts his own defense during his trial for ticket scalping. Writing on a blackboard, he makes the point that when you "assume," you make an "ass" of "u" and "me."

Unfortunately, when you assume, you're more likely to make an ass of u. That's how the great author Sir Arthur Conan Doyle managed to look a fool when he ignored his critical faculties and declared his belief that photographs showing two young girls surrounded by fairies were genuine.

When the girls were old ladies, they admitted the fairies were actually illustrations clipped from a book.

Blind faith has been described as belief without evidence. It can cause people to reject their soul's guidance, instead putting their lives in the hands of another human being. Sometimes, the consequences can be disastrous.

In 1997, thirty-nine members of the Heaven's Gate cult donned brand-new shirts, pants, and Nike trainers, put $5.75 in their pockets, and took a lethal cocktail of phenobarbital and vodka.

Their leader, Marshall Applewhite, claimed to have arrived on Earth as the reincarnation of Jesus and that he would exit this world in a spaceship following the comet Hale-Bopp—along with a chosen few. To be better prepared for this event, he and several of his followers had themselves castrated.

Why so many people followed Applewhite to self-destruction has much to do with the consequences of hiding behind the Illusion. When you adopt someone else's beliefs, especially those that are erroneous, you have to switch off the connection between your brain and your intuition. If you didn't, you'd make a poor follower. You'd be questioning everything, asking for validation, and it wouldn't be long before you lost the approval of the leader.

Instead, by abdicating responsibility and allowing that person to tell you when to get up, what to eat, and so on, you gain approval, but at a huge karmic cost.

The moment you stop taking personal responsibility, you choose beliefs over facts. "A spaceship is coming to take me to a better place? Sure, count me in." Your soul might be screaming a warning, but behind the comfort of the Illusion, the voice is muted.

It's been said many times that knowledge is power. It allows you to make sensible decisions based on facts. If Marshall Applewhite's followers had followed their souls' innate curiosity and said, "How do we know you're Jesus?" or "Spaceship? Prove it," they might still be here today.

If knowledge is power, ignorance is powerlessness. Totalitarian governments know this. Who are the first to get the chop when the coup or revolution takes place? Intellectuals.

Throughout our world's bloody past, intellectuals have frequently been the source of government-sanctioned extermination. Mao Zedong rounded up writers, students, and intellectuals and had them killed or imprisoned in reeducation camps.

Pol Pot was so determined to wipe out every intellectual in Cambodia that he executed people simply for wearing glasses or speaking a foreign language.

Intellectuals, or those who think for themselves, are the last things a dictator wants, and that's why they're the first to go. It's not even necessary to kill them all. By jailing or executing a small bunch of educated dissidents, the dictator puts the fear of death (literally) into anyone else who might be tempted to criticize the regime.

SPIRITUAL ACT 5: SPREADING KNOWLEDGE

The Spiritual Act related to healing a past-life fear of Failure is helping others to gain knowledge. There are many ways of doing this. You could support literacy projects or many of the charities that exist to help mentor and tutor children. You might consider becoming a mentor yourself.

You missed out on education from having had past lives cut short. Education is the key to healing yourself and making a difference in the lives of those who might otherwise lack the opportunity to gain knowledge.

Genuine knowledge is a threat to those whose power is based on beliefs. It doesn't just happen in dictatorships either. Teachers who refuse to toe the conventional line have historically faced the wrath of the established powers.

Socrates, the great philosopher, spent his life in the pursuit of knowledge. His criticisms of the government in Athens, however, resulted in his death after a trial in which he was sentenced to drink poison hemlock.

Those who offend the government in the present world face serious consequences, too. Pulitzer Prize–winning journalist Gary Webb discovered this when he wrote a hard-hitting series of articles about CIA complicity in helping the Nicaraguan Contras fuel the crack cocaine epidemic of the 1980s.

Though Webb's stories were eventually confirmed by the CIA itself, he was fired, discredited, and effectively prevented from working on any other mainstream newspaper again. His career destroyed, his reputation trashed, Gary Webb eventually took his own life.

Webb's fate was a warning to any journalist who might think about bucking the system, which is designed to support the existing power structure and to actively avoid uncovering the truth.

Approximately five hundred journalists are arrested every year worldwide, and another five hundred have been murdered during the last fifteen years. Many of these journalists, now, are bloggers, the new generation of inquiring minds who are rapidly filling the gap left by mainstream newspapers and television.

With little real investigative journalism being carried out by the mainstream media these days (largely the fault of the owners, not the journalists themselves), we're unlikely to see another Watergate-type exposé anytime soon.

What we will see is more of the real search for knowledge being carried out by individuals and smaller organizations—ones less likely to be intimidated by the rich and powerful.

It's by questioning perceived wisdom that we, as a species, grow. Whether you're a Nobel Prize–winning physicist or a humble blogger, you owe it to your soul to question your beliefs and use your sense of curiosity in the pursuit of knowledge.

KARMIC INFLUENCES

In the year 1900, brilliant mathematician and physicist Lord Kelvin declared, "There is nothing new to be discovered in physics now." Five years later, Einstein published his theory of special relativity.

There's a tendency for human beings to always feel they're at the cutting edge of technology. We give thanks that we don't live in the Dark Ages, never thinking how we might appear to our descendants in the year 3100.

Lord Kelvin expressed skepticism about the possibility of manned flight less than a decade before the Wright Brothers' historic flight of 1903. If Lord Kelvin couldn't envision a flying machine, he couldn't have begun to imagine the world we live in today.

It's easy to look back with amusement at Lord Kelvin's myopic view of a future without airplanes, computers, mass communication, and all the amazing technological developments that have evolved in the last century or so. Yet, his discoveries played a significant role in creating the world we know. From the temperature scale that bears his name, to the first and second laws of thermodynamics and his contribution to long-distance communication, his work paved the way for the problem solvers like him who followed.

As we progress through the Transformation, the desire for knowledge will increase as we cast off the limiting chains of the Illusion. We can each use our knowledge to improve, support, and illuminate the path of our fellow humans.

Knowledge, when used responsibly, can create a karmic legacy by improving the lives of others or even simply by inspiring them to seek out knowledge of their own. The secret is to stimulate the karmic motivation of Curiosity.

People often wonder how we have the technology to send a man to the moon—but not to cure the common cold. Had it not been for our souls' natural curiosity, we wouldn't have made it ten feet off the ground, much less to the moon and back.

Before we humans graduated to our current state of Stage Three Consciousness, our species had been evolving at a snail's pace. We'd taken tens of thousands of years to develop primitive spears and the most basic of tools. An outside observer monitoring our progress every ten, or even every hundred, years would have seen no apparent change.

It was only around 55,000 years ago, when we underwent the last Transformation, that things started to really move.

Plato said that necessity is the mother of invention. If that's the case, then curiosity is its father.

It was curiosity as well as necessity that gave us the impetus to up and leave Africa where our species had lived for millennia. And it's curiosity that has kept us moving forward in every area of our lives ever since.

It was curiosity that pushed our ancestors to keep looking for newer and better weaponry: first bows and arrows, then before you know it, the atom bomb.

It's through the continual acquisition of knowledge that the soul learns how neutrons behave in an atom, why $E=mc^2$, and why the universe we live in works the way it does. As we grow intellectually, we connect more strongly to our souls through the transformational goal of Knowledge, and that, in turn, leads to spiritual evolution.

During the Transformation, you'll find your thirst for knowledge becoming progressively stronger. As your consciousness starts to elevate, you'll develop an increased interest in learning about yourself and the world around you. (It has, of course, already begun to happen.)

• • •

The world is full of individuals whose thirst for knowledge has shaped its history. Some, like Galileo and Sir Isaac Newton, have left positive karmic legacies—ones that have benefitted humanity while simultaneously elevating the Collective Consciousness. Others, sadly, have used their knowledge to less enlightened ends.

To see how two people, both men of science, left very different karmic legacies, compare the impacts made by Dr. Jonas Salk and Dr. Louis Fieser.

Dr. Salk, as most people know, developed the vaccine for polio. In the 1950s, polio killed more children than any other disease. Salk's vaccine eventually led to the eradication of this crippling and often fatal disease.

Fewer people are familiar with Louis Fieser, a brilliant organic chemist. He was responsible for many great developments, including the synthesis of vitamin K. How Fieser really made a name for himself, though, was through the invention of napalm—a flammable, viscous liquid that was widely used as a military weapon throughout the twentieth century.

Napalm kills through burning and suffocation, and it has been used on troops and civilians since World War II. It rose to prominence during the Vietnam War when millions of gallons were dropped over the country.

You might think there would be no question about the impact each of these men had on the world. To a very great extent you'd be right. No matter how you look at it, Salk's karmic legacy is positive; Fieser's is negative.

Dr. Fieser's work has impacted the Collective Consciousness. Unfortunately, it has diminished rather than elevated us. Karmically, any positive work he may have accomplished during his career will be overshadowed by his invention of napalm. No spiritually conscious soul will look at his legacy and say, "I want to be just like Louis Fieser."

Spiritually, Dr. Fieser was blocked by the Illusion. He was unable to accept his responsibility for the deaths and terrible injuries that resulted from his invention. He once famously stated, "I have no right to judge the morality of napalm just because I invented it."

On the other hand, Dr. Salk has played a big part in elevating the Collective Consciousness, and each of us benefits as a result. When asked who owned the patent on his discovery, Salk remarked, "No one. Could you patent the sun?" He wanted the vaccine to be available to as many people as possible.

An inspiring old soul like Salk has influenced generations of doctors and researchers. We'll never know just how many spiritually conscious souls have been inspired by his example and gone on to create positive karmic legacies of their own.

You're probably familiar with the shocking image from the Vietnam War of a young girl running along a country road, her naked body severely burned by napalm. This little girl was Phan Thi Kim Phúc, and she was so badly burned no one expected her to live. She endured seventeen operations over the next twelve years, and her body still bears the scars from that 1972 bombing.

Kim described the pain of the napalm on her skin as "the most terrible pain you can imagine." Despite having suffered such horrendous injuries, Kim has forgiven all those who were responsible for the attack that killed her two little brothers and left her scarred for life.

Kim now devotes her life to helping child victims of war through her own foundation and by working as a goodwill ambassador with UNESCO. Her karmic legacy is one that will affect generations in a positive way. The gritty black-and-white image showing her fleeing the smoke and flames of a napalm attack played a large part in swaying American public opinion against the war in Vietnam.

The work Kim does—from speaking out about the importance of peace, to being a walking example of what it is to be a spiritually conscious old soul—has influenced millions. Her part in raising the Collective Consciousness has been incalculable.

THE KARMIC CONSEQUENCE OF UNFINISHED BUSINESS

Having your life end prematurely might be considered unfortunate, but if it happens a couple of times, your soul starts to get worried. When you've had a string of truncated lifetimes in your recent past, your soul may just assume that this lifetime will be little different.

Before I even spoke to Anna, my spirit guides told me she had an Achilles' heel: her past-life fear of Failure. "Anna was once a pirate who drowned many people in the course of his work," they told me. "She has chosen to spend many lives at sea."

During her session, when I looked into one of Anna's most recent lifetimes, I found she'd been the one who drowned. This time she was a sailor named Jim, a crew member on board a merchant vessel during World War II. The ship had made an uneventful trip from Southampton, England, to the United States. On the return journey, however, it ran into trouble in the shape of a German submarine.

As a highly intuitive person, Jim began to get the sense the ship would be torpedoed. His anxiety built over several days until he couldn't eat or sleep. Finally, he couldn't think of anything but the threat of going down with the ship.

In the early hours of a cold North Atlantic morning, Jim went out on deck. It was still dark, and a light rain was falling. He paced the deck until the sky began to lighten. Every so often he'd stop to scan the sea for signs of a periscope. As long as he was on deck, Jim felt he might have some chance of escape.

When the torpedo finally hit, it blew a massive hole in the hull of the ship almost directly below him. The blast threw him into the sea. The moment he went under, the shock caused him to gulp the freezing water. He was dead in seconds.

Another life was over before it had been completed. The fear of Failure was once again reinforced. And when I asked Anna if she had any issues with drowning, she didn't have to think twice.

"I think that's why I was born in the Midwest," she said. "The ocean doesn't do it for me. I don't even like looking at water that much. I'll take the prairie any day. My husband wanted us to move somewhere near a body of water. I told him I'd never sleep for worrying about the children drowning.

"My husband told me I should learn to swim. I had a kind of 'it'll kill me' reaction. It's just not going to happen in this life. I reckon I'm still going to get drowned," Anna said.

Like most people with a strong fear of Failure, Anna is drawn to learning, though the path has not been easy. "My parents divorced when I was in high school. I watched my mom clean hotel rooms for lousy pay, so I wanted a well-paying job as soon as possible.

"I knew everything at age fourteen, and it's been downhill ever since," she said with a laugh. "It's crazy to be eighteen and asked what you want to do with your life. I didn't know what I wanted to do. Instead of going to college like I should have done, I did a two-year program at a technical institute."

Now in her midthirties, Anna is devoted to learning. "I look at the world as a constant education. The more I learn, the more I see there's still so much to learn, and now I can't stop. I'm all about wellness and nutrition. I can't learn enough."

CURIOSITY EXERCISE 1

QUESTION WHAT YOU READ

There's a priceless piece of dialogue in one of my favorite movies, *So I Married an Axe Murderer*. In it, the hero, Charlie, expresses amazement that his mother refers to the *Weekly World News* (the supermarket tabloid) as "the paper," given that papers are supposed to contain facts.

His mother replies, "This paper contains facts. Plenty of facts. 'Pregnant man gives birth.' That's a fact."

But not every newspaper is such a stickler for the facts as the *Weekly World News*. Some of them get things wrong. Some even print stories that are biased or downright dishonest.

I encourage you to get in the habit of seeking out different sources, rather than relying on one place for your news. Question what you read and check more than one source to verify accuracy. If you do this, you stand a greater chance of determining what's fact and what's not.

"I'm a recovering know-it-all!" Elizabeth told me when we first spoke. It was a clear sign of the past-life fear of Failure we were to uncover in her next session.

During a past life in London, Elizabeth was a young boy who suffered debilitating migraines. His father, a greengrocer in the area of Streatham, took the boy, James, to see a cranial specialist who suggested an operation to "relieve pressure on his brain."

The procedure, known as "trepanning," involved boring a hole in the child's head with a mechanical drill. James trusted his parents. The parents trusted the doctor. Sadly, the doctor was incompetent, inexperienced, and arrogant. He used fancy words and false promises to convince the family to allow him to operate on James.

The operation was, as you can probably guess, not a success. The actual procedure was not just ineffective, it was excruciatingly painful. An infection set in, causing permanent damage, leaving James with constant seizures. It did nothing to stop the migraines.

James's mother took care of him until her death; then his father took over. James spent a great deal of his time in a semi-darkened room, rarely venturing outside.

When his father died, James ended up in a home for the insane. He was treated with callous disrespect and began to develop deep resentment toward the staff and even other patients. When he attacked a female patient who rejected his advances, he was beaten and locked in a solitary cell.

Because of his behavior, James was incorrectly judged to be insane. This impression was reinforced by his habit of quoting endlessly from the Bible.

As the years went by, James grew despondent. He began to worry that he really was insane. His moods became darker, and he developed chronic pain from stomach ulcers. Finally, in a fit of despair, he strangled himself with his own clothing.

When I'd finished telling Elizabeth about this life, I asked her if anything jumped out at her.

"I'm determined not to be sick," she told me. "As a child, I was so ill that by the time I was six years old, I'd been poked, prodded, and injected a thousand times." A big part of her recollection of childhood is her mother comforting her during her frequent stomachaches from the ulcers she developed at age five.

"When I was a little girl, I believed doctors were the enemy," she told me. "I had a seizure only once, but after that I went through a litany of tests. I felt trapped by my parents who were always taking me to doctors."

The past life in London has created several fears in Elizabeth, but it's the fear of Failure that's the strongest.

"I've always backed away from opportunities," Elizabeth told me. The problem began in her teen years. "I was born with a genius I.Q. and had every opportunity you could ask for.

"I remember being a little girl and sitting in bed thinking, 'I'm such a lucky girl to be born in this country, to have two parents, and to have more opportunities than most other people.' But in my teens, I couldn't keep things together emotionally. I developed a fear of school. I never made it through the last quarter. No one could understand it."

When I asked Elizabeth about the curiosity her soul would use to motivate her to keep learning, she told me, "I got a job in a corporation, but I always felt a sense of being an imposter, so I went back to get a GED.

"I wrote a paper on ESP, and that's when the door opened. Since then, I've read thousands of books on everything spiritual. I've studied kundalini, tarot, healing, past lives, astrology—you name it. I'm a spiritual Renaissance person!

"I used to think I knew everything. But I've learned that I don't. I spoke to a friend in the hospital where I volunteer doing reiki, and she was defending people who think that one modality is better than another. I've learned that one is no better than the next—just different."

I told Elizabeth how humility is a welcome side effect of the accumulation of knowledge. She agreed. "People get invested in their beliefs. If you can recognize that your way is not the only way, then you can open up to possibilities."

The fear of Failure surfaced in Elizabeth's teenage years as literally flunking school. Rather than risk failure, she simply refused to try.

Since we spoke, Elizabeth has become a real estate agent. She's working at an agency and taking advanced-degree certification courses.

"I'm no longer afraid of failing exams," she told me. "I'm better able to walk through situations that would have paralyzed me before I knew their past-life origins. My life has become more hopeful, less limited, and less fearful."

CURIOSITY AS THE CURE FOR INERTIA

By drawing Curiosity, the karmic motivation, out of your soul, you can overcome the curse of inertia and procrastination to launch yourself into a more purposeful future.

When I spoke to Rosemary, the life my spirit guides wanted to talk about was one in Japan, several hundred years ago.

Rosemary was a boy, the son of a temple builder. When the boy was small, he was put to work helping his father in construction. Over the years, he suffered many accidents—yet his father was unsympathetic and demanding. The boy was never allowed to fully recuperate from his injuries.

At age fourteen, the boy broke both his legs in a fall and was sent to a village on the coast where his aunt took care of him in return for his help in gutting fish.

The work was tedious, the hours long, and the aunt had even less kindness in her than his father. Having very limited mobility, the boy felt stuck, with little hope of anything ever changing. After six harsh years, he died in a typhoon.

Reliving this life stirred something very profound in Rosemary's soul. Before we began the exploration, I asked her to look for any physical changes—goosebumps, a subtle shift in temperature, or a change in her heart rate—as her soul's memory was stirred. As soon as I began telling her about her past, Rosemary felt a chill, a deep sense of anxiety, and nausea.

The fear of Failure has resulted in a huge thirst for experience in this life. Rosemary has a mission of Exploration—a need to explore the world for firsthand knowledge. Like everyone with this mission, she loves to travel. When we first spoke, she'd just returned from a safari in Africa where she'd taken a balloon flight over the Serengeti.

She also has a desire for Education. Desires are a little smaller than missions and can often get out of balance. With a desire for Education, a person will sometimes become a perpetual student, putting off being in the real world for the joy of learning.

Rosemary has a triple whammy: a desire for Education, a mission of Exploration, and a fear of Failure with all the curiosity that entails.

When we'd finished exploring her life in Japan, I asked her, "Have you been drawn to classes, workshops, anything like that?"

"I've been taking classes since my kids were born," she said.

When I asked Rosemary what classes she's taken, she said, "I've learned to drywall, landscape, and paint. I've done classes for meditation, kundalini yoga, drawing, grinding, and welding. I've learned quilting, photography, and moccasin making. (I thought that would be handy.) I've been in writing courses—one for scriptwriting, another for short stories. I learned first aid, and in a carpentry course I built a deck and a fence."

I was impressed. But it didn't end there. Rosemary suddenly remembered a few more accomplishments.

"Oh," she said, "I forgot: I've also done reflexology, reiki, and numerology. I took a parenting class, a natural medicine course, herbology, and lots of cooking classes. Then there was Pilates, basic hair cutting, anger management, accounting, dog training, astrology, understanding the stock market, and skating.

"I've learned to access my intuition, direct my own movie, and teach my baby to swim. Also, I studied philosophy, child psychology, mythology, and woodworking, and I went to Byron Katie's School for The Work.

"I learned to cook vegetarian, make tofu exciting, use herbs for healing, create tinctures from herbs, and to make my own spa products. And recently I learned to remove body hair with sugar like the Egyptians used to.

"I've met some wonderful people doing all this," she added.

"I bet you have," I said. "But removing body hair with sugar???"

This insatiable curiosity showed itself again when Rosemary's son was diagnosed with Tourette's syndrome. Upon hearing the news, she did what anyone with a fear of Failure would do: she researched the subject inside and out, looking for a cure.

"I got a big, honking book on the brain from the Mayo Clinic, and when I heard someone on the radio talking about herbal medication, I called him and asked about books on the subject," she said. "He gave me a formula for vitamins and herbs he thought would help.

"It was amazing. I sat my son down and said, 'You've got to learn to swallow pills.' He did and responded immediately—within twelve hours."

One curious resonance from the past life in Japan, in which she was forced to work so hard, is that Rosemary finds it hard to take a break. "I keep feeling someone's going to reprimand me or blame me for something. I've always felt guilty for sleeping in. Now I understand why."

STIMULATING YOUR MOTIVATION OF CURIOSITY

When a life has been cut short, there's a need to achieve maximum knowledge in this life to make up for it. Searching for knowledge overcomes inertia and the feeling that there's something out there to be done.

....

CURIOSITY EXERCISE 2

LEARN SOMETHING NEW EVERY NIGHT

Bring in your spirit guides with the following request: "I call upon my spirit guides, acting in my highest interest, to help me reach the transformational goal of Knowledge through the motivation of Curiosity."

- Use an encyclopedia or the Internet (I use Wikipedia) to seek out a subject you know little or nothing about.
- Spend five minutes researching the topic you choose.
- Spend another five minutes writing what you've learned in a notebook.
- Every so often spend the time learning something with practical use.

....

Though my spirit guides suggest this as a nighttime exercise, you can do it any time that works for you. I've been using this exercise for a while. In the last few days I've researched TV marionette puppets from the 1960s, Black Panthers, Luther Burbank, and the movie *The Great Escape*.

On a more practical level, I've learned to play the bass guitar solo from Paul Simon's "You Can Call Me Al," and the bass part for the Four Tops's "Bernadette."

My kids are always curious to see what Dad's been doing while they've been asleep. They were transfixed when I demonstrated how to fold a T-shirt in two seconds. As they chanted, "One Mississippi, two Mississippi," it was done. (Check it out on YouTube.)

My wife, who was looking on, remarked, "You won't have any excuse for not putting away your laundry now."

Knowledge is a key step toward the next goal: that of Understanding. In the following chapter, you'll see how empathy and intellect combine to create a higher level of awareness.

CHAPTER SEVEN

THE POWER OF UNDERSTANDING
Accessing Your Ability to Relate

GOAL Understanding
MOTIVATION Empathy
FEAR Intimacy

NOT JUST THE FACTS

"And then the jackass dumped me!" Diana said, looking at the floor, shaking her head like she still couldn't believe it had really happened. It was a little disconcerting to hear this otherwise gentle old soul describe her ex in such graphic terms.

One of the most common markers of a fear of Intimacy is difficulty truly understanding another person. It's why people with this fear often seem genuinely bewildered when their partners break up with them. They'll say things like, "I'm so confused," or "I don't understand why he/she left."

Diana fell firmly into this category. "We were together four years," she said. "Then he told me it was over. It came as a complete surprise."

As she spoke, my spirit guides gave me some inside information.

"She had a lot to do with it," they told me.

"He never spoke about his feelings," she continued.

"His father abused him as a child," they said.

"He was so insecure."

"She was uncommitted."

"Whenever I tried to talk to him about our relationship he got angry."

"She would provoke him."

After a few more minutes, in which "jackass" was used several more times, Diana paused to take a breath.

At the root of her problem was a past life in which intimacy with another soul was associated with pain. A typical scenario goes like this: You fall madly in love with the person of your dreams. He goes off to fight in a war. He never comes back. The grief is so profound, you choose to spend the rest of your life alone rather than risk such pain again.

In a subsequent life, your soul will associate intimacy with grief and sorrow. Instead of allowing yourself to fall deeply in love, committing yourself to someone, you hold back a little—just in case.

If you have a past-life fear of Intimacy, you may know how hard it can be to get close to someone.

Many people who have this fear choose a partner with the same fear, making it less likely they'll have to face intimacy issues in the relationship. Then they blame that person when a problem comes up rather than looking inward, which, if you have a problem with intimacy, can be scary.

I told Diana I had some observations from my spirit guides. "They feel you might have said or done things that triggered your ex's insecurity."

Diana thought for a moment. "I guess so."

"And they tell me your ex was abused by his father."

There was a long pause. "That makes sense," she said. "I always wondered about that."

"My guides tell me you might have said things that you knew would make him angry."

Diana lowered her head. "Guilty," she said softly.

Like many people with a fear of Intimacy, Diana has a block in the area of empathy. This doesn't affect her ability to be compassionate or sympathetic. She's a very kind person. It does, however, make it hard for her to fully figure out other people.

WHEN EMPATHY IS BLOCKED

Empathy is the ability to pick up on nonverbal emotional signals and get beneath the surface of another person.

When empathy is blocked, it acts as a barrier to genuine understanding, making it hard to fully relate to your partner or even your children. Not surprisingly, it's a major cause of relationship problems.

Lack of empathy doesn't mean you're not a kind or feeling person. It simply means there's a difficulty accessing the cues and signals that other people put out.

The cure for a fear of Intimacy is to find the karmic motivation of Empathy, and that connects directly to the goal of Understanding.

Even in my office, Diana's empathy started to kick in as she gained some insight into the events of the past. She experienced one of those little epiphanies that are sometimes described as "aha" moments. Suddenly everything made a lot more sense than it had.

My spirit guides asked me to emphasize that their remarks were not in any way meant to condone her ex's bad behavior.

They simply wanted Diana to look back on the events of the past through different-colored lenses.

As she was leaving my office, I asked her when she and the "jackass" had split up. I was thinking it might have been earlier that same year.

"Oh, about twenty-five years ago—just after we both left college," she said.

For twenty-five years, Diana had seen the breakup of her first serious relationship through the eyes of the young college graduate she'd been when the split happened. Now she was able to step back and use her empathy to review the event with greater understanding.

In future relationships, she can use her motivation of Empathy to help her reach the transformational goal of Understanding. When she does, she'll find intimacy like she's never known.

SIGNS OF A FEAR OF INTIMACY

The most common trigger for a fear of Intimacy is, not surprisingly, falling in love. One of the more common symptoms is the tendency to run away from a potentially viable relationship—what's often described as a fear of commitment.

If you're with someone who has a fear of Intimacy, getting him or her to express emotional feelings can be as hard as extracting teeth, and sometimes just as painful.

One of my clients has been married twelve years, and her husband has never said, "I love you." He is, however, making progress. In the last three or four years, he's been able to manage a cheerful, "I'm very fond of you," when suitably prompted.

The motto of a person with a past life fear of Intimacy is "I've never given 100 percent to anyone." At least that's been a common response when I've asked clients if they hold back a part of themselves in relationships.

Without giving 100 percent, a relationship has far less chance of working out than when both parties involved can commit without fear. And it does take two. As long as one partner is afraid of giving 100 percent, then the missing part will act as a wedge between them both.

Diana couldn't understand why her ex behaved as he did. He was probably equally bewildered by her behavior. Given his abusive childhood and her provocation, his own fear of Intimacy must have been pretty close to the surface.

How different things could have been if she'd been able to understand him a little better twenty-five years earlier.

OTHER PEOPLE'S SHOES

It was a sunny Saturday morning in London, sometime back in the mid-1980s. I was on my way to my studio when I drove past a hotel in Russell Square. At the foot of the steps was a sign that read, "Psychic Fair Today."

I'd only recently begun taking an interest in such things and was still hovering between cynicism and acceptance. I slowed down, mulled it over for a few seconds, and decided to give it a chance.

In a garishly lit basement room, I found a dozen or so assorted psychics, tarot readers, and healers. An eclectic bunch, each had a little table with various charms, crystal balls, and piles of cheap photocopied flyers.

I wandered around for a few minutes, checking out what was on offer. I tried to get close enough to a couple of readers and their clients to hear what kind of talk was going on. "He did it once and he'll do it again," I heard one say. "Do what?" I wondered.

A couple of tables away, a woman with short, red hair was finishing up with a customer. As I got within a few feet, she asked casually, "Are you a cartoonist?"

"Uh, yeah . . . how did you know?" I asked.

She didn't answer my question. Instead she said something completely out of the blue. "Your ex-wife—the blonde—she emotionally castrated you because she was so hurt by the death of both her parents."

Her remark had been spoken so casually it sounded like a throwaway; it didn't really sink in for a while.

I continued walking the room and finally sat down with an elderly psychic who ended up doing some very effective energy work for stress reduction. It wasn't until I was walking back upstairs and out of the building that it hit me.

What the red-haired psychic had said made total sense. My ex had lost her mother when she was ten and her father a decade later. And for the last three years we were together she had treated me appallingly.

Over the next few weeks, I had little flashes of enlightenment surrounding my former relationship. My ex couldn't—and wouldn't—talk about emotions. She'd never spoken about her mother, and it struck me that I'd never seen her grieve her father.

It took some time, but the woman whose neck I'd once wanted to strangle became someone I wanted to put my arms around and comfort.

The red-haired psychic's observations helped me see beyond the Physical Plane. When she described the source of my ex's anger, it was like a veil lifted. Until then I'd considered her to be some kind of evil troll with no redeeming features. From that moment on, I could see her as a complex human being, harboring deep emotional pain she didn't know how to express.

True understanding is a goal, and as such, your soul will continually urge you to embrace it. It's never enough to go by what you see. To understand, you have to add the extra dimension of empathy.

The motivation of Empathy can be awakened, in many cases, by simply taking the time to reflect and considering the world from the other person's perspective.

You've had traumatic incidents in this life and the past. It's useful to remember that your parent, partner, or child may be struggling with deep soul-level hurts that don't always get expressed particularly well.

SPIRITUAL ACT 6: PROMOTING UNDERSTANDING

When you have a fear of Intimacy, much of the healing involves learning to put yourself in others' shoes. For this reason, Spiritual Acts that help overcome past traumas involve breaking down barriers to understanding.

They include donating to or otherwise supporting cross-cultural exchange trips and organizations that promote tolerance and diversity. Another Spiritual Act is being involved in bringing different ethnic groups together in your community.

THE COMFORT OF STRANGERS

Isabella is dealing with the fallout from a lifetime she once spent in the nineteenth century American South. As a male named Henry in that life, she grew up to become a teacher in a small private school in a conservative rural area. As you'll see from her story, the fears that stem from that life include Self-Expression and Betrayal. But the one that has had the most significant impact on her present life is a fear of Intimacy.

Henry was raised by his mother near Biloxi, Mississippi, where he had a happy childhood, marred only by the death of his father. When he was eight, he and his mother moved to a small town, where she cleaned houses to support them.

When Henry grew up, his first job was as the only teacher at a small rural school. He was bored and lonely, but appreciated the security the job offered.

And then his world turned upside down. His mother befriended a woman who had recently arrived in the area looking for work. One morning, when Henry dropped by, he found her house empty. There were signs of a struggle, and blood was spattered on the floor. Neither his mother nor her mysterious friend were ever heard from again.

Henry was grief-stricken. Not knowing what had happened to his mother kept him in a state of perpetual anxiety. As the months went by, he began to vent his anger in his diaries. He cursed God for allowing this terrible thing to happen.

Henry's writings became more and more bitter, and he declared himself in his journals to be an atheist. It was around this time that he was pulled out of his depression by the arrival of a second teacher at the school, a young woman with whom he fell deeply in love.

At some point in the first year of their marriage, his highly religious young wife found his diaries. The Godless vitriol contained within their pages shocked her to her core. She couldn't believe this embittered madman was the same person she shared her life with. She ran home to her father and showed him everything.

Henry was fired from his job and ostracized from what quickly became a hostile community. With his marriage suddenly over and his safety in jeopardy, he hopped a northbound train and left Mississippi behind.

His next employer was the New York Central Railroad, where he worked as a yardman, resenting the cold weather and long hours. He suffered increasing depression over his betrayal and gut-wrenching loneliness from the loss of his soul mate's love. Henry died several years later, when he was crushed in an accident. At the time of his death, he saw the discovery of the diaries as the pivotal point in his life.

It was that incident that threw a wrench in the gears of his life plan. It had led to the loss of his home and wife, his relocation to a place of hard labor and loneliness, and ultimately to his early death.

And if Henry hadn't allowed himself to get so close to his spouse, he'd never have suffered the emotional wrench of separation.

The effects of this fear of Intimacy are ever-present in Isabella's life. Like many people with this fear, she has difficulty getting totally intimate with another person. In Isabella's case, the fear is compatible with her chosen profession: she makes her living as an adult movie star. It's partly her fear of Intimacy that makes it possible to have sex with strangers.

Isabella uses an alias in her work; it helps her to separate the two different parts of her. "In front of the camera, I go into performer mode, and I become Sonia," she said. "It's like a room I walk into. It's still genuinely me, but the vulnerable part is in another room. As Sonia, I'm an invincible goddess; as Isabella, I'm more shy and reserved. Sonia wants to be famous, but Isabella wants to stay indoors."

We talked about how blocking your Empathy makes it harder to see others as complete persons. It can create strong black-and-white feelings. In a previous session, the otherwise sweet-natured Isabella alluded to a rival for her boyfriend's affections.

"I want to know why I hate Samantha," she said.

"You only see the enemy," my spirit guides told her.

Samantha raised Isabella's hackles by making a play for her boyfriend, Jerry. It triggered the betrayal aspect of the fear of Intimacy.

When I interviewed her a few months later, Isabella was feeling considerable remorse for how she'd treated Samantha.

"What happened?" I asked.

Isabella laughed nervously. "I really tortured her. I listened in on some conversations she had with other people. Then I sent her a bunch of text messages, repeating what she'd said. I heard her tell someone Jerry really wanted her, so I texted her saying, 'What do you mean Jerry really wants you?'

"And when she confided in a friend that she wanted children, I was really mean. I texted, 'You'd make a terrible mom. Don't ever have kids!' She freaked out and changed her number. I eventually sent her an amends letter apologizing for my behavior. It was so unlike me."

The remorse Isabella felt triggered the motivation of Empathy and allowed her to see Samantha as a human being with feelings just like everyone else.

....

CLOSED BOOKS

When you have a fear of Intimacy, it can be difficult or practically impossible to communicate your innermost feelings to your partner. It's often easier to share your feelings with someone less risky, like a complete stranger or a friend. (I was going to add "therapist" to the list, but that's one person many people with this fear try to avoid.)

One of my clients who married almost thirty years ago said about her spouse, "I don't know him any better today than I did on our first date."

....

As far as intimacy goes, Isabella feels ready for it. "I've had two big relationships in my life, but they only went so far. I never felt safe to become truly intimate. I know there's a relationship on the horizon, and this time I know I can go deeper emotionally. It's like the other two prepared me for the big one."

Intimacy is emotional. Sex without emotion is not intimate. Genuine intimacy can be scary, and many people with the past-life fear prefer to find surrogates for it.

Isabella's surrogates are shopping and food. "I've had a big problem with spending," she confessed. Exactly how big was quite alarming. When we first spoke, she was more than $250,000 in credit card debt. More recently, she's been getting things under control, and is currently learning not to use her credit cards. She's working out and getting into shape for a new series of films.

Isabella joked about how she'd see someone on TV selling a new book and would feel compelled to buy it. "That's how I discovered you!"

Then she said something very significant. "I love audio books. It's like having someone read to me."

"It feels intimate?" I suggested.

"Absolutely. Yes!" she said.

THE RISK OF INTIMACY

In a previous life, Katherine was an actress named Ellen. She performed in London's Savoy Theater in the 1880s. As a young woman, Ellen's career derailed when she became pregnant, twice, by a well-known composer. After suffering the terrible loss of both her children in infancy (the cause of her fear of Intimacy), she relocated to the city of Bristol.

For the rest of her life, Ellen kept up the pretense that she was still an actress, but her dependence on alcohol destroyed any chance of continuing in that line of work.

As highly sensitive people so often do, Ellen used the alcohol to numb her emotions. In doing so, she blocked a significant part of her innate empathy. As her money dried up, she turned to men to keep her solvent.

She maintained an almost aristocratic elegance in her modest, though richly furnished home. Her men friends were regulars who regarded her more as a mistress than a prostitute.

As Ellen became increasingly alcoholic, she would go days without eating properly. She was frail and had aged prematurely. She died before age thirty from a head injury incurred in a fall in her home. It was a simple accident, but there was speculation at the time that foul play was involved. The police investigated for a while but no one was charged. (Ellen would have loved all the drama!)

In this present-day lifetime, Katherine struggles with intimacy. Her father was distant; her mother was cold and unavailable. "When my dad went away, I didn't care if he ever came back," she said. "I wanted my mom to hold and nurture me, but she never did."

In her teen years, Katherine began looking for intimacy through sex. "When I got interested in boys, I looked to them to fill a need that never got met from a father figure," she told me. "I used my sexuality to get someone to love me. I thought the attention would get me what I wanted."

Katherine never did find whatever it was she was looking for. Her past-life fear of Intimacy had kicked in by then. The situation became worse when a group of her girlfriends betrayed her most intimate secrets. "One of them is still a close friend, but I'd never share anything intimate with her again," she said.

The fear of Intimacy has prevented Katherine from connecting fully with her husband or bonding properly with her children. Like many women with intimacy issues, she married a man with the same fear. It meant she'd never have to confront her fear, but she feels deep sadness about not being closer to her kids.

"I adore my kids," she said. "I'm glad they're there, but we're disconnected somehow. I don't feel like other mothers do about their children. I didn't enjoy the baby stage at all, though I enjoy spending time, one on one, now that they're older."

I told her that's because her children were past the danger stage. "The fear meant you couldn't get close in case you went through the terrible emotional pain of losing your babies again. Now that they're a little older, the fear is losing its grip."

While we were discussing her fear, Katherine said, "I've always felt more comfortable with strangers. I can get quite close to someone I've just met, but after a while, instead of getting closer I start detaching."

Of course, what's happening is that the fear begins to surface as the stranger morphs into a friend.

A few months after exploring her past life in England, Katherine felt she'd really made progress with her fears. I told her about the movie *Topsy-Turvy,* thinking that its story of Gilbert and Sullivan, whose comic operas played at the Savoy Theater, might help connect her to that lifetime.

She made it clear she wasn't ready. "I'm afraid to watch it. I get a dark feeling about that life. It seems so full of despair and addiction, and those have been big issues in this life."

A side effect of a past-life fear of Intimacy is a block when it comes to connecting with your soul or your spirit guides. Katherine said, "I used to avoid connecting when I meditated. It was scary when I went too deep. I'd get a kind of attention-deficit disorder and have to focus elsewhere. Now, after working with you, things are opening up. I'm much less fearful."

Some time later, Katherine got in touch to tell me our sessions together had changed her life and that overcoming her fears has allowed her to move forward with certainty.

"I've spent twenty-plus years trying to figure out what I should be doing with my life," she said. "Finally, I've decided to go to nursing school to become a hospice nurse. Even though I find reasons to quit every day, I feel confident and sure of this path."

REBUILDING THE TRUST

A fear of Intimacy is a major cause of divorce and separation. It blocks connection and the warm, fuzzy feeling that comes when two souls mingle. When trust has been a major factor in the past life when the fear began, it can raise huge trust issues in the present lifetime.

For Lynne, the fear of Intimacy was created during a life as an English woman named Claire, whose father was a missionary during the early 1900s. Claire's upbringing was strict, and she had little interaction with other children. In her teens, she traveled with her father to West Africa, where they spent almost a year before he died of a tropical disease.

Returning to the family home in the south of England, Claire became a schoolteacher, not because she wanted to, but because her father had told her it was her destiny.

She married a man much older than herself, who seemed to be a good match. He was dull and pompous, but at least he had a good job. Unfortunately, he also had a severe drinking problem. He was emotionally and sexually abusive, and he would frequently get drunk and force himself on her. She told nobody, terrified by what people would think.

According to my spirit guides, what Claire ended up with would these days be described as post-traumatic stress disorder. What little self-confidence she had quickly disappeared in the early months of the marriage.

The combination of disempowerment and Victorian and religious social mores made the idea of leaving either her husband, or the job she hated, unthinkable.

Claire was in her late twenties when she died in childbirth, feeling a huge sense of disappointment with this "wasted life."

This sad lifetime is the source of a number of fears, especially one of Inferiority, caused by living her life according to the dictates of her father and husband. But most significant is the fear of Intimacy, caused by her death. The connection her soul made was that intimacy (impregnation) led to her demise and the derailment of her life plan.

For Lynne, the fear of Intimacy was triggered in this life when the other girls at school started talking about boys and dating. "I hadn't even hit puberty when I began to think the last thing I wanted was to get close to a man," Lynne admitted. "I hoped I would't get a curvy body because I didn't want to be attractive to men."

Since then, she has married and divorced, and now Lynne has no intention of finding another man. The association between sex and death made intimacy very difficult, and she's in no hurry to get close to any man again in this life. "I don't like penetration," she said. "I've always resisted it. I've always feared rape, and I have a big issue with men, especially ones who are violent or passive-aggressive."

The soul that was Lynne's father in that lifetime has again chosen to be her father in this life. Like reenacting a play, they've taken similar roles to make sure that this time the lessons are learned. What's different is that Lynne now has the karmic motivation from the fears to give her the impetus to create a better ending.

"When you told me that my past-life father is my father again in this life, it had a big effect on me. My father is highly religious. He got involved with a cult and became very extreme, alienating a lot of people and controlling everyone. He even told me to be a teacher in this life, too."

Lynne and her father had an agreement to work on the karmic issues from their last incarnation together. The intention was that he'd make it easier for her to complete her life plan this time around. But by getting stuck behind the Illusion, he slipped into old patterns instead.

SEEMING INDIFFERENCE

A person with a past-life fear of Intimacy can appear cold or indifferent when there's a problem in a relationship. The fear causes them to retreat behind a self-protective barrier.

They're not being deliberately cruel; they're simply afraid. Unfortunately, a chilly manner can cause an equal and opposite reaction in a partner if he or she also has a fear of Intimacy, resulting in a spiral that can quickly lead to the demise of the relationship.

Lynne ended up marrying someone just like her father. "Both my husband and my father had issues with openness. There was never any real intimacy with either of them."

After one of our sessions, my spirit guides encouraged Lynne to "break out of the box." She was reluctant, but she took a spiritual art course. "It was way outside my comfort level, but it was great. I loved it," she said.

Lynne is getting more comfortable creating change in her life. She does hospice work and now leads a meditation group. This involvement is helping to rebuild her trust in people—and herself.

Her fear of Intimacy used to block connection with her soul and create anxiety during meditation. "I feared letting go in meditation," she said. "It felt like not being secure. I wonder if I once abused my intuitive gift?"

What Lynne experienced was a common symptom of a past-life fear of Intimacy. She had never abused her gift; she was simply feeling the presence of her soul and getting anxious about making such a deep and intimate connection. The advice my spirit guides gave her was to "meditate, meditate, meditate" and to ask her own guides for love and empathy.

....

THE "C" WORD

It's hard to imagine that someone with commitment issues might be suffering the effects of emotional hurt from decades or even centuries ago.

The stereotypical male who can't settle down to a committed relationship is often thought to be afraid of losing his freedom. He's actually more likely to be afraid of the pain that's associated with giving 100 percent. He may deliberately choose partners who are unsuitable, which makes it easier to walk away.

A fear of Intimacy also lies behind many divorces. The tendency is to clam up emotionally and make reconciliation impossible.

For a woman with a fear of Intimacy, commitment raises huge trust issues. She may behave in self-destructive ways that push her partner away.

....

As a result of a traumatic experience in seventeenth century Spain, Erica has found herself struggling with a common effect of the fear of Intimacy—an overreliance on her intellect.

True understanding is a combination of empathy and intellect. It's only by combining the two that you can truly reach the goal of Understanding.

Many highly rational people have a tendency to dismiss their more intuitive side. In this they get full support from their teachers while growing up. Very few teachers ever tell a smart kid to go and work on his or her empathy or intuition. As a result, the left side of the brain tends to become a little overdeveloped.

In that lifetime in Spain, Erica was a servant girl named Maria, who was employed by a wealthy family. One of her jobs was to buy bread and grain from a local miller.

Maria was raped several times by the mill owner. He would have continued taking advantage of her if she hadn't become pregnant. To avoid blame, the miller accused her of seducing him with sorcery. In that superstitious and misogynistic era, no one doubted his word.

After being cruelly tortured, Maria was tied to the mill's water-wheel and drowned.

The result of that particular experience has made Erica mistrustful, especially when it comes to men. The association is, once again, that intimacy in the form of impregnation leads to dreadful consequences.

Having recently divorced, Erica is coming up against intimacy issues everywhere she looks. "I have a wide circle of friends," she told me. "I have 712 friends on Facebook alone, but I always wonder how many really know me."

When Erica and her lawyer met her husband and his attorney, she was faced with an unforeseen problem. "My ex wanted to remove me from the will. He said he no longer wanted me to have the power to pull the plug on him if something awful happened. He pointed out that with the insurance he has, he's worth more dead than alive. He knows I wouldn't do anything to hurt him, but it got me wondering.

"He doesn't want me to have the right to pull the plug, but I don't want him having that power over me, either. Then I thought, who would I trust to do that? I realized this kind of decision involves total intimacy.

"Could I ask my mother?" Erica pondered. "It would kill her to do that. My sister? She's too emotionally frail; it would devastate her. My son? He's fifteen. I just couldn't ask him. Do I open the phone book and choose someone at random?"

"How about your friends?" I asked.

"I have all these people in my life, but I can't let them get close. It's like I have a force field around me."

There was a problem my spirit guides had identified before Erica and I even first spoke: "thinking, not intuiting." It was clear that the strong Thinker part of Erica's personality was making life difficult for her. And it suggested a way to help overcome the effects of her past-life trauma.

Erica is a real intellectual. She's smart and well educated, but her empathy is blocked by the fear of Intimacy.

"I know I overanalyze things," she said. "What I find frustrating is wanting to have the right answer, but not feeling it."

When Erica used the word "feeling," I stopped her. "That's the key right there," I said. "You're playing with only half the deck. You have everything going on intellectually, but you're missing the more intuitive component."

"It seems to me that some people always know the right thing to say," she continued. "I search for it, then get tongue-tied, like I'm under pressure to get it right. When I'm away from the situation, I'll have "aha" moments. Then I don't have to worry about getting it right."

"The fear is triggered when you're under pressure, and your intuition gets blocked," I told her. "Once you're on your own, you can relax, and the fear lifts."

The solution for Erica and anyone like her is to build empathy to a point where it's in balance with her intellect. The exercise I gave her is the one you'll find at the end of the chapter.

One other small resonance still impacts Erica from her life in subjugation to the miller in Spain. "Are you allergic to wheat?" I asked her.

"Yes, it's my only allergy," she said.

DIGGING BENEATH THE SURFACE

You can't change the past, but as we've seen earlier, you can change how the past affects you. When you shift your beliefs about someone who has hurt you, you shift your reality.

In the case of someone who has deliberately violated you in some way, it can be very hard to move past the hurt. Unfortunately, by holding on to the anger, you allow that person to hurt you twice. In fact, the damage to you from the anger can be greater than the original hurt.

By bringing new awareness to bear on the situation, you help the pain to dissipate by shifting your beliefs about what happened. Understanding is a major step toward forgiveness.

....

EMPATHY EXERCISE

TEN PEOPLE WHO HAVE HURT YOU

Bring in your spirit guides with the following request: "I call upon my spirit guides, acting in my highest interest, to help me reach the goal of Understanding through the motivation of Empathy."

- Make a list of ten people who have hurt, disappointed, or angered you.
- Ask yourself what made them act that way. Think of their parents or their upbringing. Did they get all the love they needed? Did they have damaging relationships in the past? Were they bullied as children?
- Next to each person's name, write a few lines about why they acted the way they did.

Caveat: Don't sweat it! Just go with your gut feeling.

....

This exercise helps you look for mitigating factors in others, like their upbringing, past hurts, mental instability, and so on. Don't sweat this exercise. Trust your intuition. If you think someone treated you badly because he or she was bullied at school, go with it.

Understanding is a combination of knowledge and empathy. In the next chapter, we'll explore the connection between intuition and facts, and how the motivation of Honesty leads to the goal of Truth.

CHAPTER EIGHT

THE VIRTUE OF TRUTH
Overcoming Blocks to Self-Expression

GOAL Truth

MOTIVATION Honesty

FEAR Self-Expression

LIES, DAMN LIES, AND KARMIC CONSEQUENCES

In a lifetime in the Ural Mountains, sometime in the mid-1800s, Emily spoke out about the abuse she was suffering at the hands of her family. The consequences were devastating.

In that life, Emily was a boy named Dmitri who was born into a family consisting of an aggressive father, a neurotic mother, and a sickly sister. When the sister died, the grief-stricken mother looked to Dmitri to replace her.

It was not considered unusual in certain cultures in the past to raise boys for a short time in girls' clothes. In this case, it went a lot further than that. Dmitri was made to grow his hair, wear dresses, and actually pretend to be a girl. In a remote area, the family was able to keep the charade going until Dmitri was seven.

It was then that Dmitri ran away and revealed his true identity to a priest. In a few words, he ended the family's pretense—and destroyed the family itself. His father was imprisoned and his mother driven insane.

Dmitri's ability to follow his life plan, which was already jeopardized by his parents' actions, was completely destroyed. He ended his life as a farm laborer, dying alone of pneumonia. He blamed his misery on his confession to the priest.

In this life, the impact of that tragic life has resulted in a fear of Self-Expression. Emily has struggled all her life with speaking her truth.

Have you ever left a conversation thinking, "I wish I'd spoken up"? Or have you've ever walked away thinking, "Oh, my gosh! I can't believe I said that"? If you recognize either marker, or even both, then you have a fear of Self-Expression.

When you've had a past life in which expressing your beliefs or speaking your mind has led to dire consequences, a fear of Self-Expression is the result.

When you overcome the fear, you can say what's on your mind without feeling an invisible hand trying to gag you, and without blurting something that makes you groan with embarrassment every time you recall it.

Overcoming the fear lets you speak calmly and openly about even your deepest feelings, without self-consciousness or worrying how every word might be interpreted.

The resonances in this life can be distressing. I have a client whose throat closes up when she's called upon to voice her thoughts in meetings. I have another who completely loses his voice under stress.

Emily said, "I used to clam up completely if I thought there was any possible consequence to speaking out. If you asked my friends or family, they'd say I express myself really well.

But if you ask me, I'd say it's always been a struggle speaking my truth."

Emily is something of a poet. During our first session, my spirit guides suggested that a writing class would be a great way for her to develop more confidence about getting her poetry out into the world.

"When you told me that," she said later, "it scared me shitless!"

People with a past-life fear are not necessarily fearful in other ways. Emily told me how she'd been the victim of a hit-and-run accident when another car had smashed into hers. "He drove away, and I ran after him," she said. "I stopped a car, jumped in, and said, 'Follow that car!' Unfortunately I chose a rule-follower who stopped at every red light, and I never caught the guy."

BEING A GOOD LISTENER

Emily's struggle with self-expression has taught her a lesson about the importance of listening.

"Communication has as much to do with listening as it does with talking," she said. "I've learned to understand the value of listening. I believe it's truly healing when people feel validated because you've listened to them."

Emily's heroes are people like crusader Erin Brockovich: people who stand up for others and aren't afraid to speak out.

Lately, Emily's been making great progress. I asked her if she came face-to-face with her fear in her workplace.

"All the freakin' time," she said. Then she told me how much stronger she's been getting. "There was a manager who treated my coworkers badly. I was anxious about phoning her up, but I said a little prayer, brought in my spirit guides, and asked for protection.

I called her and just told her what I thought. I said her behavior had been totally unacceptable."

"And what happened then?"

"She hung up! I was still a little worried about there being consequences, but so far there's been nothing. And I know I'll be even more confident next time."

What has helped Emily is knowing why she has this irrational fear. "It's been amazing working with you," she told me. "I've learned that I'm not crazy. And now I have tools to help me get over this. That past life helped me to understand why it's been so hard speaking my own truth in this life."

INTELLECT AND INTUITION

One of the following statements is true and the other false. Can you guess which one is true?

1. Peaches originated in China and are considered symbols of immortality and unity. They're a good source of vitamins A, B, and C, and they contain 66 calories per cup.
2. A bill currently working its way through the Georgia state legislature aims to replace the state symbol, the peach, with the Krispy Kreme doughnut to give Georgia a more contemporary image.

The true statement is, of course, number 1. You hopefully didn't have to search the Internet to check it out. Your intuition should tell you when something sounds right or not.

When you connect with your soul through the goal of Truth, you'll be imbued with an enhanced B.S. detector. That's because you'll have easier access to your intuition.

Discerning the truth is a matter of using both intellect and intuition.

Emily has learned to use honesty, the motivation that inspires her to overcome her fear of Self-Expression. It's through honesty that her fear will eventually dissipate completely, and she'll connect with the goal of Truth.

When that happens, she'll be able to say what she feels without fear. She'll become a walking example of what it means to be a spiritually conscious old soul who knows the value of truth and has the confidence to express it in every situation.

AS ABOVE, SO BELOW

Fifty-five thousand years ago, honesty was expected in the tribe. The person who lied was looked on with pity. In the modern world, lies are so common that those who rigidly stick to the truth are the ones deemed unusual.

Sadly, it's the lies told by those in positions of power and influence that impact us the most because they have consequences that can be global. These liars legitimize dishonesty, and they make it more acceptable for those most in thrall to the Illusion to follow suit.

Possibly the most damaging effect of lies that originate in the corridors of power is that they polarize us. They pit those who swallow the lie against those who don't.

Remember how Saddam Hussein kicked the United Nations weapons inspectors out of Iraq in the run-up to the U.S. invasion in 2003? I'm sure you do. The phrases "kicked out" and "expelled" were used over and over again on the nightly news.

The problem is that it just wasn't true. Those in the government who perpetrated the lie knew it. And those in the media who perpetuated the lie knew it, too. The weapons inspectors were ordered to leave Baghdad by Richard Butler, head of the U.N. team. The decision was made to ensure their safety in anticipation of a joint U.S.-British military attack.

To begin with, the media happily reported something a little closer to the truth. According to Katie Couric on NBC's Today program, "Chief U.N. weapons inspector, Richard Butler, said that Iraq had not fully cooperated with inspectors as they had promised to do. As a result, the U.N. ordered its inspectors to leave Iraq this morning."

It was in the months leading up to the Iraq War that the lie began to pick up momentum. Soon, it became a commonly held belief.

The same phenomenon happened with the fib about Saddam Hussein's connections with al-Qaeda, the whopping great lie about WMDs, and the total fabrication about Iraq buying yellow-cake uranium from Niger.

Hitler knew all about the power of the big lie. It's a common propaganda technique. Repeat the lie often enough, and people will start to believe it.

The big lie was used to justify the invasion of Iraq, Operation Desert Storm, the Vietnam War, and even the Spanish-American War.

The USS *Maine,* supposedly sunk by a Spanish mine in Havana Harbor in 1898, was actually the victim of an explosion inside the ship that ignited its ammunition supply. The incident was the perfect excuse to begin the Spanish-American War.

In 1964, President Johnson ordered U.S. forces to bomb North Vietnam in retaliation for an attack by torpedo boats on U.S. warships in the Gulf of Tonkin—an attack that never actually happened.

Then there's the Gulf War of 1990–1991. An unidentified young woman testified to a Congressional Committee about how Iraqi troops threw hundreds of Kuwaiti babies out of their incubators and left them to die on a cold hospital floor. It was a total fabrication. The woman turned out to be the daughter of the Kuwaiti ambassador to the United States and hadn't actually been there at the time of the Iraqi invasion. The entire event was concocted by a PR company.

The lie worked, however. The Senate voted to go to war with the slimmest majority: just five votes. But it was enough.

Lies have consequences. The ones listed above were designed to help muster popular support for a predetermined decision: an attack on another country.

The cost of these lies can be counted in bodies. Millions died as a result of wars that were, to a very large extent, manufactured and unnecessary. The sinking of the USS *Maine* led to the invasion of Cuba and then to the invasion of the Philippines.

The Gulf of Tonkin Incident, as it became known, resulted in a massive escalation of the war in Vietnam that ultimately killed thousands of Americans and millions of men, women, and children throughout Cambodia, Laos, and Vietnam.

Operation Desert Storm in 1991, also known as the Gulf War, caused the deaths of tens of thousands.

More recently, the invasion of Iraq has, at the time of writing, led to thousands of American deaths and, according to a Lancet study, the loss of approximately a million Iraqi lives.

....

TRUTH AND KARMA

Lies diminish us. No one respects a liar because of his or her ability to tell lies.

Thanks to the effects of karma, if lies diminish you, then conversely, the truth will elevate you. The more honest you are, the more you'll gain the respect of others.

....

The citizens of a country are often the last to know what is being perpetrated in their name. Whether you live in America, Russia, China, or anywhere else on the globe, what you're told about your government's actions is supplied to you through a filter of censorship, spin, obfuscation, and downright lies.

Governments know that if you're going to launch a war, you have to avoid being seen as the aggressor. Lies are created to justify actions that would otherwise be unlikely to gain popular support.

There are two major reasons big lies work successfully. The first is because of the need for those in thrall to the Illusion to have security. Tell them they have reason to be afraid, and they will be.

The second is that younger souls and those more caught up behind the Illusion identify with their country. (It's why nationalism is a conservative rather than a progressive phenomenon.) These souls need to believe what they're told for the sake of their own personal self-esteem.

DEATHBED CONFESSION IS
GOOD FOR THE SOUL

Lee Atwater was a U.S. politician whose karmic legacy is, sadly, not one to be envied. After a short but bloody career in which he dragged political dirty tricks out of the gutter and into the sewer, he died of a brain tumor at the age of forty.

In 1988, Atwater successfully destroyed Michael Dukakis, who was running for president against George H. W. Bush, by linking him to Willie Horton, a convict who raped a woman while on a weekend furlough from prison.

Dukakis's wife, Kitty, was accused of flag burning, and Dukakis himself was the victim of rumors of mental illness. The lies and manipulations that Atwater was involved in led to Bush's election as president.

It was his deathbed confession that showed something more approaching the true Lee Atwater. The damage to his brain had one curious side effect: as it negatively impaired his conscious mind, it positively increased his ability to connect with his soul.

The closer he got to facing his own mortality, the more Atwater questioned the way he'd conducted his life. He said, "My illness helped me to see that what was missing in society was what was missing in me: a little heart, a lot of brotherhood."

When Atwater was a child, he watched his little brother die in agony after scalding himself with hot oil from a deep fryer. This incident traumatized him. He said that he heard his brother's screams every moment of every day for the rest of his life.

That awful experience caused this surprisingly old soul to retreat behind the safety of the Illusion. Cut off from his soul and his emotions, he became a cynical manipulator.

Knowing he didn't have long for this world changed all that. It helped Atwater to separate what was real from what was part of the Illusion.

"The 1980s were about acquiring," he said. "I know. I acquired more wealth, power, and prestige than most. But you can acquire all you want and still feel empty. What power wouldn't I trade for a little more time with my family?"

"I was wrong to follow the meanness of conservatism," Atwater told *Time* magazine. "I should have been trying to help people instead of taking advantage of them."

Lee Atwater left a trail of destruction behind him. His negative karmic legacy has made it easier for those who have followed him to use similar tactics. His push-polling techniques, for example, have become standard procedure for political operatives in America.

....

PUSHING AND POLLING

In telephone push-polling, a political party operative will call a potential voter pretending to conduct a poll. He or she will ask questions designed to turn a potential voter against a particular candidate.

One example from George W. Bush's 2000 presidential primary campaign against fellow Republican John McCain was "Would you be more or less likely to vote for John McCain for president if you knew he'd fathered an illegitimate black child?"

McCain hadn't, of course, but the poll was designed to suggest he had and influence a particular minority of voters.

....

Though Atwater was hardly the first to use such dishonest tactics, his legacy is evident in the continued use of smears and lies in American politics—and in the way such behavior has entered the mainstream.

You can see Atwater's influence in the people behind the "Swift Boat" ads that attacked John Kerry during his run for the presidency, or in those who made sure they used Barack Obama's middle name, Hussein, whenever possible during his election campaign.

In 2008, when vice-presidential candidate Sarah Palin told crowds that presidential candidate Barack Obama was "palling around with terrorists," she was using a smear that the young Lee Atwater would have been proud of.

The karmic legacy of Lee Atwater has been destructive on all levels. It has impacted both the individual and the Collective Consciousness.

A major effect of the Transformation is to give those on the outside of the Illusion a sharper nose for dishonesty. It will help you to discern lies and make you more conscious of the importance of your own personal honesty.

Lee Atwater's soul was crying out for him to speak his truth. When he finally expressed his true feelings, he aligned his conscious self and his soul.

It's been said, many times before, that no one on his or her deathbed ever said, "I wish I'd spent more time at the office." Similarly, when it comes to deathbed confessions, people use the opportunity to speak from the heart. No one on their deathbed ever said, "I wish I'd been more dishonest."

LEARNING TO SPEAK YOUR TRUTH

In a past life, Sabina's strong opinions about her beliefs led to a very unpleasant death. In this lifetime, the motivation of Honesty has been triggered, and now she's learning the importance of truth by undergoing huge lessons related to self-expression.

"My parents would always criticize me for speaking my mind. I grew up too afraid to say what I really thought," she said.

The fear may have been triggered in childhood, but it has its origins in a life in France many centuries ago.

Sabina was a young man named Bernard who joined the priesthood at an early age. He was heavily influenced by Huguenot thought before entering the Catholic monastery. My spirit guides described him as someone who "had never heard of being discreet" and "was blunt to the point of rudeness."

It was this bluntness that led to Bernard's demise. He spoke out in favor of the Huguenots, offending his superiors. After he shocked them by refusing to do voluntary penance, the other priests took his case to the church authorities. Bernard was eventually judged to be Satanic. His punishment was having his tongue slit, among other tortures, and he was made to live outside the monastery. He died soon after of hunger, exposure, and injuries sustained from a wild boar attack.

No wonder Sabina has problems speaking up in this life. When I asked if she had any physical resonances from Bernard's life, she gave me a litany of symptoms.

"When I was younger, I had issues with my throat. My thyroid would act up, my throat would close up when I tried to speak out about something, and a vocal cord would sometimes stop working."

Like many people with a fear of Self-Expression, Sabina hated being called on to speak in class. "From the time I was in elementary school, I'd never raise my hand in class," she said. "I was afraid of getting things wrong and having people know how stupid I was."

....

JUDGMENT AND SELF-EXPRESSION

Many people with a fear of Self-Expression also have a phobia of Judgment (something I'll discuss in Chapter Ten).

If Judgment impacts Self-Expression, you get a kind of double whammy. It can make the fear twice as hard to deal with.

The cause of both the fear and the phobia may stem from the same event. The difference is that the fear is associated with having your life plan derailed; the phobia is associated with death.

In her thirties, Sabina went back to school to study massage therapy. She felt intimidated by the other, more qualified, students. "I was working so hard and barely scraping a C," she recalled. "Then one of the teachers called me into her office. She asked me a few questions; then she said, 'Look at this test: you got everything backward.' It was the first time anyone realized I had a learning difficulty."

A student teacher administered the next test to Sabina orally—and she aced it.

Sabina continued: "When I went back to the class, one of the students began ridiculing me. 'You can't be taking the same test as us if you got an A,' she said. I was shocked. I began to feel the old fears come up, and my throat began to close up, but this time I stood my ground. 'I took the same test as everyone else,' I said confidently."

Sabina has long faced self-expression issues when it comes to her parents. "They're so prim and proper when it comes to things like punctuation and spelling," said Sabina. "One time, my aunt said in front of everyone, 'I love Sabina's e-mails; they really crack me up.'

"My mom said, 'Even with all the misspellings and mispunctuation?' My aunt answered, 'I'll take Sabina's e-mails over ones with correct punctuation any day!'

"After that, I realized I no longer needed my parents' approval. And since understanding where the fear came from, I feel like I've broken some kind of pattern. Now I'm teaching my daughters to speak from their hearts. I told them that when you speak from your heart, there are no periods or punctuation. You just have to say it with love, and hope the person accepts it."

....

SPIRITUAL ACT 7: GIVING A VOICE TO OTHERS

There was a time, in another life, when you had no voice, and no one to speak for you. The Spiritual Act connected with the fear of Self-Expression is concerned with redressing the balance.

There are many people in the world who need a voice or someone to be an advocate for them. And there are many organizations that do just that. By supporting them in small ways or large, you can use your motivation of Honesty to help others and yourself.

Your past-life experiences will influence how you express a Spiritual Act. One of my clients was abandoned as a child in the past and has been motivated to become a vocal defender of children's rights this time around.

....

SEEKING TRUTH

As your soul traverses the Transformation, truth will become a bigger issue than ever. As the Collective Consciousness accelerates toward Stage Four, you'll become hypersensitive to lies, whether they come from official sources, your nearest and dearest, or even yourself.

As the motivation of Honesty emerges to fight the fear, any personal violation of your soul's goal of Truth will create an unpleasant dissonance between your conscious self and your soul.

Other souls—especially those whose own motivation of Honesty pushes them toward the Transformation—will hold you to a higher standard of truth telling. When this happens, you may wonder why another person can get away with telling a whopping lie, while you get raked over coals for a tiny little white one.

This came up in a session with Francesca, a nurse who recently returned to the profession after several years of child rearing. She now works in a small clinic in California.

"It seems so unfair," she began. "I work in a private clinic with two doctors and several other nurses. There's also a student nurse there. Her name is Marisol. She and I have become really good friends over the last year.

"Shortly after we first met, there was an incident. Marisol made a mistake. It was not a life-threatening one, but it was certainly careless, and it might have reflected badly on her. She asked me to pretend I hadn't seen her do it.

"One of the doctors found out about it. He demanded to know who was responsible. I told him I didn't know. So did Marisol, but later she went to the doctor and confessed. You'd have thought he'd have been mad with her, but he wasn't. He was furious with *me*.

"I felt guilty and wished I hadn't covered up for Marisol, but what really hurt was that the doctor didn't seem concerned that she'd lied, too. He's a very honest person and very easy-going, too. I've never seen him react to anyone else like he did to me."

"The good news," I told Francesca, "is that the doctor wouldn't have reacted so badly if you were not such an honest old soul. He held you to a higher standard of honesty than he did Marisol."

"It still doesn't seem fair," she said.

"Consider it a reminder that you need to be very conscious of your soul's need to tell the truth," I said. "That way, you can avoid the shame you felt when you were found out."

When your soul wants you to tell the truth and you tell a lie, the incongruity comes across as unsettling. People sense something's not right, even if they can't quite put a finger on it.

But when your soul wants you to tell the truth, and you *do* tell the truth, you'll act according to the expectations of others. The result is harmony.

....

WHITE LIES

There are times when lying is acceptable. If you had to lie to save a life, you'd be supported by the universe.

And guys, the answer to the question, "Does this dress make me look fat?" is always "No." (It's a question of diplomacy and self-protection!)

....

When someone holds you, as a spiritually conscious old soul, to a higher standard of honesty, a lie breaks the trust between you. Francesca recognized that right away.

"It really affected my relationship with the doctor," she said. "Things are back to normal, but it took a while."

By sticking to her goal of Truth, Francesca will gradually restore the doctor's trust in her. There's a reciprocal aspect to this, too. When you act with congruity, it helps others trust you. That in turn makes you feel good about yourself.

THE BIGGEST LIES

You know when you're being lied to. At least you do on a soul level. As you get closer to the transformational goal of Truth, discerning the truth is going to become a piece of cake.

All you'll have to do to get beneath the surface and recognize what's true and what's not is to look for incongruity. It's simply a matter of using your intuition, your internal B.S. detector.

As I've already pointed out, lies polarize us. We end up split between those who detect something fishy and those for whom the truth is either too hard to see or too difficult to accept.

Younger souls, the ones who are most likely to find themselves stuck behind the Illusion, look to authority with a kind of innate respect. Not yet able to see those in power as souls no different from themselves, young souls imbue authority with a respect it doesn't necessarily deserve.

As long as that authority shares their values (or at least makes a pretense of it), these less experienced souls will look to it as a child would its father.

When a government lies, especially when its lies are echoed by a compliant media (as happened in Soviet Russia and Mao's China), those behind the Illusion don't generally recognize it. They have no desire to question what they're told. They want easily digestible information and assurance that they'll be protected from the evils of the world.

It's easier to accept that Saddam Hussein had weapons of mass destruction—or that some guy in a cave on the other side of the world could mastermind an attack that outwitted the defenses of the most heavily armed country in history to bring down three of the most structurally sound buildings in the world—rather than question the official stories.

In the short term, government-inspired lies are not going to dry up overnight. But as the Transformation builds, an increasing number of ordinary citizens are going to expect a much higher level of honesty from those who are expected to serve them.

There's a reason why learning to use your internal B.S. detector is so important. By questioning perceived wisdom, you'll separate your consciousness from that of those who prefer to bask in the comfort of assumption. By reaching for truth, however unpleasant, you will touch the transformational goal of Truth.

By thinking for yourself, you'll no longer be victimized by the lies of others. Seeking out the truth will elevate your consciousness—and along with it, your level of personal happiness.

During the Transformation, increasing numbers of individuals will lose confidence in governments and other bodies who, until now, have had little to fear from inquiring minds.

As more people embody the goal of Truth and learn to look beneath the surface to discern what's really going on, the pressure will be on those institutions to change.

....

HONESTY EXERCISE 1

TEN PEOPLE AND TEN TRUTHS

Having a past-life fear of Self-Expression sometimes makes the truth a little hard to get out. This exercise will engage your karmic motivation of Honesty.

Bring in your spirit guides with the following request: "I call upon my spirit guides, acting in my highest interest, to help me reach the transformational goal of Truth through the motivation of Honesty."

- Make a list of ten people you've lied to, been less than honest with, cheated on, or otherwise behaved shamefully toward.
- List the ten things you did that were less than honest.
- Beside each one, write what you'd like to say to that person if you were to tell him or her the truth about what happened.
- Picture the first person in front of your third eye, about a foot away.
- Apologize to him or her, telling the truth about what you did.
- Let that person's image evaporate, and move on to the next.

I once made an ass of myself when, during the early 1990s, I made the mistake of ignoring my intuition altogether. On a visit to London from my new home in New York, I had a reading with Bettina, an extremely gifted psychic I'd known for years.

Bettina told me I'd meet a man and a woman who would help my career as an illustrator. "She will fade out after a year or so, and he will continue to work with you," she told me. "He's older than you—like an uncle. When you ask him a question, he'll want to make sure you understand."

I had an agent at the time, but she was something of a crackpot and was driving me nuts. Bettina warned me not to sign a contract with her. I would have taken her advice, but when I returned to New York, the agent had met a couple who liked my work and wanted to do business. I assumed they were the ones.

My agent was convinced they were the key to riches, but insisted there could be no negotiation without the two of us having a contract in place. On the day I agreed to sign with the agent, I turned up three hours late. I'd been pacing the streets, putting off the inevitable. I signed my name on the dotted line and immediately wished I could have taken it back.

I was introduced to the couple and liked them, though the guy was hardly how Bettina had described him. He didn't seem at all interested in answering my questions.

Things finally got so bad with the agent that I had no choice but to fire her. It meant losing the other two as well. This was not how I'd expected things to work out.

I spent the next week sending samples of my work to licensing agents. I had several people call me back, but one, a woman, wanted to meet me the next day. When I turned up for the meeting in the lounge of a midtown hotel, she had someone else in tow. "This is my associate, Josh Brand," she said, introducing me to the man beside her.

A year later, the woman dropped out, and Josh and I continued working together for the next decade. He was honest, upfront, and the most business-savvy person I've ever known. When he went to bat for me, I knew he was going to get me the best deal he could. And when I called him, he always had time for a chat, no matter how busy he was.

Josh was also a soul mate. And when he died of a heart attack several years ago, I felt the loss like he was a brother. For more than a year I couldn't talk about him without tearing up.

What this experience taught me was that you have to use your intuition at all times. My signature on that contract cost me a lot of money at a time when I was broke. When I met the first couple, they certainly didn't seem to be all Bettina had led me to believe they'd be, but I took those two square pegs and insisted on trying to fit them into a preimagined round hole.

In the interim between my session with Bettina and meeting Josh, I felt something was not right. I wasn't sleeping well, and I couldn't see a happy future as long as that agent was in my life. Looking back it's clear that my soul was yelling a warning, and I was putting my hands over my ears and refusing to listen.

By using all your faculties, including your intuition, you'll be well on the way to embodying the goal of Truth. The following short exercise is designed to help you stimulate your intuitive muscles.

....

HONESTY EXERCISE 2

DEVELOPING YOUR INTUITION

Bring in your spirit guides with the following request: "I call upon my spirit guides, acting in my highest interest, to help me reach the transformational goal of Truth through the motivation of Honesty."

Developing your intuition is an essential part of learning to discern the truth. This simple exercise will help you recognize when your intuition is guiding you.

- Make a list of ten times your intuition served you well.
- Make a list of ten times your intellect has let you down.

....

The next chapter explores your soul's fundamental need for the freedom to be itself. The past-life fear to be overcome is one of Powerlessness—a fear more common than you might imagine.

CHAPTER NINE

THE PURSUIT OF FREEDOM
Manifesting Your Personal Destiny

GOAL Freedom

MOTIVATION Empowerment

FEAR Powerlessness

DON'T TELL *ME* WHAT TO DO!

A fear of Powerlessness is created when you've had a lifetime in which your life plan has been derailed by others. The most common causes are imprisonment, slavery, and being disempowered to an extent where you have no ability to change your circumstances.

If this is one of your fears, any attempt to clip your wings or curtail your freedom is likely to cause a strong reaction in you.

Sometimes the fear of Powerlessness will imbue a person with feistiness. If you try to guide this person or, worse still, tell him or her what to do, you'll be met by what I consider the motto of someone with a fear of Powerlessness: "Don't tell me what to do!"

At the extreme end of the spectrum, a fear of Powerlessness creates what's often known as a "control freak."

The cure for a past-life fear of Powerlessness is found in the motivation of Empowerment. It's through becoming empowered that the fear dissipates and the goal of Freedom is reached.

The goal of Freedom is a real two-way street. It's about ensuring that you have maximum freedom to live the life your soul intended, but it's also about recognizing that right in others.

For this reason, many people with this fear of Powerlessness are members of organizations like Amnesty International or Oxfam. They remember only too well when they were disempowered through imprisonment or poverty, and that gives them the impetus to empower others.

The payoff for overcoming a fear of Powerlessness is enormous. Self-empowerment will give you the impetus to overcome blocks to fulfillment in this life, and it will keep you in a healthy state of autonomy. By recognizing that you have the freedom to make huge changes in your life, you can make radical shifts toward personal transformation.

In the tribe, everyone had the ability to live their lives with maximum freedom. In this world, the freedom to live your own life can become a battle between you on one side and the forces of commerce and coercion on the other.

THE POWER OF SUGGESTION

Back in the fifties, a poster for Ireland's famous beer declared, "Guinness Is Good for You." Around that time, the following exchange took place in a pub between a TV interviewer and an old bloke with a pint of Guinness in his hand.

> **Interviewer:** "Does advertising influence your choice of beer?"
>
> **Old Bloke:** "Not at all."
>
> **Interviewer:** "So why do you drink Guinness?"
>
> **Old Bloke:** "Because it's good for you."

Advertising is a highly sophisticated form of coercion. It is designed to manipulate you on an emotional level. It's how a cigarette company can take a bunch of addictive, toxic chemicals, put them in a cool-looking package, and sell them for hundreds of times what it costs to make.

Whether we know it or not, we're all impacted by advertising. Advertising works. If it didn't, then a corporation like Coca-Cola might spend its estimated 2.2 billion-dollar annual ad budget elsewhere.

Being coerced into drinking Coke rather than Pepsi may not seem particularly serious—and maybe you do prefer the taste of one over the other. But all those billions of marketing dollars have resulted in a huge lack of choice.

Companies like Coca-Cola spend a small fortune coercing cash-strapped schools into putting their products in vending machines, in what are called "pouring rights." "The school system is where you build brand loyalty," a senior Coca-Cola executive once explained.

You might want your kids to have a healthier choice, perhaps something produced locally. But in virtually all cases, your kids will have to settle for whatever the major corporations decide.

At the far end of the coercion scale we have slavery, a hugely damaging assault on the soul. Being clapped in irons and transported to a distant country to be worked to death is never a part of anyone's life plan.

For anyone held captive in a Southern plantation, a Soviet work camp, or a salt mine in Mali, the effect is the same. The original life plan is derailed, and a fear of Powerlessness is created.

During the Vietnam War, young people were selected for active service regardless of how much they opposed the war.

Forcing someone to join the military, sending them to a far-off land to kill and be killed is simply another form of slavery.

A more subtle form of slavery exists, and it doesn't require conscription to achieve its ends. Called the "poverty draft," it happens when a young person is faced with unemployment or few opportunities for meaningful employment. Joining the army may be the only viable option. He or she might seem to make the decision without coercion, but often there's little other choice.

According to the Associated Press, "Nearly three-fourths of [U.S. troops] killed in Iraq came from towns where the per-capita income was below the national average. More than half came from towns where the percentage of people living in poverty topped the national average."

Under economic slavery, immigrant workers are forced to labor on America's farms for what essentially amounts to slave wages. Often forced to live in conditions that would be considered unfit for animals, they work long days and are exposed to toxic chemicals and other dangers.

Even in the more visible part of the working world, you can spot coercion. Impossible deadlines, unrealistic expectations, and bullying by superiors can make the workplace one that damages the soul.

Without unions, many major employers force workers into ten-hour days with mandatory overtime. Refusal can result in sanctions, loss of advancement, and even dismissal.

....

THE HIGH COST OF "EVERYDAY LOW" ETHICS

A major corporation, Walmart disempowers individuals and communities. By paying low wages, preventing workers from forming unions, and putting small retailers out of business, they diminish the quality of life for everyone.

Walmart is, at the time of writing, the world's biggest company. Its profits are measured in the billions. Yet, many of its employees earn below the national poverty level.

The company has undermined labor standards in America and abroad. In what has been described as a "race to the bottom," Walmart has forced suppliers to cut costs to the point where U.S. factories have closed, and manufacturing has moved to countries like China. Competitors have been forced to slash costs and cut jobs to compete.

Walmart senior executives are some of the richest in the world, while its U.S. workers are among the poorest in the country. Former CEO Lee Scott took home over $30 million in 2008. (*Forbes* magazine lists four members of the Walton Family, whose patriarch, Sam, started the company, in its list of the top twenty richest people on Earth.) Meanwhile, the average annual salary for Walmart employees is a little over $19,000.

According to a report from the National Labor Committee, some workers in China slave for as many as 130 hours a week making toys for Walmart, at an hourly rate of 16.5 cents.

Because of the low wages paid by the company, U.S. taxpayers have to pick up the slack—to the tune of around $2.5 billion a year for such things as Medicaid, housing assistance, and food stamps.

A spokesperson for the company accurately observed that if you're the sole breadwinner, then maybe Walmart is "not the right place for you."

After the Transformation, Walmart will be shown to our grandchildren as the worst example of corporate greed and economic slavery imaginable.

Your soul came here to learn all about being human. It started out a little afraid of the world, but after a few incarnations, it grew more comfortable with being here. Now you're an old soul, and you probably get the sense you've been around the block more than once.

The more times you've been here, the more you want to run things yourself. In your first few lifetimes you might have been happy to have people tell you what to do. In a strange new world, letting a priest or some other authority figure tell you when to get up, when to pray, what to eat, and how to make love made things easier for you.

But now, in the second half of your journey on the earthly plane, you don't need strict rules to keep you on the right track.

The older your soul becomes, the more it rejects intrusion into its business. It wants to be left alone to make its own decisions and even its own mistakes.

The very young soul is afraid of those it sees as different from itself, and it will sometimes isolate itself from the outside world. The older soul, who simply wants to be left alone to get on with his or her own life, will sometimes detach itself from the mainstream.

Superficially, the two may appear similar. But there's a big difference between "Get the hell off my property," and "Excuse me, but I'm trying to find a little tranquility here. Thank you."

Your soul wants you to experience the joys of human existence with the least interference in its life plan.

It has multiple "destinies," each of which is a part of, or consistent with, your life plan. Your partner might be your destiny. So might your work or leisure activities. You might have any number of destinies.

Being prevented from achieving any one of those destinies can be a serious matter. It can derail your life plan and create anything from mild dissatisfaction to severe unhappiness.

REBELLIOUS SLAVES

One of my clients, a healer, was having difficulty giving up smoking. Though she'd cut down over the years and could get through the day with just five or six cigarettes, she couldn't completely quit.

"You're a healer," I pointed out. "Don't you think it's a little incongruous to be healing people and poisoning your own body at the same time?"

Megan sighed. "I know. I know. I really should quit. But there's something else going on."

"What's that?"

"I've always been a rebel. Smoking makes me feel more independent."

"The tobacco companies spend billions of dollars in marketing every year to make sure you think of smoking as being rebellious. Maybe it's time you began rebelling against them?" I suggested.

Like a mythical hero on a quest, your soul sets out to achieve its destinies. With each setback and distraction, it recalibrates its internal guidance system to give you every chance of completing your life plan.

Your soul highly values its freedom. It resists attempts to restrict it, and it urges you to take responsibility for your own life. It wants you to recognize the reciprocal aspect of freedom. If you want freedom (and trust me, you do), then you have to remember that others have the same right to freedom that you have.

Your soul has learned a great deal about freedom from not actually having any. Throughout your many previous incarnations you've been a slave, a prisoner, a serf, a servant, and you've had many other opportunities to learn what it's like to have no say over your own destiny.

THE KARMIC CONSEQUENCES OF INCARCERATION

Few things create a fear of Powerlessness like having been locked in prison. The moment the hand of authority comes down on your shoulder, your life plan stops. You no longer have the freedom to make your own decisions.

When Brenda called, she told me how she's been wrestling with food issues for years. She was eighty pounds overweight and diagnosed as prediabetic. "I would eat forever," she told me.

During our second session, I found the source of the problem. Brenda had been imprisoned more than two hundred years ago, and the trauma was still with her.

....

A *NOT* SO HYPOTHETICAL EXAMPLE

Years ago, my spirit guides asked me to imagine I was a prisoner in an Egyptian jail cell, with only a tiny window near the ceiling to let light in. "What," they asked me, "would you want people in America, an affluent and relatively free country, to do for you?"

My answer was, "Something."

"Precisely," they said. "That's why you should remember people who are suffering like that."

They inspired me to renew my membership in Amnesty International.

What I didn't realize until more recently was that the example from my spirit guides was not hypothetical. I really had been locked up in an Egyptian prison cell in another life.

....

The moment you're thrown into a cell, your life plan comes crashing to a halt. No one deliberately chooses imprisonment as part of his or her life plan. Having your freedom curtailed is always contrary to your soul's wishes.

It was in Revolutionary France at the end of the eighteenth century that Brenda had the experience that most scarred her soul. In that life, she was an architect and engineer named Claude. This unfortunate young man had strong political views that led to his appearance before a Revolutionary Court.

What shocked Claude was the suddenness of the sentence handed down. He was given no opportunity to negotiate or plead his case. In a state of shock, he was taken from the court and thrown into a dungeon known as an "oubliette," which comes from the French *oublier,* meaning "to forget." It refers to a dungeon with an entrance, usually in the ceiling, but no way out.

Injured from his drop into the darkened hole, Claude lay for days in total darkness, unsure whether he was asleep or awake. All around him were the dead and decaying bodies of other prisoners. As he slowly starved to death, he was eaten alive by vermin.

Such a terrifying end to any life has to have strong resonances. The first thing my spirit guides said to me was, "Ask Brenda about the unexplained itching."

I did, and her reaction was immediate.

"All my adult life, I've had unexplained itching," she said. "I've checked myself into clinics. No one can find anything wrong with me. It drives me crazy."

"Do you have a fear of the dark?" I asked.

"I sleep with a night light. I always have," she said.

The slow starvation she underwent explained much about her compulsion to eat. By overeating, she's avoiding the risk of dying of hunger. Sadly, this overreaction is creating a host of problems for her in this lifetime.

A few months later, I asked Brenda if the fear had subsided since our exploration.

"Absolutely," she said. "A lot has changed since we last spoke. I've relocated to a great little apartment, and I started working with a trainer. Remember how your spirit guides suggested I needed an exercise expert and a good nutritionist? Well, she's both. I'm also getting hypnosis for weekly reinforcement."

I couldn't wait to ask the big question. "So, how much weight have you lost?"

I weighed in today at twenty-six-and-a-half pounds less than I did two months ago," she said. "I never used to feel full or satisfied. Now I eat well and don't have any cravings."

Brenda was eager for me to know just how much impact her past life had on her present. "You told me I'd been an architect," she said. "I've always loved design and architecture. Even as a child, I was always designing furniture and rooms. My sister has often commented, 'What is it with you and buildings?' I never knew where the desire came from. I probably missed my calling by not doing something like architecture or interior design."

There was something else Brenda felt I should know. Shortly after our sessions, she took a trip to Europe with a friend. "Marcy was never into spiritual things, but I was still processing the work I did with you and eventually shared some of it with her. We bought a copy of *The Instruction,* and she was able to identify everything you told me: my soul age, soul type, all the influences, missions. And she had it in exactly the same order. She nailed me on every single thing. Up until then I didn't think she really got me!"

I had one last question for Brenda. "Do you still sleep with a night-light?"

"Marcy likes a darkened room at night. Since we had to share, I let her have her way. I was okay with it, but I still prefer to be able to see the room at night. I guess it's just habit."

I was just about to put the phone down, when I thought of something else. "The unexplained itching," I said, "Does it still bother you?"

"Oh my gosh," she said, "It's so much better. I don't wake up with bloody legs from scratching anymore."

Another person still feeling the effects of a past-life imprisonment is Amber. She was an early-American colonist, a man named Samuel, who worked as a fisherman and preacher. Like the young man in Mississippi I wrote about earlier, Samuel began questioning his belief in God after suffering a terrible loss.

Samuel and his son were fishing in squally winter waters. As their boat lurched in the waves, Samuel's son lost his balance and fell overboard. There was nothing his father could do. The boy simply disappeared beneath the waves forever.

Samuel was heartbroken. He became increasingly angry, especially at those who would tell him it was God's will. He began cursing God in the presence of his immediate family. They were terrified. At a time when simply questioning the Trinity was enough to have you put in the stocks, whipped, and even worse, they were afraid for Samuel *and* themselves.

Sure enough, Samuel's blasphemy was his undoing. Several witnesses heard him taking the Lord's name in vain, and he was tried and thrown into prison. He was forced to recant, which he did only under extreme duress. A short time later, in a squalid prison cell without proper bedding or heat, Samuel died of hypothermia.

The death in that life has left a resonance with Amber. When I asked her if she had any issues with the cold, she told me an astonishing story that's directly related to what happened all those lifetimes ago.

"A couple of times I've become so cold I thought I was going to die," she told me. "One time I was at home. The temperature in the house was normal, but I started to feel really cold. I ran a hot bath and called my sister. I said, 'If you don't hear from me in the next half hour, call 911.' After lying in the bathtub for a while, I went to bed wrapped in blankets. It took me all night to fully warm up again."

The major fear that resulted from Amber's death in Virginia was Powerlessness. After experiencing what it was like to be completely disempowered in that and other lives, she came into this one fully prepared.

"I chose my parents well," Amber told me. "They were both on their own at fifteen, and they expected us children to be totally independent at an early age, too. They said the world was our oyster and encouraged us to go out and explore it.

"My friends couldn't believe how liberal they were. There were no curfews, but we were expected to act responsibly. The other kids were so confined they were always trying to break out. My brother and I never got in any trouble, but the other kids certainly did.

"I was in sixth grade when I flew on my own to visit a friend for six weeks. Independence was so natural that I bought my first home at twenty-five and started my own business two years later. I didn't need anyone's help."

....

RUNNING HOT AND COLD

Though several of the examples I've used in the book describe people who have issues with the cold, one of my clients has the opposite problem.

She was once a pale-skinned Brit who was transported to Australia as punishment for theft. After months at sea below deck, she landed in the penal colony and was immediately put to work in the scorching sun. She suffered terrible burns and eventually died from sunstroke.

Though she lives in a cool part of the globe in this life, she has relatives who live in Spain. Her visits there are not at all to her liking.

"I hate the heat," she told me. "When I'm there, I spend the whole time indoors." And it's not just the weather that affects her. "I don't like hot showers, and I'll never use a hot tub."

....

Empowerment, the motivation related to Powerlessness, links you to your soul's goal of Freedom. A few months after our sessions, I asked Amber about her need for personal freedom.

"Working with you opened my eyes to see that everyone has the right to choose what they do in this lifetime," she said. "I discovered that I had the freedom to learn so many lessons, but other people need freedom of choice, too. I really didn't recognize that before. I've become more accepting of people's need to follow their own path.

"I hate it when anyone tries to disempower me, and I get really fired up when I see someone else being disempowered. I was in the supermarket recently, and this big guy was screaming at his wife. I walked up to her and said, 'Are you okay? Do you need some help?' The woman with me said, 'Are you crazy? He could have had a gun or a knife.' I didn't care. I just saw someone in trouble and had to do something."

Recognizing the importance of freedom has inspired Amber to help those who have had theirs radically curtailed.

"I want to help children who are sex slaves. I've been finding like-minded people from all different backgrounds to join me. We're starting small, but each one of us knows a couple of others who might join us. It's a great little group, and it'll soon grow."

There was one thing I had to know. "Do you still have issues with the cold?" I asked.

"I live in Minnesota, for crying out loud!" she laughed. "Of course, I have issues with the cold. I sometimes wonder why I've chosen to live in such a cold climate, but I love winters. As for the cold I thought would kill me, I still feel it in my heels and upper arms, but there's been a huge improvement since we uncovered that past life."

DREAMS OF THE PAST

During our first session, Jessica told me about a vivid dream she'd had as a very small child. "I was shot by a firing squad," she said. "Was it real?"

"It was most definitely real," I told her. "It happened in Barcelona about a hundred years ago. You were caught up in some kind of a revolution."

Jessica had sensed the dream took place in Spain but thought it might have been somewhere farther south. I checked with my spirit guides, just to make sure it had actually been Barcelona.

"We do know our geography," they assured us.

"I can remember being wanted by the authorities," Jessica continued. "My wife tried to protect me, but there was nothing she could do to stop them."

We both agreed that the man she'd been in that life was something of a fugitive. When the authorities finally caught up with him, they wanted to silence him as quickly as possible.

"You were a very proud man in that life," I told her.

Jessica agreed. "When I stood facing the firing squad, I refused a blindfold. I looked each one in the eye with defiance. After I was shot, I felt myself leaving my body through the top of my head. I was consumed by feelings of love. I remember thinking, 'Shakespeare was right—life's a play, and we're all playing our parts.' I wanted to share my revelation with my wife. I was saying, 'It's okay. It's okay,' but she couldn't hear me.

"It was a horrible feeling to touch her but know she couldn't feel me. She was distraught, and I wanted her to know she hadn't done anything wrong."

THE CIRCULO ECUESTRE

I could see the interior of a grand building that seemed to have some significance in Jessica's life in Barcelona. When I described it to her, she told me she'd seen it in her dream. In fact, she'd drawn a picture of it recently. There was a word associated with this story. I told her it was something like "equestri." I assumed the man was an equerry, an officer in charge of horses.

The next time Jessica and I spoke was a few months later. In that time, she'd had the chance to do a little research. She'd found the building. It was the Circulo Ecuestre in Barcelona.

But there was more. She'd found the person she was in that life. When she saw a photograph of him, she recognized herself right away. "He had the same short-cropped hair I saw in the dream."

In her life in Barcelona, Jessica was Francisco Ferrer y Guardia, a humanitarian and educator who founded the secular Modern Schools and fell out with the establishment over his progressive views. He was arrested during a popular uprising know as Tragic Week, when troops killed hundreds of rioting citizens. Though innocent, he was charged with being a ringleader and executed.

On the eve of his execution, Ferrer y Guardia, a very old soul, wrote on his prison wall, "Let no more gods or exploiters be served. Let us learn rather to love each other."

When you've suffered a sudden interruption to your life plan (arrest and execution are prime examples), you're a perfect candidate for a fear of Powerlessness.

Jessica's soul came to Spain in that life to learn important lessons about being on the Physical Plane. When the life it was experiencing came to an abrupt close, any opportunity of completing its various missions and lessons also ended.

The vivid execution dream was a sign of a highly intuitive person. I asked Jessica if she'd been aware of her psychic abilities when she was growing up.

"When I was twelve years old," she said, "I answered a call from my older brother's best friend. He asked me if Jeff was there.

"'No, Jeff's dead,' I told him. It was totally untrue, and to this day I have no idea what made me say it. But the next day, the same guy called. This time it was true."

The previous night, Jeff and his buddies had been drinking beer in a field beside a construction site. They'd found a bulldozer and started it up. Jeff was crushed beneath its tracks.

The loss of Jeff devastated the family, especially Jessica, who felt terrible guilt. "Jeff was not a nice guy. He liked to hurt people. I used to wish he *was* dead. Then when he died, I thought I really had the power.

"There were people at school I didn't like, and I'd wish them away. Then a few months later, they'd say something like, 'My dad got a new job and we're leaving.' So, when Jeff died, I thought it was because I'd wished it to happen."

Jessica was experiencing precognition, the ability to sense the future. She didn't will anything to happen. She simply sensed events before they happened.

EMPOWERING OTHERS TO EMPOWER YOURSELF

My first session with Sophia revealed a past life as a nurse in a field hospital during World War I. She fell in love with a patient who recovered from his wounds, only to die in battle a few months later. This tragic experience has given Sophia a fear of Loss ("I've always had a sense of impermanence—that everything could change") and a fear of Intimacy ("I don't think I've ever known what intimacy is"). Both of these fears are big issues in her life now.

It's the fear of Powerlessness, however, that has played the biggest role in making Sophia who she is today. Much of Sophia's current life plan has to do with completing what went unfinished in her soul's past. "My life has been all about preventive health care," she told me.

Feelings of powerlessness that get triggered by circumstances beyond your control can be a massive source of soul-level frustration. The impetus for change is designed to ease that frustration.

It's through the motivation of Empowerment that the goal of Freedom is reached.

"I set up a community program to offer free physicals to school-age kids with no health care," she said. "It felt such a meaningful thing to do. People were really surprised. Their perception of health care was that it's all profit driven."

Sophia sees prevention as empowerment. "What I did for others impacted me. When I got into prevention, I started going to the gym, eating whole foods, and taking antiaging meds. It made me ready to empower others."

During another session with Sophia, a past life in Hong Kong came up. It followed from the last one we looked at and is her most recent past life.

Following our first session, Sophia met Kevin, someone it turned out she'd been with in her life in Hong Kong. The roles were reversed then. In that life, Sophia was a man, married to a woman who is now Kevin.

Their time in Hong Kong was one of constant struggle. With nine children and two grandparents in the home, they worked hard to feed to all those hungry mouths. The husband (Sophia) would have liked to have been a doctor or nurse, but he ended up as a kind of hospital orderly, augmenting the family's income by baking buns to feed other hungry mouths.

Sophia's life in Hong Kong ended with a long battle against the effects of emphysema and lung cancer after her partner died in childbirth. Leaving the children behind was a major source of the fear of Loss in this life.

As we've seen, the motivation stemming from her life in Hong Kong pushes her to empower others. And since this life is a completion of that one, her death from cancer is significant.

"It explains why I've been drawn to work with the American Lung Association and the Cancer Society," Sophia said. "I developed an asthma screening program and a project for cancer education, and I coordinated volunteer services for people with cancer.

"I also developed a program to offer free mammograms to people with no means. I got the hospitals to donate the machines, the technicians, the film, and the radiologists—all of it free of charge."

The motivation of Empowerment is working overtime in Sophia, making her an active part of the Transformation, and taking her on a very fast track to Stage Four consciousness.

"I'm always trying to empower people to be healthy," said Sophia. "I could never make doughnuts or run a hot-dog cart. I just feel compelled to help others. It began when I started nursing, and I took a class on prevention. It hit me like a ton of bricks that I needed to work in community health."

SPIRITUAL ACT 8: GIVING POWER TO THE POWERLESS

Many people have their life plans cut short by unexpected disasters. People might suddenly be imprisoned or lose their jobs and their homes.

You've been there. You know what it's like to have it all come crashing down on you. For that reason, Spiritual Acts related to Powerlessness reach out a helping hand when it's needed.

Though Spiritual Acts are often voluntary and unpaid, your work may also offer the opportunity to help others. A Spiritual Act is not necessarily less spiritual just because you get paid for doing it.

Sophia and her husband, Kevin, met late in life, and are completing something that began in their previous lifetime together. One big difference this time is that now that their children have left home, neither feels any need to have family around them.

I told Sophia in our first session that she needed to work on being a little more warm and fuzzy. Later, after she'd met Kevin, I mentioned that the life in Hong Kong was the last of several in which she'd been male. "Kevin will help you develop your fuzziness," my guides said.

Sophia laughed. "When he does something for me, he'll wait for me to say thank you. And when he tells me he loves me, he'll pause and then add, ' . . . and you say?' He's helping me to be more gracious—more warm."

REMEMBERING THE PAST

Many children come into this life with a fear of Powerlessness. It can make them extremely hard to handle. They'll often resent what they see as an attempt to disempower them.

Their anger can be triggered by being pinned down to have a diaper changed or being told to tidy their room.

Sometimes a past-life fear can be combined with something more physical to create a complicated set of symptoms that require more than a session with me to overcome. My spirit guides are quick to tell me when a client needs a therapist, a doctor, or some other kind of help.

When Victoria asked me about her daughter Kimberly, I warned her that I could only do so much. Not only did Kimberly have a fear of Powerlessness to contend with, but there was something else going on.

When we first spoke, Victoria told me how Kimberly would totally overreact whenever she couldn't get her own way. "Kimberly ran away from home when she was still in kindergarten.

We took her home and talked to her about it. We asked her what she'd do for money and how she'd manage to eat. The next time, the little stinker raided her piggy bank and the fridge, and she took a suitcase with wheels. After that, anytime she disagreed with me or was asked to do something, she'd say, 'I'm outta here!'"

WHO DO YOU THINK YOU ARE?

A common problem raising a child you've known in previous incarnations is that they can find it hard to adjust to their new role.

Kimberly revealed her innermost feelings back when she was still in kindergarten. During an argument with her mother, she yelled, "You can't tell me what to do. I used to be your mom!"

As Kimberly grew older, she became increasingly difficult to deal with. She had what appeared to be ADD, she was angry, and at age fourteen, she was getting into drinking, drugs, and boys. Her mother was severely stressed out.

"I can't talk to her," Victoria said. "She's doing really badly at school. She's so convinced she's dumb that she'd rather not do a project than do it badly. It's really hurting her self-esteem. If I try to help her, she just yells at me.

"Kimberly will stay out all night, delete her friends' numbers from my phone, and switch off her cell phone as soon as she leaves the house.

"A couple of months ago, I had to call the police after she hit me. The cop read her the riot act. It finally seemed to get her attention."

My guides had already given Victoria some tips about dealing with Kimberly. This time they recommended a doctor: not just any doctor, but a specific one. "My guides suggest you check out Dr. Amen's clinic," I said. "Have you heard of him?" (Daniel Amen, MD, is an author and brain-imaging specialist.)

"I know Dr. Amen," Victoria said. "I've been looking into his work. He has a clinic not far from here. I'll get in touch with it right away."

The next time Victoria and I spoke, Kimberly had been to see Dr. Amen and was a new person. "It turned out she had irritation in her frontal and temporal lobes that's been causing severe depression and anxiety. It mimics ADD.

"We're treating her naturally and conventionally. You wouldn't believe the change. In three months she's 90 percent better. She's stopped hanging out with the wrong crowd, she's learned to say 'sorry' when she gets angry, and she's got a boyfriend who's a sweetheart!"

Victoria learned to use her own motivation of Empowerment to get help for Kimberly. This in turn has had a healing effect on both mother and daughter.

Together, Victoria and Kimberly are shifting out of Stage Three into a Stage Four Consciousness.

....

EMPOWERMENT EXERCISE 1
THE FACETS OF YOUR LIFE

This exercise will help you focus on the parts of your life that need the most work and ensure you have the support of your spirit guides behind you.

Bring in your spirit guides with the following request: "I call upon my spirit guides, acting in my highest interest, to help me reach the transformational goal of Freedom through the motivation of Empowerment."

Rate each of the topics listed below from one to ten according to how much that aspect of your life is fulfilled.

- Life partner
- Location
- Recreation
- Work
- Social life
- Creativity
- Health
- Service to others
- Family
- Other activities

In your journal, write a paragraph or two describing each facet of your life listed above.

When you've done that, go through the list again, describing the changes you'd like to see take place in each area. Once a week, review the list and ask your spirit guides to help you make the changes you've described.

....

CONNECTING WITH YOUR OWN FUTURE

One night, a few months before I began writing this book, I was sitting in my office chatting with my spirit guides about concepts they wanted me to cover in it.

They said, "The past affects the present."

I said, "Of course it does."

"In that case, the present affects the future."

Yes," I agreed. "That follows."

"And the future affects the present."

I was tired, so I said, "Let's pick this up in the morning when I can get my head around it."

The next morning I got a call from my friend Dr. Daniel Rubens, an anesthesiologist at Seattle Children's Hospital.

"I thought you might be interested in this paper I've come across," he said. "A couple of researchers have discovered that the future affects the present."

I read the paper. It was full of statistics and arcane symbols. It made as much sense to me as ancient Sanskrit.

Fortunately, I got a chance to meet up with the two authors of the paper over dinner a few months later. "We know the future affects the present. We just have no idea why," Michael Franklin, the lead researcher, told me.

What I could tell them was that the key is the soul. "Time is more fluid on the other side," I explained, "so your soul often experiences events before they happen. It's why you think about someone, and then the phone rings, and it's them."

My explanation didn't really help. As scientists they have to work with empirical data. Still, their results are astonishing.

I asked Michael to explain the tests as you would to a child. Even then I still had to get him to repeat everything more than twice. I'll do my best to explain what he and his associate Mike Zyphur did in the simplest terms possible (because that's about all I can do!).

In phase one of the "forward" test, you teach fifty people, group A, to practice pushing buttons to separate cards on a computer screen depending on whether the number is above or below five.

Group B, meanwhile, practices pressing buttons depending on whether a card is red or blue.

Then, in phase two, you put both groups together and give them a task in which they have to do a mixture of both tests.

It's hardly surprising that the ones who practiced with numbers above and below five do better in that part of the test, and the ones who separated red and blue cards do better with that.

So far so good.

In the "backward" test, everything is reversed, using a new set of subjects. In phase one, the whole group begins by separating cards both by color and by number.

Then, in phase two, the people get split into two groups at random. Half practice separating cards by color, the other half by number.

You'd think the results would be like flipping a coin.

Well, you'd be wrong!

Michael can predict who did best with the colored cards and who did best with the numbered cards by which test they're assigned to do afterward.

So, if you're chosen to practice separating the red and blue cards, you'll have already done that test better in the first round.

"It should be like a coin flip," Michael told me. "But what you get is much better than chance—usually more than 60 percent."

This is the principle of retrocausality: the future affects the present.

And what does this have to do with the next exercise? The answer is everything.

The following written exercise is designed to connect you with your own future. By doing so, you'll become more emotionally attached to your goals than you would otherwise.

The motivation for change, once stimulated, will help you to set tangible goals and find the impetus to achieve them.

. . . .

EMPOWERMENT EXERCISE 2

WRITE YOUR LIFE STORY

Bring in your spirit guides with the following request: "I call upon my spirit guides, acting in my highest interest, to help me reach the transformational goal of Freedom through the motivation of Empowerment."

- Picture yourself at age one hundred. You might be relaxing on a beach somewhere or dangling your great-grandkids on your knee.
- Look back on the glorious life you had: all the places you went, the people you met, the things you did. Include everything you can think of that would make you say at the end of your life, "I have no regrets!"
- Don't include anything that has already happened. You're looking back on your future.
- When you've done the exercise, slip back into the present and ask yourself, "If I'm going to do all this stuff, what's the plan?"
- If you say in your life story, "I learned to play the trumpet and joined a band," then your plan might include: Buy trumpet. Get trumpet lessons.
- Your life story doesn't have to be long. A couple of pages perhaps. And it doesn't have to be great prose. Mine began with bullet points that I expanded to a paragraph or two.
- Think of this as a work in progress. As you and the world change, you can keep coming back to it, adding and subtracting where appropriate.

I had an e-mail from a client who found this exercise particularly useful. She wrote, "One major item that came to light was that I wanted to develop my talent for healing. I began taking action to start the ball rolling, and everything lined up to help me explore that path.

"I wrote the intention in my journal, searched the Internet for classes, found a reiki teacher I connected with, started learning, and I'll become a reiki practitioner in a few weeks' time. I plan to work with oncology patients later in the year. It all unfolded effortlessly and has helped me fill a void I've felt for years."

Thanks to the principle of retrocausality, it's a lot easier to make plans when you can already sense having achieved them.

From a spiritual point of view, the freedom to live your life the way you choose is essential, but with that freedom comes responsibility. If your freedom comes at the cost of another person's freedom, there can be serious karmic consequences.

Your soul wants you to be free to choose your own relationships. But if you were to abuse that freedom by choosing to have sex with a minor, for example, you'd be acting irresponsibly, not to mention illegally and immorally, too.

Freedom and empowerment are principles that appeal to older souls, who tend to be more open to change. Those who most strongly resist the change that the Transformation brings are younger souls and individuals or organizations in thrall to the Illusion. They will strive to maintain the status quo. Their fear of change is a symptom of their fear of Powerlessness, and they'll be driven to control, coerce, and disempower others.

As we move through the Transformation, expect to see a reaction to the shift in consciousness in the form of more coercive behavior from governments and fear-based organizations. Attacks on freedom are on the rise, and the Internet, for example, offers a prime target for those who wish to maintain traditional power structures by limiting access to information.

The tendency among less-enlightened souls is to coerce others into doing as they're expected. Coercion is, however, always doomed to failure. You might keep a lid on freedom for a while but, as history shows, it never lasts for long.

When you coerce anyone into doing something contrary to his or her life plan, you risk setting the karmic ball in motion, which can have an impact on all concerned for lifetimes to come.

To leave a positive karmic legacy, it's your job as a spiritually conscious soul to empower and be empowered. The key is to recognize that every soul needs maximum opportunity and freedom.

In the next chapter, we'll explore one of the most significant causes of negative karma: untimely and premature death.

CHAPTER TEN

THE PASSION FOR PEACE
Healing Your Karmic Wounds

GOAL Peace
MOTIVATION Nonviolence
FEAR Death

THE BUCK STOPS HERE

In the early morning of August 6, 1945, an atomic bomb exploded over the Japanese city of Hiroshima, killing 70,000 men, women, and children. It's estimated that by the end of that year the same number again died from horrifying injuries incurred in the blast.

A few days later, another nuclear bomb wiped out as many as 75,000 people in the city of Nagasaki, with thousands more to die in the following months and years.

The official justification was—and still is—that dropping these two bombs shortened the war and saved a million American lives that would have been lost in a ground invasion.

The spiritual view is that the killing of a child is a crime regardless of whether that child's parents are American or Japanese. The same goes for the citizens of any country, regardless of age.

The records from the U.S. Strategic Bombing Survey following the attacks state that Japan would have surrendered, regardless of whether or not the bombs were dropped.

Some involved in the decision to use the newly created atomic weapons hoped that such a massive display of force would curb Russia's imperial ambitions. Others wanted to see the effects such a weapon would have on a heavily populated city. There are even suggestions that after spending huge amounts on developing the bomb, it was politically imperative to actually use it.   *

Many people participated in the bomb's creation and ultimately in the decision to use it. Each has some degree of spiritual responsibility, or karmic debt, as a result. The final decision to drop the bombs on Japan came from President Harry Truman, and that's why his karmic debt is the most significant.

Truman once proudly declared, "The buck stops here." Though it's unlikely that he was thinking about karma when he said that, in spiritual terms he couldn't have been more right.

As we've seen, karma is created by interfering with another person's life plan. It can happen as a result of disempowering children by giving them limiting beliefs about themselves. It can happen when you steal someone's money, leaving that person without the financial means to follow his or her life plan.

But the big one is always murder. Nothing prevents a person from completing their life plan more than having the plug pulled in the middle of it.

. . . .

REMINDERS OF DEATH

The symptoms of a fear of Death are varied. Actual death itself is rarely the fear (at least in older souls). It's more likely to be an irrational fear of something your soul associates with violent death.

By far the most common death-related fears are a phobia of Judgment and a phobia of Sickness. The resonance most often associated with the former is a fear of public speaking; with the latter it's a fear of doctors, dentists, hospitals, blood, and vomiting.

When I saw that Patrick had a past-life phobia of Sickness, I asked him if he had a problem with blood or vomiting.

His response was emphatic. "I puked once when I was four. I will never, ever throw up again. I've never been so scared in my life."

....

Killing another human being, whether it's with a knife in the ribs or with a nuclear device, is considered murder, and therefore it has karmic consequences. The degree of culpability depends on the degree of responsibility as well as mitigating circumstances.

Leo Szilard, the scientist who came up with the chain reaction that led to the bomb's development, tried to convince Truman to abandon his plan to use it and therefore incurred less of a karmic debt than he might otherwise have.

Human beings throughout the ages have always found ways to mask the reality of war. The images of war that make it on to the nightly news show shattered bunkers and flattened buildings, but never, as happened in Hiroshima, children with their charred skin trailing from their fingertips and eyeballs hanging from their sockets.

From a spiritual point of view, no amount of spin changes the reality of what happened. The myth that dropping the bombs on Hiroshima and Nagasaki saved a million lives is often presented as justification for its use, yet it has no bearing in truth.

The bombing, from a soul's perspective, was cruel and unnecessary. What counts against Truman karmically is that he knew the cities of Hiroshima and Nagasaki were filled with civilians (which was why they hadn't previously been bombed), that there were alternatives to using the bomb (Japan was already asking for peace), and that it was his finger on the button.

....

ONE PERSON'S HERO IS ANOTHER'S WAR CRIMINAL

Leo Szilard's recognition of the immorality of the bombing of Hiroshima and Nagasaki led him to say, "If the Germans had dropped atomic bombs instead of us, we would have defined the dropping of atomic bombs on cities as a war crime, and we would have sentenced the Germans who were guilty of this crime to death at Nuremberg and hanged them."

....

When Truman learned of the horrors unleashed on the citizens of Hiroshima by the first bomb (too late to stop the destruction of the people of Nagasaki), he put a halt to any further nuclear attacks, expressing concern for "all those kids." Sadly, it was too late for tens of thousands of "kids," not to mention Truman himself. Karma was created along with the first mushroom cloud.

Truman's opinion of the "Japs" (whom he described as "beasts" and "savages") might be considered less than enlightened. And that's something that played a big part in his ability to order the destruction of so many people.

The demonization of the enemy is an essential part of every war. It's hard to shove a bayonet in the stomach of another human being if you consider that person an equal. But once that person is dehumanized, he or she is no longer a sentient being like yourself.

On a larger scale, it's easier for whole groups of people to inflict atrocities on those who are physically and culturally different from themselves. In the 1930s and '40s, dehumanization facilitated the persecution of Jews in Nazi Germany, the murder and torture of the Chinese citizens of Nanking by Japanese troops, and the massacre of the 200,000 civilians in Hiroshima and Nagasaki.

Would Truman have dropped the bomb on a city of Caucasians? Perhaps. But it was certainly easier to do so on an alien culture like Japan's. The dehumanization of the Japanese people is evident in war correspondent Ernie Pyle's remarks that "In Europe, we felt that our enemies, horrible and deadly as they were, were still people, but out here, I soon gathered that the Japanese were looked upon as something subhuman and repulsive—the way some people feel about cockroaches and mice."

For the soul that was once Harry Truman, the karmic consequences of his actions mean that many lifetimes will be spent undergoing a kind of karmic payback.

Everyone must have a soul. You couldn't survive without one. And it's your soul that makes the decision about who you'll be in each incarnation. Left up to our conscious selves, we'd all be chasing after affluent, comfortable lives located as far away from potential war zones as possible.

But as long as your soul is making the big decisions about who you'll be and where you'll live, you'll go from one lifetime to the next ensuring that karmic debts are paid and balance is restored.

One of the ways you'll do this is to "see the other side of the coin," or to understand the consequences of actions taken in the past.

The other is to take an active part in preventing violence. The motivation of Nonviolence helps us take positive steps toward the goal of Peace.

Since karma rarely gets balanced in the same life in which it was created (except for "instant karma," where there's time or opportunity to make sufficient amends), it usually takes another lifetime (and sometimes many lifetimes) for the lessons to be learned and equilibrium restored. What you sow in one life will generally have to wait for another to be reaped.

The soul that was Truman spent the first incarnation following the life as president of the United States in the Ural Mountains in Russia, where it chose to be a young girl living in the Techa River area. The province of Chelyabinsk in which she lived was severely contaminated by radioactive waste over a period of decades. (In fact, Chelyabinsk has been described as "the most polluted area on Earth.") She was poisoned by strontium 90 and died around the age of seven.

Truman's soul chose this life to see firsthand the effects of radiation poisoning. It made this choice in the pragmatic way all souls plan their upcoming incarnations. The decision was based on the desire to explore certain circumstances rather than individual events: to grow up in an environment contaminated by radioactive waste, not simply to die at an early age.

Truman's soul is currently back in the former Soviet Union, this time working in a technical capacity in the area of Chernobyl with a view to ultimately being involved in nuclear safety.

Since the decision about how karma will be balanced is made on a soul level, the person who once was Truman may be totally unaware that the motivation that will push him to help others is the result of past-life actions.

When it came to karma, the buck truly stopped with Harry Truman. Causing the death of several hundred thousand human beings resulted in a soul-level trauma that will take many lifetimes to balance.

By hopping from one part of the world to another, frequently seeking opportunities to help others, Truman's soul will gradually learn the big lesson that all life is sacred.

WHAT'S SO FUNNY 'BOUT PEACE, LOVE, AND UNDERSTANDING?

When Elvis Costello sang, "What's so funny 'bout peace, love, and understanding?" the sentiments hit a nerve with many old souls. The question I want to explore here is what's so *hard* about peace, love, and understanding?

How many people died in wars in the twentieth century? One estimate puts the total number of lives lost through battle and war-related famine, pogroms, genocide, and suchlike at over 250 million.

You might think from those kinds of numbers that our history has always been one of violence and bloodshed. Yet in the tribe, violence between humans was virtually unheard of, at least in our first 45,000 years.

As previously discussed, it wasn't until the Illusion took hold 10,000 years ago that inflicting violent death on each other became common practice.

THE CORRUPTION OF THE HUNTER

Armies are full of Hunter soul types. These physically active individuals are task-oriented and loyal, and they make good soldiers. Yet not a single one of them is in this world to deliberately take another human life.

Hunters are not warriors. Their original purpose was to protect and provide for the tribe, not to wage war on other humans. Their purpose has not changed. When a Hunter type becomes a soldier, the only spiritually acceptable role is one of defense, and then only with minimal force.

When a soldier takes a life, he or she will be traumatized on a soul level. It may cause stress disorders or depression that will vary in intensity depending on the circumstances and the degree to which the individual is caught up in the Illusion.

Healing depends on pushing through the Illusion and confronting the actions. Guilt and remorse are emotions that lead to an awareness of the universal principle that all life is sacred.

....

No soul comes into the world planning to be blown to bits by a bomb, starved to death in a work camp, or shot for being the "wrong" ethnic type.

And no soul comes into the world with the intention of killing another human being.

Your soul wants to complete its life plan in peace. It seeks to avoid a premature end to its life at all costs. When you die in an air raid or on the battlefield—or as a result of violence of any kind—a major karmic consequence is a fear of Death.

No one is immune from the karmic consequences of premature death through acts of violence. Every single violent death is an assault on the soul and its core value of peace.

In Chapter Three, when I discussed the importance of cooperation, I expressed my spirit guides' opinion that we'd never have survived as a species without all pulling together. Similarly, we'd have been in a sorry state if we'd kept annihilating each other.

Your soul is intrinsically peaceful. When you act aggressively toward someone, that impulse never comes from your soul; it is always a result of the Illusion.

To put it in the simplest terms possible, your soul will never choose to kill another human being. It can be hard to fully understand the implications of such a statement. What it means is that all willful killing is karmic and is always against the wishes of your soul.

I've had many debates with my spirit guides about the significance of this. No matter what scenario I throw at them, the answer is always the same: your soul will never choose to kill another human.

"What if armed intruders are attacking my family?" I'll ask them.

"Your soul will never sanction the taking of a life," they'll reply. (They're not saying one shouldn't defend one's family, but they make it clear that the choice to kill will never come from the soul.)

When we kill, or when someone kills us, it's a violation of the universal principle that all life is sacred. And because it's the ultimate interference in your life plan, it always results in karma, though just how much depends on the circumstances and the choices available to us.

THE WILL TO LIVE

In his inspirational book *Man's Search for Meaning*, author Viktor Frankl wrote about what gave people the will to survive in a Nazi concentration camp. He recognized that those who refused to give up were the ones most able to find meaning in their lives, however desperate their circumstances.

The soul's will to survive has helped many people make it through adversity. Yet no soul will choose to survive at the cost of another human's life.

If you ever end up in such awful circumstances, your soul will look for every way to keep you alive—except by killing another person.

Aggression as a solution to a problem is never mutual. A soul who has violence foisted upon it never accepts it by agreement.

On a soul level, there's always the desire to work things out peacefully.

Individuals who push for war are, to varying degrees, stuck behind the Illusion. They lack the ability to connect with other souls, especially, as we saw in the case of Harry Truman, those of a different culture or ethnicity. What they'd willingly foist on other people is never what they'd wish for themselves.

In 2003, George W. Bush ordered U.S. troops to impose "shock and awe" on Baghdad, or more specifically, the people of Baghdad. The initial attack killed more than 6,000 Iraqi civilians, many of them women and children. Would Bush have ordered the attack if his mother had been there at the time? Would having a person close to him—a blood relative—on the ground have made a difference? Would he have ordered the attack if the citizens of Baghdad had been English-speaking Caucasians?

Being caught behind the Illusion made it simple for Bush to order the deaths of thousands of civilians. Being disconnected from his soul made it easy to detach himself from their suffering.

THE KARMIC CONSEQUENCES OF SHOCK AND AWE

In the past, when a nation went to war, its leader would get out in front and, as his (or occasionally her) title suggested, lead.

We'd see a lot less enthusiasm for militaristic adventures abroad if the politicians and generals who advocated these wars had to be out there on the front line for the duration.

Yet, whether a leader charges into battle on a horse, like Genghis Khan, or issues orders from the Oval Office, the karmic consequences are the same.

PAST-TRAUMATIC STRESS DISORDER

It's not just taking a life that creates soul-level trauma. Having been the victim of a violent death can cause what I call *past*-traumatic stress disorder. You won't find it in any of the books (apart from this one, of course), but it may explain why some people carry around the symptoms of post-traumatic stress without there being any obvious cause to explain it.

Children often come into the world with the traumas from the past still highly visible. (You can spot past-life fears in most children if you look closely enough.)

....

A PHOBIA OF STRANGERS

In Claire's past is a death in Normandy, France, during the D-day landings in World War II. She was a young, male, British infantry soldier, who made it past the beachhead and was later crushed beneath the tracks of a Panzer tank. Death was not instantaneous, and my spirit guides added that the sound of German voices increased the fear the young man experienced.

Much later, Claire wrote to me. "What you told me was very significant. I grew up in Switzerland and had to learn German at school. I'd always had an aversion to Germans and their language, so I resented being forced to learn it. I've had a few short verbal encounters with Germans that have left me unable to utter a word in response.

"I always felt so bad about disliking someone for no apparent reason and about feeling so uneasy and stressed in their presence.

"The exploration we did was so incredibly helpful to me. It cleared up a three-decade long misconception I had about myself. Knowing what happened has helped me find peace with who I am and enabled me to work on letting go of those hindering emotions."

....

When Grace was a little girl, she was terrified of two particular uncles and one of her grandfathers. She made a very telling comment when she told me, "I was scared to death of them."

What Grace feared in these three men was their size and their overt masculinity (what my spirit guides would refer to as "testosterone"). "They were all big guys. I was five or six before I would go near my grandfather," she said.

"There's a picture of him trying to hold me when I'm about nine months old. I'm pulling away, giving him a stiff arm and bawling."

Grace was petrified of her Uncle Bill. When she was five, she had to stay with her aunt and uncle while her mother was at a three-day workshop. By the afternoon of the second day, she was crying, vomiting, and wouldn't leave her aunt's lap. "Poor Mom had to cut her workshop short and come and save me," she said.

Sleepovers were another source of fear. "I dreaded mealtimes when I had to sit at the table and be seen by the dad," Grace said. "I always felt that if I could stay out of his sight, I'd be okay. Bedtimes were just miserable. I was scared, wanting to go home, and I had this overwhelming sense of dread in my gut."

The discussion about large men followed a past-life exploration that took us to World War I Belgium. Grace had been a small boy named Paul, whose father owned a bar in a village outside of Brussels. In this small family business, one of Paul's jobs was to bike to a nearby farm and collect eggs from an elderly widow.

What struck both of us as I told Grace about this was that we each felt an ominous sense of doom. There was an inevitability of death, even though we still knew little, at that point, of what had happened.

When Paul reached the farmhouse, it was clear something was wrong. Yet, despite having a strong feeling that he was about to die, Paul walked inside to look for the old woman. When I got to this point in the story, Grace interrupted me to say, "From that moment on, I knew it was over."

Inside the house were two very large and extremely drunk German soldiers. Paul, who had developed a fear of loud noises as a result of the war, was terrified by their size and bellowing voices.

The soldiers spent hours bullying, beating, and ridiculing the boy. They'd force him to do impressions of a chicken, then pull him close to their faces and yell obscenities at him. Throughout this terrible experience, Paul was resigned to his fate. He knew he'd never survive, so it seemed pointless to protest or try to run away.

Later in the day, as it was getting dark, the soldiers gave Paul one last beating and threw him outside. He died a few minutes later from internal bleeding.

When I'd finished describing the events of this life, my spirit guides suggested that Grace might find it useful to research the events surrounding that time in history.

When we spoke a few weeks later, Grace was excited about all the changes she'd undergone since we first talked. "I can't begin to tell you how much that session has freed me. I used to feel permanently beaten. I realized that I was terrified as a child by all the events from that life.

"I did what your guides suggested and researched what happened in Belgium during World War I. The first twenty-four hours was exhausting. In fact, it was devastating. But I started to get some visual images from that life, and it helped me gain a better understanding of what happened.

"Then, just recently, I felt inspired by it. I called a friend and said, 'Wouldn't it be fantastic if, as parents, we knew all the fears our children bring into this life?' My friend has been actively helping her son who has autism. She's learned all she can, but I thought it would really help her to understand her son's past-life fears."

Like almost every old soul who has died violently in a recent past life, Grace is committed to nonviolence in this life. "My mantra is all around nonviolence," she said. "I look at the war in Iraq, for example, and wonder why anyone thinks violence is a solution."

After they've explored a past life with me, many of my clients find they've overcome a fear without noticing it happen. Grace has always feared explosive sounds, a result of being close to the sound of artillery fire in her life in Belgium.

"I've always hated loud noises like fireworks or thunderstorms. They make my neck stiffen up, and I get an intense headache," she'd told me.

"How's your fear of loud noises now?" I asked her a few weeks later.

"Oh, my gosh! I hadn't thought about it," she said. "But last night we had a thunderstorm, and my husband called me outside to look at the sky. It was pretty cool—a lot of dramatic clouds and colors. I was so intent on watching the sky I never even noticed the thunder. Normally I wouldn't dream of going outside."

Grace expressed relief that the life we explored wasn't one in which she'd hurt someone else. "It took a lot of courage for me to let you uncover that past life," she said. "I knew my heart was blocked, but I was afraid to find out why. I was scared in case I'd been responsible for the death of lots of people.

"I can't describe how healing this work was. I feel like a different person. And one thing I'm very aware of is that I don't want to drag anything negative into my next life. I mean, what if I can't find you next time?"

• • •

Camille has, like many of us, learned the horrors of war the hard way: by being a victim of its inevitable brutality. In our sessions together, we exposed two disturbing lives that have shaped how she views war.

Camille is one of millions of people who have been drawn to do something to actively help victims of war. The impetus comes directly from her personal experiences and the karmic motivation of Nonviolence.

The first life we explored was in Moravia where Camille was a young girl in a comfortable, middle-class home. Though she suffered from a form of what we might call autism, she learned reading and music from her brother. She wrote song lyrics to help her better process her thoughts.

The girl and her brother were in their home when Prussian troops broke in. They killed her brother and kept her captive while they repeatedly raped her over a period of several days. After that event, the girl was unable to eat or speak. She died from the effects of malnutrition and grief.

LOSING THE WILL TO LIVE

My spirit guides will sometimes describe a past-life death as having been caused by a combination such as "cholera and grief" or "influenza and a broken heart." It means that the physical ailment might have been overcome, but the will to live was no longer there.

Many of my clients have died of cholera in previous incarnations. This terrifying disease can cause a person to lose up to a third of his or her body weight in just a few hours. Watching family members die before their eyes was often enough to make them give up hope.

Camille's second significant past life was in France during World War I. In this incarnation, she was a teenage boy named Thomas. Her soul's earlier incarnation in Moravia was fresh in Thomas's experience and was having a strong impact. When Germany attacked France, the boy's family urged him to join the army.

Thomas, who considered himself a pacifist, resisted. But under pressure from everyone around him, he finally agreed to fight. He went through the process with a heavy heart, knowing he'd never return alive.

At the front, the war was being fought in trenches. It was cold and wet, and thousands of rounds of shells were being fired from both sides every day. From the moment Thomas reached the battlefield, he saw death everywhere. Most of his comrades died within days of their arrival.

Rotting corpses and body parts would be blown out of their makeshift graves by the shelling. The stench was appalling and the noise unbearable. Within a week, he was almost completely deaf.

One evening, Thomas was ordered to help take a group of wounded soldiers to a field hospital. It was a welcome break from being in the trenches. Later that night, as he walked back to the front lines along a muddy road in a torrential rainstorm, he died after being hit by a truck he didn't hear coming. As his soul left his body, he felt an overwhelming feeling of pointlessness about the whole experience.

And that's very much how Camille feels about war in this life. "When I was younger I was influenced by others who believed that war is sometimes necessary," she told me. "Where I stand now feels like a progression. I recognize that when you let war out of the box, you can't control the outcome. It's so often the civilians who get caught in the cross fire."

The way to heal the battle scars from wars in your soul's past is to be involved in redressing the balance. Camille is karmically drawn to nonviolence. "The life in Moravia definitely impacts my current life," she said. "Always, in the back of my mind, there'd been a fear of being attacked that way. There's nothing in my current life to explain the intensity of my response to rape. What you told me finally explained feelings I couldn't understand."

The way Camille has chosen to heal her wounds is to support the International Rescue Committee (IRC), an organization that helps refugees of wars.

"I became involved with the IRC after my husband went to Rwanda during the conflict. When he told me about the atrocities he'd seen, I found it shocking," she said. "I really like the fact that 90 percent of the money the IRC raises goes to help people in dire need. It's a wonderful way to contribute and make people more aware of what's happening out there."

Camille told me how much she wishes she could do more. "Helping the IRC has made me look at my life in a very different way. It's made me realize that we live in a relatively stable country, and we should be thankful for that. I think we need to remember how lucky we are and do more to help others."

PAST-LIFE PHOBIAS

As I described earlier, phobias are death-related fears. A phobia of Judgment can make a person hypersensitive to what others are saying or thinking about him or her. At least eight out of ten people with this phobia have a fear of public speaking.

Alicia, the woman whose aversion to the cold I told you about earlier in the book, was once a jobless Lebanese teenager named Hassin, who joined an "anarchist" street gang when his family relocated to Paris at the turn of the twentieth century. He very quickly became disgusted by the violence he was caught up in. But the gang, fearing he might be a security risk, was not prepared to let him leave.

His sister, who occasionally worked as a prostitute, was known to the gang. They threatened her to put pressure on her brother to stay, but it backfired on them. When the young woman was slashed with a knife, her brother became even more adamant about leaving. Unfortunately, the gang still wasn't prepared to give up on him.

Hassin was abducted by the gang. They tied him to a chair in front of a kind of "court," and interrogated him for hours. He was tortured, not so much for information as sadism, until he finally died.

The result of this traumatic death is a particular death-related fear: a phobia of Judgment. Like most people who have this phobia, Alicia is terrified of public speaking.

....

PUBLIC SPEAKING AND JUDGMENT

When Pam, a business analyst, walked into my office for her third session, she was an embodiment of the cliché "grinning from ear to ear." The reason for the smile was that she'd overcome a huge past-life phobia of Judgment in the previous week.

Pam's phobia had first manifested at school when she froze in the middle of a gymnastic performance as she felt everyone's eyes on her. After a car crash in which she suffered post-concussion syndrome, it began to surface more strongly.

When she was called upon to speak in front of a group of people, she would freeze both physically and verbally.

"In staff meetings I'd get tongue-tied," she said. "It was so frustrating because I had all this information I wanted to get out. I would be okay one-on-one, but in a group, my heart would start racing, I'd start breathing rapidly, and I'd just shut down verbally. I'd feel a huge sense of embarrassment and inferiority. I couldn't understand why it was happening to me."

Pam used the Identify and Annihilate technique for a month. "I just kept focusing on my eyes," she said. "It was like they really were the windows to my soul."

For details about the Identify and Annihilate (I&A) exercise, see the Appendix on page 325.

Soon after practicing the I&A technique, Pam started a new job and had to get up in front of 140 academics. "I talked for four hours," she recalls. "When it was over I received so many accolades. People kept telling me what a great job I'd done."

"The I&A exercise was incredible. It gave me self-esteem. Now I feel that I have something to say, and I can say it. I've become a new person. And it's helped me get over other fears, too."

Pam has even started helping other people use the technique, too. "I have a friend who was going through the same fear. I told her how to use I&A. Now she feels incredibly confident."

What's exciting about what happened to Pam is that we didn't even explore a past life. We went straight to I&A knowing that she was suffering from a phobia of Judgment by the symptoms she described.

....

What brought Alicia's phobia of Judgment front and center was an event that would cause anyone to feel at least a little intimidated: her boss was indicted on twenty felony counts, and despite knowing nothing about his crimes, Alicia was called before a grand jury.

"I had nothing to hide," she said, "But the more nervous I got, the more I worried that they thought I was lying. And the more I worried, the more nervous I got. It totally spiraled. I got so stressed beforehand that I thought I'd have to leave the country."

Any situation in which Alicia is being "judged" is going to act as a trigger for her fear. Her soul is going right back to the time she faced the gang in Paris.

When we first spoke, Alicia was facing the prospect of going back in front of the grand jury again. After we'd explored her past life, I'd suggested she use the Identify and Annihilate technique I previously discussed to attack the fear, rather than simply trying to suppress it.

When I talked to her a few weeks later, she'd noticed some big shifts. "The technique you gave me really helped," she told me. "When I imagine being in front of the grand jury again, I don't get the same feeling of terror I used to. I feel more like an average person."

Alicia is learning to overcome a fear that affects millions of people. Uncovering the source of her terror was the first big step toward healing the past and changing the present.

....

SPIRITUAL ACT 9: GIVING PEACE A CHANCE

There are many ways to carry out Spiritual Acts related to overcoming the fear of Death. The most fundamental is to be vocal about your opposition to violence.

There are many organizations devoted to peace and the opposition of various wars. And there are also charities and nonprofits whose purpose is to help victims of violence. You should have no problem finding one that triggers your motivation of Nonviolence.

....

Many people who have died of injuries sustained in war are dragging a phobia of Sickness around with them, as are those who've died of terrifying diseases like cholera.

Nicole called up for her session, apologizing for being a few minutes late. "I had to pick up my boyfriend from the hospital," she said.

We were near the end of the session when I asked Nicole if she had any other questions.

"Can you tell me anything about my boyfriend, Chris?" she asked.

I expected my spirit guides to say something about his soul age or his connection to her. Instead, they described a past life, set, once again, during the First World War.

"Chris was a French pilot," I said. "He flew a biplane called a SPAD." (I consider it a triumph of my knowledge of trivia that I could tell Nicole the acronym stood for Société Pour L'Aviation et ses Dérivés.)

"Chris lost his foot when he crashed his plane," I continued. "He recovered in a hospital where he became sufficiently mobile to help other patients. Unfortunately, his doctors decided he needed another operation. This time he developed gangrene and died in a great deal of pain soon after."

I remembered what Nicole had said about picking Chris up from the hospital earlier. I said, "I bet he doesn't care much for hospitals."

"He hates hospitals!" she said.

Chris, it turned out, had been to the hospital to get a pin taken out of a recently broken ankle, an injury he incurred in a car accident. Not only was he terrified of the procedure, but he'd worked himself into a state of near panic by watching a program about staph infections on the morning of the operation.

"You'd have thought he was having open-heart surgery," Nicole said. "He kept saying, 'They're going to cut me open! They're going to *cut me open!*'

"It explains so much," she said. "When my sister was in the hospital, I was appalled at his behavior. He kept going on and on about how he hated hospitals. I asked, 'Why don't you take the focus off you and start thinking about my sister?'

"When he had his accident, I was with him day and night. I never left his bedside. But when I spent several days in the hospital for a small operation, he didn't feel he needed to do the same for me. When he did come to see me, he kept saying, 'I gotta go!' I hardly saw him the entire time."

....

NONVIOLENCE EXERCISE 1
VISUALIZING WAR

Bring in your spirit guides with the following request: "I call upon my spirit guides, acting in my highest interest, to help me reach the transformational goal of Peace through the motivation of Nonviolence." The purpose is to connect you with a time when you've been on the receiving end of armed aggression.

- Close your eyes and relax for a minute or two.
- Ask your spirit guides to take you to a life in which you learned the truth about war.
- Go wherever your guides take you. Remember, if you get anxious, just open your eyes and try again later.
- When you've finished, open your eyes and write a few paragraphs about your experience.

The second part of this exercise is a prayer. You can use it daily if you like. It goes as follows:

"I ask the universe to surround me with loving, peaceful energy so that I may become a beacon of peace and higher spiritual values."

Thank your guides, and don't forget to tell them, "Session over."

This exercise is simple, yet it can reveal fascinating insights into your soul's past. You might get a sense of being in the midst of battle somewhere. You might even get images. Try not to force it. If nothing happens, just try it again later. As my spirit guides would say, "This is not a test."

It might appear that having died in wartime is the only source of a past-life fear of Death, but any sudden and violent death can be its cause.

Jill is a riding instructor in Kentucky who has always been surrounded by horses. Recently she became too afraid of being thrown to get in the saddle.

"When I was a kid," Jill told me, "I'd just get back on and keep riding. Now I'm too afraid."

"I've never had any really serious falls," she said. "But I've begun to worry about a fall resulting in a back or neck injury, and that if I ride alone, no one will find me until it's too late. The fear doesn't seem grounded in reality—it is out of proportion to the experiences I've had when riding in this life."

Usually I explore a client's past life first; then I make the connections with this life. In Jill's case, I had the cart before the horse, so to speak. I knew already that her fear must be related to a fall from a horse.

"You were the twelve-year-old son of a Prussian cavalry officer. You went riding on your own in a forest when the horse fell and rolled on top of you, crushing your lungs and breaking your neck," I told her.

Uncovering the cause turned out to be the cure. A few months later I asked Jill how she was getting on. "I immediately started feeling the need to ride again," she said. "Something really shifted after we talked. I realized that I'm in this physical body to enjoy the freedom of riding. It struck me that if I never rode again, there'd be such sadness."

As a result of her past-life death, Jill's soul has a heightened sense of the need for her and others to avoid violent death. "I began finding peace within myself. Then I read that when you change yourself, you change everyone around you. It inspired me to become an active member of a peace ministry."

A few months later, I e-mailed Jill to see how she was doing. She had good news. "I was ordained as a Minister of Peace several months ago," she wrote. "And not three weeks after that, through a series of synchronicities, I was invited to speak at an international peace celebration. So today, I gave my first official speech as a Minister of Peace."

PEACE IN THE AGE OF TRANSFORMATION

I was about fourteen years old when something happened that triggered my karmic motivation of Nonviolence. I was walking home from the local supermarket with a bag in each hand when I spotted the three most notorious bullies in the area standing in a huddle on the other side of the road.

I knew the best thing was to avoid eye contact and hope they'd ignore me. It didn't work. They spotted me and immediately began planning their attack. I expected the worst, but instead of all three going for me, the two bigger ones sent the little guy over.

He crossed the road, walking purposefully toward me. He looked me straight in the eye, and without breaking his stride or even speaking, he punched me right on the nose.

I'd always been something of a pacifist, but that incident helped convince me that violence is as mindless as the cowardly little jerk who hit me.

I didn't know it then, but my past as a victim of violent death came to the surface after that encounter, and it's still with me. It inspired me to join the British pacifist organization the Peace Pledge Union. I must have been one of its youngest members ever.

My convictions have stayed with me. I still believe that war solves nothing. It never has; it never will. In wartime we can see examples of extraordinary bravery in our fellow humans. Yet war itself is a cowardly response to threats, and it more often than not brings out the worst in human nature.

The Transformation is bringing out the motivation of Nonviolence in a lot of older souls. Those behind the Illusion are having to work a lot harder these days to drum up popular support for wars than they once had to.

In an attempt to whip up fear in support of the Iraq War, Secretary of State Colin Powell's superiors put him through a degrading charade before the United Nations in which he was made to lie through his teeth.

This incident might have left an ugly stain on an unblemished career had his credibility not already been irreparably tarnished by his complicity in the cover up of the My Lai Massacre during the Vietnam War.

....

THE WAR ON TRUTH

They say that truth is the first casualty of war. Colin Powell's role in covering up the atrocities committed by U.S. troops in My Lai during the Vietnam War is a prime example. In this case, the truth was so ugly that every attempt was made to bury it.

In an early morning rampage, U.S. soldiers under Lieutenant William Calley massacred a village of Vietnamese civilians. By the time the slaughter was over, more than five hundred men, women, and children were dead. Young girls were raped and their bodies mutilated; babies were bayoneted and shot; many of the villagers were herded into a ditch and machine-gunned.

When news of these atrocities came to light, it played a big part in pressuring the government to end the war. And the news wouldn't have come to light if Powell and others had had their way.

To the U.S. military, however, the lesson of Vietnam was not so much to ensure such things never happened again, but to make sure they never come to light again.

That's why journalists these days are embedded: they only see what the authorities want them to see. It ensures compliance. It's also why images of wars are strictly controlled. Even taking photographs of coffins has been made illegal. War has been sanitized as never before—at least for domestic consumption.

In an obscene example of injustice, Calley, the officer responsible for ordering the massacre in Vietnam, spent just three-and-a-half years under house arrest for his crimes. His soul, however, will spend many lifetimes working off the karmic debt created in My Lai.

. . . .

Someone once said, "The problem with violence on TV is not that it's too graphic; it's that it's not graphic enough." If pictures of raped and mutilated children were shown on TV, it might make people think twice about cheering on the troops.

Casualties remind humans of the horrors of war and trigger deep recollections of lives cut short by brutality and violent death. They stir the motivation of Nonviolence. And since that often leads to an outspoken opposition to war, those who run wars know intuitively that showing its reality doesn't help their case.

Body bags, pictures of children with missing limbs and agonizing burns, footage of grieving parents—all highlight the truth about war's indiscriminate brutality.

Even when injured troops return to America, their pictures are kept out of the media. Having risked their lives for those in power, they become an embarrassment. They get hidden away out of sight for fear their presence will scare the support for the war out of the populace.

This fear is not unfounded. Every person who turns his or her back on war impacts the Collective Consciousness. And if enough people do it, then waging war is going to get increasingly difficult. Already recruiters are having to stoop to some pretty dirty tricks to lure new cannon fodder to the forces.

Recruits are promised more than $70,000 for scholarships to college when they leave the service. The average payout from the G.I. Bill has actually been just a little over $2,000. Fifty-seven percent of soldiers have received no benefit whatsoever.

There was a time when young men thought there was nothing as noble as dying for their country. Thanks to the transformation of the Collective Consciousness, dying in battle has a lot less appeal these days than it did even fifty years ago.

As the Collective Consciousness grows, resistance to military interventions will grow, too. In the 1960s the question was posed: "What if they gave a war and no one came?" It's a question that may have renewed relevance as we enter the Transformation.

There will come a time when the idea of solving problems through aggression will no longer find popular acceptance. A more enlightened population—one that sees through the usual bogus arguments for war—will not so easily allow themselves to be whipped into a frenzy by the fearmongers.

As the Collective Consciousness evolves and more souls start to recognize their common humanity, taking up arms against one's brothers and sister will become unthinkable.

The West was once terrified of Communists. Now the big fear is terrorists. What happened to the Communists, by the way? Have they all been killed? Or were they never that much of a threat anyway?

Terrorists offer a great new reason for armed intervention—and a justification for "preventive" war. Which means anyone can be attacked at any time—just in case.

....

SPOT THE TERRORIST

A woman named Sally Cameron was arrested under the UK's antiterrorism laws for walking on a path designated for cyclists only.

In Maryland, police put the names of nonviolent peace protesters and anti-death penalty activists on a terrorist watch list.

At the same time, Luis Posada Carriles, who admitted blowing up a Cuban airliner killing seventy-three people, is at the time of writing a free man living in Miami. The U.S. government has refused to extradite him to Venezuela where he faces terrorist charges. (Suggested reasons for this apparent double standard include a fear he would spill the beans on covert CIA activities and a reluctance to upset some Cuban exiles who consider him a hero.)

As long as Carriles is smart enough to avoid walking on a cycle path or attending a candlelight vigil outside Death Row, he should be safe.

....

Spiritually conscious older souls recognize that killing and maiming huge numbers of foreign citizens doesn't so much stop terrorism as help recruit more terrorists.

Your soul, as I've said before, will never sanction the taking of a human life. And even if you tacitly stand by and let others take a human life, you bear some karmic responsibility. It's easy to criticize German citizens in the 1930s for not speaking out against the persecution of Jews. It's a lot harder to accept that staying silent while hundreds of thousands of humans are killed and tortured in places like Iraq, Gaza, Pakistan, and Afghanistan is essentially no different.

We all have a choice whether to be part of the problem or part of the solution. Being part of this particular solution is to recognize and honor your soul's commitment to peace and, at the very least, to speak out against violence when you see it.

Your soul is apolitical. It has no nationality. It simply wants all humans to live together in harmony, recognizing our common connection through the Collective Consciousness.

It doesn't matter the rationale: killing is always wrong. Every person on the planet has the right to live his or her life safe from the threat of shooting and bombings. You don't want to have missiles dropped on you, and neither does anyone else.

Once you embrace the transformational goal of Peace, and especially its reciprocal nature, you can truly consider yourself to have elevated your consciousness.

A Stage Four soul will never fight or sanction a war. It is not only nonviolent, but it will also vocally oppose aggression and actively work to prevent war and to help its victims.

CONNECTING WITH A PEACEFUL FUTURE

The impetus for Peace, as we've seen, lies in the motivation of Nonviolence. It's this energy that inspires people to take to the streets to protest wars or to help the victims of armed conflicts.

The urge to achieve peace will increase in all parts of the globe as the Transformation builds momentum. Achieving peace, however, requires more than just high hopes and good thoughts. It's incumbent upon spiritually conscious souls—those who recognize the importance of peace—to play an active part in achieving that goal.

Recognizing that passivity is not the way to achieve peace will help you and older souls like you to become part of the shift toward a less violent world.

One way to stimulate the motivation of Nonviolence is to visualize the goal: a world without conflict. Though it may seem hopelessly idealistic in these violent times, connecting with a more peaceful future will help inspire you to do your part to achieve the goal.

....

NONVIOLENCE EXERCISE 2
VISUALIZING PEACE

Bring in your spirit guides with the following request: "I call upon my spirit guides, acting in my highest interest, to help me reach the transformational goal of Peace through the motivation of Nonviolence."

The purpose of this exercise is to help you see the potential for peace in the world.

- Close your eyes and relax for a minute or two.
- Ask your spirit guides to take you to a life in the future in which there is permanent peace.

- Spend some time in the future exploring what it's like to live without the threat of war.
- When you've finished, open your eyes and write a few paragraphs about your experience.

Like the previous exercise, the second part involves a prayer. Again, you can use it daily. It's a reminder that you are a part of the Transformation and that nonviolence is not passive. The prayer is as follows:

"As a Stage Four soul, I recognize the right of all souls to live in peace and will actively work to embody the transformational goal of Peace."

Thank your guides, and don't forget to tell them, "Session over."

....

The motivation for peace lies within you. It's the desire to live your life free from the threat of violent death. And, of course, it applies to those you love. The key is to broaden that desire beyond those closest to you and apply it to every other soul on the planet.

The next chapter explores the fear that most acts to separate us and how the goal of Love leads to the recognition that we're all one.

CHAPTER ELEVEN

THE FULFILLMENT OF LOVE
Recovering from Rejection

GOAL Love

MOTIVATION Forgiveness

FEAR Rejection

THE NEED FOR ACCEPTANCE

The most common symptoms associated with a past-life fear of Rejection are loneliness and a sense of not fitting in or belonging to the community, culture, or society to which you were born.

The source of a fear of Rejection is having been abandoned by your community or family. Perhaps, many lifetimes ago, you were ejected from your town or village for some crime or other. Maybe you were disrespectful to the monarch or caught committing adultery or some other crime that offended the sensibilities of the community.

In some cases the fear goes back to a time when you were considered a second-class citizen due to your ethnic origins, religion, or family background.

Whatever its cause, a fear of Rejection has its origins in a life where your ability to complete your life plan was severely compromised as a result of your expulsion, physically or spiritually, from the community.

....

THE TERROR OF ISOLATION

Rejection in a previous life often lies dormant until a trigger awakens it. One of my clients had a life as a Native American woman who was rejected by her tribe. She was taken deep into the wilderness and left on her own, where she died after being attacked by bears in the dark.

In this lifetime, my client went into a panic in a Boston subway station at night when she realized she was the only one on the platform.

....

The common triggers for a fear of Rejection include being overlooked for promotion, being passed over for a job, being slighted by someone you trust, or having a partner dump you for someone else. And it can surface if parents separate, especially if one or both of them no longer shows the same level of interest in you.

Not surprisingly, a person with a fear of Rejection finds it extremely hard to ask someone for a date, given the high risk of being rebuffed.

A sadly common marker for this fear can be seen in those relationships where one partner prematurely dumps the other, as if trying to make sure he or she is the one doing the rejection rather than vice versa.

Like a fear of Betrayal, a fear of Rejection can make it hard to forgive and forget. Even when you can barely recollect an incident, a slight like not being invited to a birthday party in third grade can linger with you throughout adulthood unless you deal with it.

The cure for a fear of Rejection is the motivation of Forgiveness. By forgiving those who've hurt you, you can push any feelings of loneliness, abandonment, or alienation into the past where they rightly belong.

Once you overcome your past-life fear of Rejection, you'll feel a comfortable sense of belonging. You'll have less anxiety about a partner leaving you, and you'll never have to worry about feeling lonely again.

Forgiveness leads directly to the goal of Love—the highest aspiration of every soul. It allows you to create a more compassionate world for yourself and to influence others.

Souls are, for the most part, social creatures, which is why we humans are drawn to relationships, friendships, and communities. When you feel a sense of belonging with other souls—whether in a golf club or a church—your soul experiences connection with the Collective Consciousness.

Those who are detached from others, unless it's part of their life plan (which is very unusual), tend to suffer internally as a result of their disconnection from the Soul World.

A widowed spouse who becomes isolated after his or her partner's death is most often wrestling with the combined symptoms of loss and rejection.

THE FEAR OF BEING DISOWNED

After her son and daughter-in-law were imprisoned for drug-related crimes, Anita took on the role of raising her two grandchildren. Though the kids' parents have been out of jail for several years, their mother never phones or even sends a birthday card.

When seventeen-year-old Mike called home late one night from the back of a police car, he was in tears. He'd rolled a friend's car after getting drunk. They were lucky to be alive. But what was stressing him out was not the car or the drinking. Mike was terrified of being disowned.

"I had to keep reassuring him that I wasn't going to kick him out," Anita said. "He was a kid who never cried, but now he was hysterical. He kept repeating, 'You really love me that much?' as if he couldn't believe I wasn't going to reject him."

Mike's fear of Rejection goes back to a past life in which he was ostracized by his family. Now, after being abandoned by his mother in this incarnation, the fear is just beneath the surface. It took a sudden trigger to make it the only thing on his mind.

Anita is a spiritually conscious old soul who recognizes Mike's need for unconditional love and reassurance. "I made it clear that nothing he does will ever cause me to disown him," she said.

Detachment is the state of being separated from others on a soul level. It can occur in childhood when mistreatment from an adult causes a retreat behind the Illusion for protection. It can happen as an adult when your heart is broken by a callous lover.

Deep hurts to the soul can push an individual so far behind the Illusion they lose all connection with their soul or the Collective Consciousness. When that happens, they'll see the world purely in terms of how it affects them. In extreme cases, they may show signs of narcissism or sociopathic behavior.

A fear of Rejection originates not so much from being dumped by a partner (that tends to be more of a trigger than a cause), but from being excluded from the tribe or community in some way. Being excommunicated or shunned can be traumatic in the modern world. In the past, you might have been unable to survive. And that's why rejection triggers such strong reactions in so many of us.

THE PAIN OF REJECTION

When Kelsey got her fear of Rejection, she was a young Russian woman, thrown out of the home in which she worked by her master, the father of her unborn child.

My spirit guides had told Kelsey that the barrier to her dream of having children was related to trauma from the past. And as they revealed the details of the story, it became clear where the problem lay.

In that Russian lifetime, Kelsey died alone during childbirth at the edge of a river. From then on, she would associate childbirth with rejection and the terrible loneliness she felt at the end of that life.

The symptoms of the fear were classic and came out of nowhere. "I would feel a horrible, deep loneliness and despair," Kelsey said "It would hit me at very odd times."

Six months later, Kelsey contacted me. "Your guides advised me to use the Identify and Annihilate technique to overcome the fear," she said. "They told me at the time that I'd overcome the fear in weeks, not months. They were 100 percent correct.

"The fear rose up strongly at first, coming on every fifteen minutes or so. I'd just yell at it and tell it to go away, which made me feel so silly, I'd end up laughing. After a couple of weeks, the fear had no power."

Since she was a teenager, doctors had told Kelsey she'd have problems having children. In her twenties, her hormones were at a menopausal level. She was on a list for a fertility clinic but wasn't even ovulating, so she didn't hold out much hope.

Yet, she'd always felt maternal and had a huge yearning to have a baby. When we had our first session, she asked me if she'd ever have a baby. My spirit guides felt confident that if she could overcome the block from that past life, she would be able to have a child.

Well, three weeks after the session, Kelsey got pregnant. The doctors were astonished.

"I knew I was pregnant after just two days," she said. "I started talking to my belly. And I knew it would be a girl."

At Christmas, she was at her great-aunt's house. She was just about to announce her pregnancy, when her great-aunt said, "I know you're pregnant. You came to me in a dream three nights ago and told me it's a girl."

"I told everyone I was having a girl," Kelsey said, "but no one believed me, so I got a scan and, sure enough, it's a girl."

We talked about how the fear of Rejection affected Kelsey when she was around water. "I was fine *in* the water," she recalled, "but near the water, I'd get this deep loneliness. If we were at the beach and the family was around, I'd feel totally disconnected, like there was no one I could count on."

The fear of Rejection was triggered at puberty when Kelsey became fertile. It caused her soul to overreact by closing down her system, so she wouldn't have to face the fear again. By overcoming the fear, she no longer had the need to avoid becoming pregnant, and her system was switched back on.

This story speaks volumes about the soul's ability to impact the physical body. As my spirit guides say, "Healing is always spiritual as well as physical."

THE TERROR OF ABANDONMENT

When you're the partner of someone with a big past-life fear of Rejection, you may learn how little it takes to trigger the fear.

Martin was involved in a long-term relationship with Sue, a woman who a hundred years before had been his daughter. He had rejected her by throwing her out of the house when she got pregnant. Like any karmic relationship, theirs was fraught with difficulties. Due to her fear of Rejection, Sue wasn't going to move in with Martin until he'd proven himself.

Martin's part of the karmic agreement was to balance the debt by giving Sue his support. But when Sue was moving into a new apartment, Martin wasn't there for her.

"She used to ask me, 'How do I know you'll be there when I need you?'" Martin told me. "And when she needed me for the move, I wasn't around."

For a while, Martin and Sue saw each other sporadically, but Sue had been burned and refused to let it happen again. "She's like a cat that creeps in, drinks its milk, and creeps out again," Martin said.

The couple stayed in a holding pattern for a while, until Sue rejected Martin in what he described as a "violent and despising way." They may have to wait for another incarnation together before the karmic debt gets repaid.

....

The firebombing of Dresden, Germany, in World War II was, from a spiritual point of view, a crime against humanity. Over several nights, more than 1,300 British and American bombers dropped high explosives and incendiary bombs on the civilian population of the city.

In the firestorm that followed, tens of thousands of men, women, and children burned to death. Many who tried to escape were sucked into the flames by the high winds created by the inferno.

In the aftermath of the bombing, the city was reduced to a pile of rubble and burned-out buildings. It was here that Laura had her most recent past life and death as a ten-year-old boy who lost his entire family and home.

The boy, Karl, was left to survive on his own. In the army greatcoat that had once belonged to his father, he scavenged for food in outlying areas, always returning to the part of the city that had once been his home. As the war ended, he continued to scour the city in vain, looking for a familiar face.

As I described this bleak setting to Laura, we both intuitively understood what was going on in the boy's mind. "I couldn't believe my family was gone," she said. "I felt I couldn't leave without someone to take care of me."

Some time later, during a hunt for food, Karl was shot by an American soldier after refusing orders to stop. In his father's coat, he may have been mistaken for a real German soldier. His death was instantaneous and welcome.

In this lifetime, Laura has suffered deeply from what happened in Dresden. When I asked her if she'd ever suffered from loneliness, her answer was emphatic.

"Ever since I was thirteen, I've had abandonment issues—like the sky's going to fall," she said. "That was when my mom got in a terrible car accident. I felt like I'd totally lost her when that happened. I lost a lot of confidence and began to fill the loneliness through relationships with guys. I was always looking for love."

Like many older souls who suffer from a past-life fear of Rejection, Laura has found herself drawn to help others in the same position she was once in.

"I had a relationship with a woman who was rejected by her family when she came out of the closet. She was suicidal over it. The fear of losing her made me want to walk away, but my spirit guides told me, 'Laura, you're here to help her. We'll support you through it.' I stopped her from killing herself. I realized even back then that there was something karmic going on.

"We were together for four years after that. Now she's married to a woman and expecting their second child. The other good news is that her family is finally beginning to accept her."

A DOUBLE-EDGED SWORD

Jacquie began our conversation by saying, "You might not want to use my story for your book. It doesn't have a happy ending." We both agreed, however, that telling a story that might help someone else is more important than any happy ending.

I'd asked Jacquie if I could interview her about a significant past life we'd uncovered in a session a few weeks earlier. It was one in which rejection featured strongly.

It turned out that in someone as empathic as Jacquie, being the one doing the rejecting had turned up some unexpected karmic consequences.

The past life in question was in Oxford, England, during the latter part of the nineteenth century. Jacquie was a young man named Rupert, an undergraduate at one of the city's famous colleges. His girlfriend, Lucy, is, in this life, Jacquie's boyfriend, Dylan.

Rupert was an average student. In fact, there was nothing remarkable about him other than a quirky sense of humor. As a prank, he sent a letter, purportedly from his professor, to the *London Times*. The letter, which made the professor look like a fool, was published, causing a minor scandal.

The prank caused Rupert to be "sent down," which meant being asked to leave the university. The severity of the sentence came as a complete shock to him. He received little support from his family, and worse still, Lucy refused to marry him until he had a decent job.

Finding a job turned out to be harder than Rupert expected. He was not particularly bright, and being sent down from Oxford had all the cachet of a dishonorable discharge from the military. Even his closest friends avoided him for fear of having their own reputations tarnished by association.

Rupert began drinking heavily, often going days without food. The more he slipped into alcoholism, the more Lucy retreated from the relationship. Ashamed of his past behavior and his very public drunkenness, she told him it was over.

From that point on, Rupert lost the will to live. On a sunny summer's evening, he was stung by a bee. Weakened by alcohol, he had no resistance to the allergic reaction he suffered. At the age of twenty-four, he died in a hospital alone, feeling abandoned by his friends and family.

I thought it might be a bit of a long shot, but I asked Jacquie if she had any problems with bees.

"I can't go on picnics because of my fear of being stung by a bee," she said. "The funny thing is that I've never been stung by one in this lifetime."

I asked her if she could draw any other dotted lines between her present life and the past. The strongest resonance was something that could only have come from the past.

In this life, Jacquie is an alternative healer. "It seems crazy, because I'm good at my work and really conscientious, but I always feel like an imposter. I worry people are going to think I'm a fraud." This feeling seemed to be directly related to the experience of passing herself off as her professor.

When Jacquie and I first talked about her partner, Dylan, my spirit guides described the relationship as strongly karmic. They were referring to the baggage the couple has brought into the relationship as a result of multiple past-life experiences together.

In Oxford, Lucy left Rupert because she was embarrassed to be with him in his alcoholic state. In this life, Dylan (who was once Lucy) is seeing the other side of the coin. His long-term drug problem has resulted in him losing every job he's ever had. He currently lives in his car.

Jacquie, too, is experiencing life from the opposite side. As Rupert, she was on a path of self-destruction; in this life, she is highly responsible and committed to helping people.

It's this desire to support others that's causing deep sadness in Jacquie. As a healer, she wants to help Dylan. As someone wrestling with a challenge of Self-Destruction, he doesn't want anyone interfering with his suffering.

"I've supported Dylan for years," Jacquie said. "My friends have always criticized me for being codependent, but I can't just abandon him."

After fifteen years, Jacquie has finally had enough, but though she's finished with Dylan, she can't let go.

"In that Oxford life, he abandoned me because he was embarrassed by me," she said. "I hate to say it, but in this life, *I'm* embarrassed by him. He looks totally disheveled—like a homeless person. Now I'm finding it really hard. Dylan won't speak to me, and it's making me so unhappy. I know I'm doing the right thing, but I can't understand why, when I'm the one leaving him, I'm suffering like this."

The problem is that as a highly empathic person, Jacquie identifies with Dylan strongly—so it's like she's the one being rejected.

I told Jacquie the fear of Rejection must have been triggered strongly in this life. Sure enough, she had a major incident in her past.

"I've always had a huge fear of being ostracized and excluded," she began. "I wanted so desperately to be a part of the crowd that I joined every group they had at school." Then Jacquie described an incident that happened in sixth grade, when a classmate became jealous and turned Jacquie's friends against her.

"I was devastated," she remembered. "I stayed home for a week. From then on, I was so afraid of being ostracized that I played down all my abilities. Nothing has ever impacted me like that event.

"A friend once pointed out that when we play board games, I'm really competitive with guys. But when it comes to women, I try not to beat them. I'm not threatened by men—just women."

Jacquie feels that being afraid of excelling has impacted her career. "I could have been a doctor, but it became more important for me to be loved than to achieve," she said. "I want to bring other alternative healing into my work, but I'm terrified of being seen as too 'woo-woo' and being ostracized."

Jacquie described her work with me as being "in progress." My spirit guides agreed. They recognized that healing would take a considerable length of time given her depth of connection with Dylan and her huge fear of Rejection. They gave her a technique for sending soul-level healing to Dylan and encouraged her to e-mail him, offering her continued support. "Moving on," the spirit guides said, "does not preclude friendship."

"Working with my past lives has been really fruitful," Jacquie told me. "I've gained a lot of insights. Things that make no sense on the physical level make sense on the soul level. People say I'm codependent, but you showed me it was something deeper. Compared to all those people criticizing me, you were like a loving light. It's been very healing."

THE FEAR OF THE WOO

I have a lot of clients who are doctors. Many of these caring old souls are interested in alternative practices, such as energy healing, craniosacral therapy, and acupuncture.

Traditional medicine, however, has been slow to embrace alternative, and often preventive, medicine. In such a conventional world, many of these doctors are conscious of not wanting to appear too "woo-woo."

The Transformation will eventually bring many alternative practices into the mainstream, and it will be progressive, old-soul doctors who lead the way.

Though Jacquie carries deep sadness about her relationship with Dylan, she agreed with my guides that she was being dragged down by his problems and had little choice but to break up with him. Though their karmic agreement on a soul level was to be together, this time around it was to support each other. "Dylan," they said, "has not upheld his part of the agreement."

I looked back on my notes from our first session and found a cryptic note from my spirit guides. They said, "Rejection is a double-edged sword," meaning that for someone with this fear, rejecting someone else is as bad as being rejected yourself. For an empathic old soul like Jacquie, this couldn't be more true. She'd told me, "I wish he'd rejected me. I could have handled that so much better."

THE ABILITY TO FORGIVE

One of the biggest blocks to experiencing the goal of Love is the difficulty, or even the inability, to forgive. What every person with a past-life fear of Rejection really wants (whether they know it or not) is love. By embracing the motivation of Forgiveness, healing is most quickly accomplished and the goal of Love achieved.

During the Transformation and beyond, forgiveness will become a recognized means of achieving a higher level of consciousness. If you suffer from a fear of Rejection (and we all do to some extent), then it's critical to learn this important skill.

Since your soul is always trying to alert your conscious mind to the existence of the karmic motivations you need for healing, most of us have the ability to draw on it when we need it. It may, however, take some work to fully engage it.

It can be hard to forgive someone who has really hurt you. If your soul has its way, however, you'll eventually feel the urge to forgive. It allows you to move beyond that person and the painful memories.

Christine knows all about rejection. It happened to her when she was a priest named Edmund in twelfth-century England. (This lifetime is one of the oldest I've come across that still has a significant impact on the present.)

As part of a monastery, the young man enjoyed the companionship of the other priests and the sense of protection from the outside world it offered. The work was hard and the living conditions austere, but being part of a community more than made up for it.

In those days, smallpox was endemic. Most people had it in childhood and were immune to it. In the remote area surrounding the monastery, however, smallpox was still something to be feared.

When Edmund started showing symptoms of the disease, he expected to be nursed through it by his fellow priests. It came as a shock when they decided he had to leave the monastery.

Edmund pleaded for compassion, but the older priests were adamant. Several of his brothers begged their superiors to show mercy, but their minds were made up.

As disturbing to Edmund as the rejection was the attitude of the older priests. Those he'd always looked up to as father figures were suddenly cold and indifferent, and some were even angry, blaming his condition on his lack of piety.

In the early hours of a bitterly cold winter morning, Edmund found himself outside the monastery walls with only a blanket and a loaf of bread to help him survive.

The inevitability of his death terrified Edmund. He was sick, lonely, and chilled to the bone. The smallpox might have been survivable had he been allowed to stay in the monastery. In the end, however, hypothermia killed him.

At the time he left the Physical Plane, Edmund's strongest impression of monastery life was not of the happy times he'd had. All he could see in his mind were the snarling faces of the priests who'd dragged him, begging for mercy, into the wind and snow.

Not surprisingly, there are lingering resonances of this trauma in Christine's present life. She hates the cold, has chronic skin issues, and fears angry men.

When I asked her, a few months later, how this past-life exploration had affected her, she couldn't contain her enthusiasm.

"It was transformative," she said. "I processed the trauma for weeks and cried so much. It hit on every single fear in this life. I don't really have words to describe what happened, or how I managed to transmute the fears, but now I can truly say I live without fear."

One thing that resonated strongly with Christine was the connection between the events in the monastery and her present-life fear of angry men. "My ex-husband, Dan, could be so mean to me," she told me. "I'd get so scared I had to call the police a couple of times."

Even after the divorce, the anger and violence continued, culmintating in what Christine calls the "Christmas Day Massacre of '08." "We had joint custody of our daughter," she said. "I met Dan at a gas station to hand over our daughter, and that's when something set him off. I was trying to tell my daughter to call me if she needed me. He said, 'She won't.' Then he grabbed her out of my arms and spat at me. I followed them to the car trying to say good-bye, and my daughter was screaming for me. Dan threw me to the ground twice.

"When the police came, they asked if I wanted to take out a warrant for assault. I didn't. I found out later Dan actually went to them the next day, accusing *me* of assault.

"My transforming lesson has been about forgiving and letting go," Christine continues. "I've used Dan's antics to develop tolerance and forgiveness. I consider him to have been one of my biggest teachers. I had years of being put down and criticized all the time. Now I can just say 'okay' and let it all go."

It took Christine a long time to get to a place where she could forgive her ex. The process was made harder by having to maintain contact with him for the sake of their daughter. It's a lot easier to "wash that man right out of your hair," as my guides (and *South Pacific* composers Rodgers and Hammerstein) put it, when you don't ever have to see that person again.

HEALING THE PAIN OF REJECTION

Monique is forty-seven years old, married with two teenage sons, and has a career in sales.

"I'm a black sheep, a loner, and an outcast," she told me. "I've always felt I work in a very male environment, but I don't fit in—even in groups of women. I wanted to join a book group, but once I was there, I felt I didn't belong. I'd go home feeling confused about it."

When I delved into one of Monique's more traumatic past lives, I saw a massive past-life fear of Rejection. "The life we're about to explore may cast light on the issue," I told her, "but I have to warn you that it's not pleasant." Monique assured me she wanted to explore it no matter what came up.

Before we began, my spirit guides made an observation. "This is the first of several lifetimes in which abdominal injuries have been an issue," they said.

In the early 1700s, at the time of Europe's Great Northern War, Monique was a woman named Mathilde who worked in a small town in Denmark packing salt fish in barrels. She lived alone for most of her life, having lost her closest relatives to war and sickness. The biggest tragedy, however, happened when her fiancé fell victim to cholera. From that point on, she lost all interest in the outside world.

Losing the only real relationship she'd ever had embittered Mathilde. As she aged, she became increasingly bad-tempered and uncommunicative. Word was that she practiced sorcery. Her neighbors kept well away from her, fearing any association with her might reflect on themselves.

A gang of local boys would taunt her while she worked. Every so often she'd catch one and give him a good beating.

Mathilde's life changed on a chilly spring morning when Prussian troops came through the town. They spotted her hiding from them and dragged her to a secluded place where they beat and raped her. Before the soldiers left, they stabbed her in the stomach and left her to die.

She staggered back to the center of town begging for help, but her neighbors refused to help her. It was the young boys who had, until then, been so mean to her who helped carry her home. They laid her on a table and ran away before she could put a curse on them. She died alone a few hours later.

Before she died, Mathilde actively forgave her neighbors, particularly the boys who'd been so cruel to her throughout much of her life.

At the time of her death, she felt a bitter sense of loneliness and disappointment. She'd spent years on the fringe of the community, and even after suffering terribly at the hands of the soldiers, it was only the boys who'd helped her. This event was the beginning of a fear of Rejection that has followed her soul over many lifetimes.

The first question I asked Monique was, "Have you ever had any unexplained abdominal pains?"

Monique's response shook me in its enormity.

"All through my childhood and teens I had unidentified stomach pains. When I was little, I'd curl into a ball at night, clutch my stomach, and roll by the bedroom door for hours," she explained.

"I never called out for help. I just lay there until I cried myself to sleep. My parents took me to doctors to check for ulcers, but they never found anything wrong."

The trigger for Monique's fear of Rejection in this life happened in her first few months as a baby. Being forced to sleep in her own room, rather than her parents' bedroom (effectively being rejected again), brought the fear rushing to the surface. Suddenly her soul was back in Denmark, experiencing the pain and isolation all over again.

Exploring this traumatic lifetime in Denmark was healing for Monique. "I've often felt I have big issues, but they've never had an obvious cause. Someone who's sexually abused—they have obvious issues. Mine were always so subtle. I never had any excuse for the way I am."

I asked Monique if she'd found that forgiveness comes as easily in this life as it did in her past.

"Oh, yes," she said. "Forgiveness comes naturally to me. I don't stay mad for long."

Why did Monique feel compelled to forgive those who'd rejected her in that past life? She was dying, and at that time she connected more strongly than ever with her soul. Forgiveness is a loving act, and her soul wanted her to leave the planet with as much love inside her as she could muster. That love would help to mitigate the effects of the fear in the future.

BEING THE REJECTER, NOT THE REJECTED

When I spoke to Martha, she began the session by telling me how she was currently dealing with cancer for the second time. She was distressed by the lack of concern shown by her thirty-year-old son, Robert. "He's been disinterested in me since he was a teenager," she said.

My spirit guides corrected her. "It began when he was ten."

"That's exactly when I first got cancer," she said. "He was never the same after that."

Robert has a past-life fear of Rejection. When his mom had to go to the hospital and leave him with a relative, he was overwhelmed by being left alone. The reason he acts so cold toward his mother now is that he's terrified of losing her. He deals with the fear by "rejecting" her just in case she "rejects" him.

Kayla has been accused of being a social butterfly. She would disagree with that characterization; she considers herself to be simply a good hostess.

In her recent past, Kayla was an Australian soldier who died in battle somewhere in Europe during World War II. At the time of his death, the young soldier felt abandoned by his comrades, his superiors, and even his country.

In this life, the fear of Rejection was triggered by a move to a new home when Kayla was seven. "On our old block there were at least a hundred kids, but when we moved there was no one," she said. "My sisters found new friends, but I didn't. Eventually I met a girl who'd been ostracized and no one would play with her—so I did. I felt isolated and yearned to be included, but I always felt left out. I'm not shy, but I can be reserved around people, and I didn't always connect well.

"At some point I began taking responsibility for being included. Instead of waiting for others to include me, I came out of my shell and became the one to organize events. I would throw a party or get a group together to go to the movies.

"When I get people together, I make sure everyone is included, and I always try to match people together. It's simply good etiquette. I truly believe we'd have a better society if we had better etiquette."

....

SPIRITUAL ACT 10: REUNITING WITH THE TRIBE

During the Transformation, those who are overcoming a fear of Rejection will be drawn to bring people together as they connect to their goal of Love.

Unity is the Spiritual Act associated with this goal. It means getting proactive about surrounding yourself with other souls. It will get you off the sideline and into the game. And though it can be a little scary at first (it puts the fear of Rejection front and center), once you get the ball rolling, you'll never want to go back.

The degree to which you get involved is, of course, your choice. You could organize a coffee morning with a few friends, or you could bring a million people together to create a movement for change.

As we reunite with the tribe, you'll find that an increasing number of people will be switching off the TV and putting the computer to sleep in favor of becoming more involved in the community.

Detachment from others is not the natural state of being for you and your soul. It can be hard, however, to get through life without encountering the triggers that remind your soul of past-life rejection.

When you were young, were you ever excluded from a game by the other kids? Did your best friend dump you to play with someone else? Later, were you ever passed over for the school team or did you ever have a job application rejected?

If you didn't experience rejection of some kind, you're one of the lucky few. It's much more likely that you did. And how you react to abandonment and any other kind of rejection depends on your soul's past.

The stronger the past-life fear, the more you're going to suffer when you face rejection—especially if the fear has been triggered multiple times.

The bigger the fear, the more important it is to become a uniter. It doesn't necessarily mean opening your home to a crowd of strangers, but it does mean recognizing that you, as someone who has suffered the pain of rejection, should be the first to make sure others around you feel included.

It's a major step toward healing the trauma from the past.

....

RANDOM SPIRITUAL ACTS OF KINDNESS

One of the Spiritual Acts associated with the goal of Love is to write a letter of forgiveness. Another is to be a friend to someone in need. You might want to send an e-mail to friends you haven't heard from in a while, telling them you've been thinking about them.

....

THE POWER OF FORGIVENESS

In Chapter Four, I told you about Karen and how her past life in Prague created a huge fear of Inferiority in this life. Well, something triggered that fear (and others) in the early part of this life. It was having been sexually abused by a neighbor.

Karen told me, "When we talked about past lives, it opened a door, and I walked through. I then discovered more past lives in dreams and meditation. Around that time, I woke up in the middle of the night. The room was pitch black—no light at all—but a fuzzy ball of light floated around. I watched it for about ninety minutes until I fell asleep.

"Then I had a vivid dream. I was visited by the guy who'd abused me. He'd died a few years earlier, and I have to admit I was glad. I had a lot of hate in me, and I knew I wasn't his only victim.

"His spirit asked me a question. It said, 'How do you forgive someone who has done something terrible to you?'

"I said, 'It's not the act you're forgiving, it's the soul.'

"The man said, 'What I did was learned behavior.' I realized immediately that he meant it was a case of the abused becoming the abuser. I felt nothing but compassion for him. What he went through was awful. I felt a sudden release of all the anger and woke with a jolt, crying, 'I forgive you—I understand—I forgive you.'"

In an earlier chapter I wrote about the girlfriend who threatened to stab me with a pair of scissors. That incident happened in 1991, a very long time ago.

In some ways, the events of that period of my life seem like a distant memory—almost as if they happened to someone else. Yet, as I described in my previous book, *The Instruction,* her malfeasance cost me the business I financed for her, my savings, my home, and even a little bit of my sanity!

I was determined not to let her affect me, but I found it impossible not to feel angry. I handled my anger by masking it with humor. I had a host of amusing stories of her various excesses that I could entertain people with. Unfortunately, all I was doing was sweeping her under the rug.

Some years ago, I was telling a group of friends how she'd ripped me off, threatened me, and so on. While I was talking, I found my cheeks were reddening. I'd learned to make these stories funny, but a spark of anger still burned inside. It alarmed me that she could still affect me after so long, and I recognized that something needed to be done about it.

The next morning, I spoke with my spirit guides. "I thought I was done with her," I said.

"Almost," they replied. "But you still hold anger within you."

I knew what was coming. I feigned resistance. "No," I pleaded, "Please don't ask me to forgive her!"

My guides went along with the joke. "Resistance is futile," they said. "You are at our mercy."

What followed was a brief reminder of something I already knew: forgiveness doesn't mean condoning someone's actions.

"She should be in jail," I said.

"We agree," they said, "but this is not about her; it's about you."

That's when my spirit guides gave me the following exercise. It's simple, it's easy, and I can't tell you the effect it had on me.

....

FORGIVENESS EXERCISE
RELEASING THE PAST

Bring in your spirit guides with the following request: "I call upon my spirit guides, acting in my highest interest, to help me reach the trans-formational goal of Love."

- Write the names of ten people who have hurt or betrayed you.
- Beside each person's name, write a line or two about what they did to hurt you.
- Close your eyes and visualize the first person on your list about twelve inches from your third eye (the spot in the middle of your forehead, between your eyes).
- When a clear image forms, say the following words: "I love you and forgive you."
- Repeat: "I love you and forgive you."
- Let the image crumble or fade away.
- Do this nine more times, or as often as you need to.

....

When I did this exercise, I pictured my ex-girlfriend as I remembered her, said the words, and let her image turn to dust.

And that was it. Months would go by without her entering my consciousness, and if I did bring up one of her stories, I'd get no emotional or visceral reaction whatsoever.

In fact, writing about her in this book hasn't triggered the slightest twinge of anger. It hasn't been cathartic or healing, because no catharsis or healing was necessary.

I've taken many people through this process (which is similar to what the Hawaiians call *ho'oponopono*). The reactions have been astonishing. It can trigger deep feelings. Some people feel immediate relief—like a weight has been lifted. Others find it happens more slowly and requires a little repetition.

Sometimes an event can be too close in time for this exercise. You might have to wait until your initial anger has subsided. But we're all different. You won't know without trying.

Your soul wants you to know the power of love. If you're paying attention, you'll find it's continually pushing you in the direction of love. To be truly fulfilled, it's essential to have love in your life.

Having love is not simply about finding romance. It goes much deeper than that. Though it includes romantic love, it also means love in the spiritual sense.

When I was a teenager, I used to visit an old man with multiple sclerosis once a week. He would regale me with stories of Scotland during the early twentieth century, and I would do little more than make him a cup of tea and listen. To be honest, my visits didn't seem such a big deal, and I'd pretty much forgotten about the old man until my spirit guides reminded me.

"Your company was appreciated more than you'll ever understand until you return to the Astral Plane," they told me. "Spiritual Acts do not have to be big. Your weekly visits significantly impacted the old man's happiness, and he helped you become the person you are today. His impact was subtle, but significant."

If you ever feel the absence of love in your life, extend a hand and help someone. Spiritual Acts are always loving, and love is always reciprocal.

CHAPTER TWELVE

THE EMBODIMENT OF TRANSFORMATION
Inspiring Change Through Example

BEING A HERO

As you reach the ten goals, you'll naturally embody your soul's highest values. And when you do, you'll become a hero—not the kind with a cape and the ability to stop a runaway train with one hand, but one who acts as an example to others.

Your example will show those you come into contact with what it is to be a spiritually conscious older soul who embodies the Transformation.

The good news: you just have to be yourself. By going through life acting according to the ten goals, others will look to you for inspiration and guidance.

You don't have to lead a movement for social change or sell your worldly goods and devote the rest of your life to healing lepers—although you could. All you really have to do to be an inspiration to others is to live an authentic life: one of purpose and meaning.

I spent the first twenty years of my working life as a cartoon illustrator. Like every artist, I didn't just pull my style out of thin air; I had my heroes.

I was particularly influenced by a curious character I knew little about back then, but whose humorous drawings of classical musicians used to crack me up: a man by the name of Gerard Hoffnung.

Hoffnung was born in Germany in the 1930s. His family, who were Jewish, relocated to England to escape Nazi persecution, and young Gerard immediately began turning into an eccentric in the great English tradition.

He smoked a pipe and affected the voice of an old curmudgeon. It worked, in part, because he always looked much older than his age. He was unable to serve in the war due to his German origins, which probably wasn't a hardship as he was a committed pacifist. Instead, he trained as an artist.

Hoffnung got his first job as an art teacher at the age of twenty-one. On his first day, he told the class to take out their pens and start doodling. Meanwhile, he serenaded them on the bassoon. Halfway through the period, he got up and walked around the room, looking over each student's shoulder saying, "That's not doodling. I said, *doodle!*" He didn't last long in that job.

At the time, Hoffnung was already a well-known cartoonist, and he went on to publish a best-selling series of books on the subject of orchestras and their musicians. He illustrated books for children, as well as one for adults based on one of his favorite operas.

Hoffnung was a BBC broadcaster, a debater at the Oxford and Cambridge Unions, and he taught himself the tuba sufficiently well enough to play Vaughan Williams's Tuba Concerto at the Royal Festival Hall.

It was there that he produced a series of humorous concerts with pieces by some of the top composers of the day. The events were a huge success, and orchestras still play many of these quirky compositions today.

In one performance, *The Piano Concerto to End All Piano Concertos,* the pianist is under the assumption she's been hired to play Grieg's Piano Concerto. The rest of the orchestra is committed to playing Tchaikovsky's Fourth Piano Concerto. With neither side prepared to give an inch, they race to the finish, each determined to have the last note.

Another piece is played on vacuum cleaners and dedicated to President Herbert Hoover (Hoover being the generic name for vacuum cleaners in Britain).

As a socially conscious old soul, Hoffnung became a Quaker and participated in a prison visitor program. He supported nuclear disarmament; vocally opposed the death penalty, racism, fox hunting, and injustice of all kinds; and spoke out on behalf of gays and other minorities (at a time when homosexuality was illegal in Britain).

Hoffnung was married with two children and had an active social life, entertaining many of the great artists, writers, and musicians of the day in his home.

He died, of a coronary embolism, a gravelly voiced, balding old man of thirty-four.

What I admire about Gerard Hoffnung—apart from inspiring me to be a cartoonist—is how he managed to cram so much into such a short time. His brief but meaningful life is a reminder that we can all leave some kind of a karmic legacy from our time here.

Hoffnung died while TV was in its infancy, but I'd be willing to bet that if he were still around, he wouldn't be spending every night slouched in his recliner, watching reality shows. And I don't think he'd be continually filling notebooks with plans for the future or always talking about what he was one day going to do, without following through. Instead, I think he'd be participating in the true reality: the one we call real life.

You can see in Hoffnung an embodiment of old-soul values. He saw injustice in the world and did something about it. Becoming a prison visitor, for example, was a way of being of service to some of society's less fortunate souls.

It takes a lot of energy to be a Hoffnung, and most of us would be considered human dynamos if we accomplished in our lives half of what he did.

If there's one thing to be learned from Hoffnung's example, it is that life is what you make of it. You can sit on your butt waiting for your life to happen, or you can get up and start getting involved.

Life, as it has often been said, is not a rehearsal. This is it: a live performance with you in the lead role. You can take the play of your life in any direction you choose.

And to paraphrase again the well-known adage: no one on his or her deathbed ever said, "I wish I hadn't had such an interesting life."

REPRESENTING THE TRANSFORMATION

I looked for inspiration for my earlier career in the world of cartoonists. As you move into the Transformation, it's important to look for inspiration for your life. (You may be a hero, but you need heroes of your own.)

Inspiration can be found in people who are already beginning to embrace the Transformation: souls, just like you, who are living their lives according to higher spiritual values.

I talked in Chapter Seven about the kind of karmic influence a person like Jonas Salk would have on future generations of doctors and researchers. Thanks to the example of Salk and thousands of others whose actions have elevated the Collective Consciousness, spiritually conscious old souls are popping up all over the place.

Amazing, inspirational people are living among us now, impacting their fellow humans simply by their example. Some are highly visible, like the Dalai Lama and the poet Maya Angelou. Others, like family members or particularly influential teachers, are not.

It will enhance your spiritual development to find others whose example you can use for guidance. By learning to recognize the signs of elevated old souls, you can see how the ten transformational goals work in their lives and learn to apply the same principles to your own.

You can do as I did and choose a role model in your field, or you can look around and find inspiration from people in all walks of life. It's useful to do both.

A perfect example of someone who embodies the principles of the Transformation is my friend, the singer India Arie. When I saw her perform in Seattle, I was moved beyond anything I could have expected by the overwhelming feeling of love in the auditorium.

What I was witnessing was the effect of an old soul in the process of elevating her consciousness from Stage Three to Stage Four.

The love India projects from the stage is a reflection of her deep and genuine spirituality. The audience responds with love (which is a two-way street, of course) because they intuitively recognize India's authenticity.

This is no diva spouting "I love you, Seattle" platitudes before going backstage to bitch about the lighting guy and the shape of her sandwiches. She's someone who genuinely connects with every person in the room through her spirituality.

India's songs express the heartfelt beliefs of a spiritually conscious soul. They're about empowerment, love, truth, and her personal journey of transformation.

India began writing songs when she first went to college. "I'd just arrived in Savannah," she told me. "I could feel all kind of emotions, especially with it having been the first slave port. It was as if I was sensing my ancestors.

"I always wanted to sing and play guitar—to be James Taylor, Stevie Wonder, or Bill Withers. My boyfriend had a broken old guitar, and I just started writing songs. Three months later, I got a standing ovation in a coffee shop.

"I was never the kind of person to ask for help, but I would sit down to write and say, 'Billie, Nina, please be with me now.' I wrote 'India's Song,' which is about spirits, and when I called Billie Holiday and Nina Simone in to help me, I realized they were really there."

After that, India began to invoke her spirit guides all the time. "Calling in my guides became as natural as singing," she said.

India sees a big part of her mission as helping people get out of bad situations—ones she's been in herself. "I created a mission statement for myself: to spread love, healing, and peace through the power of words and music."

To get where she is now, India had to get over some big insecurities. "I wasn't sure I could really be a professional singer," she told me. "I worried about the birthmark on my tongue or that my voice was too deep. I worried that no one would buy my albums.

"But that all changed when I started to grow spiritually. It's why I write songs about body image, like 'I Am Not My Hair.' Young women come up to me and say, 'You made me see I'm beautiful.'

"I used to hold back a part of myself, but now I'm expressing old soul values—I have nothing stopping me. On my most recent tour, I made a commitment to be more of myself. It meant talking about spiritual ideals. I went on the road truly being myself—being authentic.

"When I was performing, I could feel a higher spiritual energy. I was in the middle of an ocean—singing, dancing, crying, and laughing. It was like being lifted off the ground. Sometimes, I'd close my eyes and forget people were there.

"I wasn't thinking about what I looked like or what people thought of me. I'd just start talking or singing a certain song if the audience started singing it. It would take me a long time to come down after a show. It was a totally spiritual experience."

India has become aware of the profound impact her past lives have had on her. "I understand now what has shaped me, and particularly why I write about respect and women. It's made me feel even stronger. I got so much understanding on a very deep level that I know I'm going to keep writing those songs."

It's impossible not to be touched by the beauty and integrity of India's songs. Her lyrics are positive and empowering. They come from the heart of a loving old soul.

Simply by being true to herself, she's elevating the consciousness of all those who come in contact with her and her music. Without the slightest element of coercion, she's showing kindred spirits a way to embrace the values that are the mark of the Transformation.

A SACRED CALLING

But you don't have to be a star to make a difference. The next person I want to talk about is an old client of mine. She's a spiritually conscious soul who's making a profound impact on people's lives—or more specifically, their deaths.

Susan James is a hospice social worker. As she puts it, "It's like being a midwife at the end of life. It's a lot of work to come into this life, and it can be a lot of work leaving."

In ancient times, shamans and priests helped us die. The Celts had *anam ćaras,* "soul friends," to usher people out of the world. Susan's work is recovering something developed centuries ago.

"In the past, death was not to be feared," she explains. "It was simply a natural transition. If you go back long enough, you'll find that every culture had rituals and prayers for the dead and dying.

"Many people of my generation have left organized religion to search for something more spiritually meaningful. But now, when people like us reach the end of life, where do we go for comfort? For many of us, hospice care becomes much more than a medical presence in our lives.

"People in hospice see it as a sacred calling. When you're with someone at the end of their life, you're in a sacred bubble. They're partly in this world and partly in the next. Even a person who was never spiritual will start having conversations with people on the other side."

I told Susan how my great-grandmother was unconscious for days at the end of her life. Then she suddenly sat up and spoke to a crowd of relatives who'd gone before her. "That happens all the time," Susan said.

I wondered if everyone finds a peaceful way out of this world.

"The amount of fear and resistance correlates to the struggle a person went through in life," Susan said. "Not everyone gets the Disney ending, especially if he or she lived life in fast-forward. People tend to die the way they lived. Fast-lane people often die fast: 'I've bought my ticket; let's just get on the plane.' It's a way of honoring their spirit.

"The ones who have the hardest time are those who have regrets or don't have enough time to process what's happening to them. Sometimes they may have unresolved business with their loved ones."

I asked Susan if she ever found her work a burden.

"I consider what I do to be a calling, not work," she said. "It's never been a burden to be with people at the end. The dying remind us how to live: loving people, telling them often, having no regrets, seizing life, living with joy. They become teachers at the end. They see what's important, and everyone around them gets that lesson, too. They truly give me as much as I give them."

What unites two seemingly different people like India Arie and Susan James is that they both embody the ten transformational goals of Equality, Cooperation, Respect, Justice, Knowledge, Understanding, Truth, Freedom, Peace, and Love. There's no hypocrisy, no ego. Both women want to live a good life: one of meaning and service to others. And they're doing it.

One is impacting thousands at a time, while the other is doing it more modestly. Each is creating a karmic legacy, and each is impacting the Collective Consciousness in a big way. Simply by being authentic—being who they really are—their souls are touching the souls of everyone they come into contact with.

The most influential people you'll encounter in the Transformation are those like India and Susan, who lead by example. The good news is that you may be one yourself. And if you're not, you can be.

If you choose to represent the Transformation and be a hero, you can join those other spiritually conscious souls simply by embodying the ten transformational goals.

To use one of my own expressions, which my spirit guides frequently throw back at me: "You don't have to reinvent the wheel."

There are spiritually conscious old souls out there doing what spiritually conscious old souls do: living their lives with integrity, being of service to others, and helping raise the Collective Consciousness to a higher level. You just need to look to them for guidance.

TRANSFORMING THE TRIBE

So what will the world look like after we've undergone the Transformation and the Collective Consciousness is manifesting Stage Four Consciousness?

The answer is that it's a little hard to say. There are so many variables involved that painting an accurate picture of life in the Stage Four tribe is impossible.

One thing we can be sure of is that our society will become more fair. The goal of Equality imbues all those who reach it with the awareness that wealth and opportunity are commodities that should be more fairly distributed.

In the tribe of the future, there will be fewer underdogs, thanks to a system that will take care of the sick, the unemployed, the homeless, and the less fortunate. Identifying with the circumstances others find themselves in will motivate us to create genuine equality. Seeing beyond color, religion, gender, and social class, we'll recognize only fellow souls.

As we embody the goal of Cooperation, we'll be naturally drawn to work together with one another. We'll see more community-based ventures and businesses, along with more active participation from all of us.

Many hierarchies we take for granted will break down. And as unlikely as it may seem from our current vantage point, the three branches of government—executive, legislative, and judicial—will work on behalf of the people, not their wealthy patrons.

For-profit health care, overpriced homes, and credit cards with rates of interest that would embarrass medieval moneylenders will all eventually bite the dust.

Through the goal of Respect, we'll feel better about ourselves, not because someone tells us we're the greatest nation on Earth, but because we act that way. We'll recognize that each of us has the right to self-determination and work that gives our lives meaning.

The goal of Justice will ensure that we treat one another more kindly and that those who violate society's (much fairer) laws are rehabilitated, not simply punished or forgotten.

A major focus of Stage Four souls is the pursuit and the synthesis of facts through the goal of Knowledge. It's hard to imagine how different things will be when the money that's spent on feeding the currently insatiable appetite of the military is channeled toward education.

A combination of knowledge and responsibility will result in huge advances in science and technology, without the current lack of concern for its long-term ramifications.

As a result of billions of souls reaching the goal of Understanding, divisions between nations and cultures will evaporate. As empathy builds within us, we'll actively work to understand our species' amazing diversity.

In our current world in which propaganda frequently masquerades as news, you can expect to see a far greater emphasis on the importance of honesty. The goal of Truth will impact how we interact with one another as the expectation of honesty increases.

Recognizing that we're here to fulfill our souls' purpose, the goal of Freedom will impel us to empower and be empowered. It will become increasingly important to live free from arbitrary rules and unjust restraints on our ability to complete our life plans in safety.

We can expect a huge reaction against wars and other acts of violence as the Collective Consciousness rises and we embody the goal of Peace. Far from passively avoiding conflict, we will each feel motivated to play a part in achieving peace.

As violence subsides, we'll look to forgiveness as a means to overcome the desire to perpetuate aggression. Bringing outsiders into the tribe will help remind us that we are all souls beneath the skin. We can expect to see a return to more community-based activities, in which connections and friendships are made and maintained.

A future in which we can each realize our soul's full potential is not just some impractical utopian dream, but a realistic expectation of what we can expect from our species' future.

The world we live in is, to a very large extent, one rooted in the Illusion. We don't have to have inequality. There's no universal law that says we can't share what we have with one another. We managed for tens of millennia without Wall Street, multinational corporations, and nuclear arsenals—and we can do it again.

It's the job of Stage Four souls to begin remaking the world according to our souls' highest values: the ten transformational goals.

EMBODYING THE TRANSFORMATION

Each chapter of this book has described the source, the symptoms, and the cure for a trauma that impacted your soul somewhere in its richly textured past. Now, as you move forward into the future, you have a chance to do so unencumbered by the baggage from all those ancient incarnations.

This is an opportunity to reinvent yourself: to create a new you, one devoid of fears and limiting beliefs and full of energy and a desire to start living a more meaningful and purposeful life.

And to help you do this, I have one more exercise from my spirit guides. It's very simple, yet like all their suggestions, highly effective. I know, because, like all the others, I've done it myself!

....

TRANSFORMATIONAL EXERCISE 10
BUILD AN ALTAR TO YOUR HEROES

- Think of nine people you admire—individuals who you feel embody the goals (or as many of them as possible). They don't have to be alive today.
- Beside each name, write a few lines about why you admire them, using terms from the Transformation. An example might be, "Harry Belafonte is my hero because he embraces the transformational goals of Peace, Freedom, Equality, and Respect."
- As a reminder, the ten goals, once again, are Equality, Cooperation, Respect, Justice, Knowledge, Understanding, Truth, Freedom, Peace, and Love.
- Build an altar. This can simply be a piece of paper that you pin to the wall, or it can be more complex, with candles, incense, and personal objects.
- On your altar, put a picture of each of your heroes.
- Below each picture, write your reasons for admiring this person.

When you've listed all nine names, add your own name to the list and write a few lines about why you can be a hero, too.

My list of ten names currently includes John Lennon, Mohandas Gandhi, Martin Luther King Jr., Helen Keller, Cindy Sheehan, Richard Feynman, John Pilger, Paul Farmer, Nelson Mandela, and of course, myself.

You can see from my list that if there's a theme here, it involves the goals of Peace, Love, Freedom, Justice, Truth, and Knowledge. It just so happens they correspond to some of the strongest fears I've had to deal with in this lifetime.

When you sit before your altar, take time to reflect on the fears you've recognized from reading this book, and think about how the past has made you who you are.

Look to your heroes for inspiration, and ask yourself how you, too, can bring the ten goals into your life.

I want to leave you with some thoughts from spirit guides on the Causal Plane. But before I do, let me wish you the very best of good fortune as you make your way through the Transformation. Though you may encounter some turbulence on your voyage, when you elevate your consciousness and reunite with the tribe, you'll find a whole new world stretching out before you—one of greater meaning, fulfillment, and connection.

And remember that as you leave your Stage Three Consciousness behind and shift into Stage Four, other souls wanting to transform will look to you for direction. All you have to do to be a positive example is to embrace the ten transformational goals—and to simply be your true self.

And now, let me pass you over to the Soul World.

A TSUNAMI OF CHANGE

Through its distorted lens, the Illusion gives the impression that the physical world must be the way it is. It creates the belief that change must be gradual and incremental.

The Transformation, however, is a tsunami of change waiting to pick up momentum. It will bring healing to an ailing planet and the impetus for each individual to create a new reality.

Change is coming, regardless of how strong the opposition to it. The fear of change is an aspect of the Illusion, and it will be swept away as the Transformation clears out the old to make room for the new.

Personal transformation is the key to creating a better world. The changes you undergo will affect those around you. Eventually the ripple effect of individual transformation will positively impact the Collective Consciousness.

The Transformation is an opportunity for you to seek out a better future in the company of kindred spirits. The voyage will take you to new and unexplored territory. When you arrive, you will wonder why you didn't set out sooner.

We will support you every step of the way. We will answer your questions and offer guidance and reassurance when you need it. You only have to ask.

Remember that you are an ambassador for the Soul World. You lead by example and have the ability to influence those who choose to follow in your footsteps.

Your soul is ready to take you to the next level of consciousness. Transformation is within your reach.

We wish you the best of good fortune on your journey.

—The author's Causal Plane spirit guides

APPENDIX
Identify and Annihilate Technique

The first step is to identify the past-life fear. The second is to annihilate it. Begin by entering a meditative state. Bring in your spirit guides with the following words: "I call upon my spirit guides, acting in my highest interest, to help me annihilate my fear of
_____."

Stand facing a mirror, look straight into your eyes, and tell your fear you're not going to put up with it any longer. Show it no mercy. (Imagine you're a professional wrestler railing against your opponent.)

Here's a suggestion:

"Listen up, fear of _____*! I've had it with you, you little punk! I'm going to murder you. I'm going to be your assassin. You'd better get out of here while you have the chance. I'm done with you. I want you gone . . . NOW! I will annihilate you. . . . " and so on.*

When you've finished, thank your spirit guides and tell them, "Session over."

Give yourself a couple of minutes a day to do this exercise. Wait until you notice a shift in one fear before moving on to the next.

The exact words don't matter as long as you identify the fear by name. You don't have to yell—you can grit your teeth and hiss the words through them. Use emotive words. Have fun with it.

ABOUT THE AUTHOR

For more than a decade, Ainslie MacLeod has used his psychic abilities to explore the influence of the soul on human beliefs and behavior. More recently, his investigations have led him to focus on uncovering past-life trauma to heal unexplained fears, phobias, and other blocks to happiness in the present moment.

Ainslie has been a featured guest on Oprah's Soul Series and is a faculty member at the Omega Institute and Kripalu Center. He was the recipient of a gold medal from the Independent Publisher Association for his previous book, *The Instruction*. He lives on a tranquil island in the Pacific Northwest with his wife and two young children.

ABOUT SOUNDS TRUE

Sounds True was founded in 1985 with a clear vision: to disseminate spiritual wisdom. Located in Boulder, Colorado, Sounds True publishes teaching programs that are designed to educate, uplift, and inspire. We work with many of the leading spiritual teachers, thinkers, healers, and visionary artists of our time.

To receive a free catalog of tools and teachings for personal and spiritual transformation, please visit SoundsTrue.com, call toll free at 800-333-9185, or write to us at the address below.

P.O. Box 8010
Boulder, CO 80306